IMPRISONING

AMERICA

IMPRISONING
AMERICA

The Social
Effects of
Mass
Incarceration

Mary Pattillo
David Weiman
Bruce Western
Editors

Russell Sage Foundation, New York

The Russell Sage Foundation

The Russell Sage Foundation, one of the oldest of America's general purpose foundations, was established in 1907 by Mrs. Margaret Olivia Sage for "the improvement of social and living conditions in the United States." The Foundation seeks to fulfill this mandate by fostering the development and dissemination of knowledge about the country's political, social, and economic problems. While the Foundation endeavors to assure the accuracy and objectivity of each book it publishes, the conclusions and interpretations in Russell Sage Foundation publications are those of the authors and not of the Foundation, its Trustees, or its staff. Publication by Russell Sage, therefore, does not imply Foundation endorsement.

Library of Congress Cataloging-in-Publication Data
Imprisoning America : the social effects of mass incarceration / edited by Mary Pattillo, David Weiman, Bruce Western.
    p. cm.
  Includes bibliographical references and index.
  ISBN 0-87154-652-3 (cloth)   ISBN 0-87154-654-X (paper)
    1. Imprisonment—United States.   2. Imprisonment—Social aspects—United States.   3. Criminal justice, Administration of—Social aspects—United States.   I. Pattillo, Mary E.   II. Weiman, David F.   III. Western, Bruce, 1964–

HV8705.I455   2004
365'.973—dc22   2003066871

Text design by Genna Patacsil.

RUSSELL SAGE FOUNDATION
112 East 64th Street, New York, New York 10021
10 9 8 7 6 5 4 3 2 1

Contents

Contributors

MARY PATTILLO is associate professor of sociology and African American studies and faculty fellow at the Institute for Policy Research at Northwestern University.

DAVID WEIMAN is Alena Wels Hirschorn '58 Professor of Economics at Barnard College, Columbia University.

BRUCE WESTERN is professor of sociology and faculty associate of the Office of Population Research at Princeton University.

KATHRYN EDIN is associate professor of sociology and research associate at the Population Studies Center at the University of Pennsylvania.

HARRY J. HOLZER is professor at Georgetown Public Policy Institute, Georgetown University, and visiting fellow at the Urban Institute in Washington, D.C.

ELIZABETH I. JOHNSON is a doctoral candidate in social work and developmental psychology at the University of Michigan.

LEONARD M. LOPOO is assistant professor of public administration at Syracuse University.

JAMES P. LYNCH is professor and chair of the Department of Justice, Law, and Society at American University.

JEFF MANZA is professor of sociology and associate director of the Institute for Policy Research at Northwestern University.

SARA MCLANAHAN is professor of sociology and public affairs at Princeton University.

TIMOTHY J. NELSON is assistant research professor at the Institute for Policy Research and senior lecturer in the Department of Sociology at Northwestern University.

ANNE M. NURSE is associate professor of sociology at The College of Wooster.

RECHELLE PARANAL is project coordinator at the Institute for Policy Research at Northwestern University.

STEVEN RAPHAEL is associate professor at the Goldman School of Public Policy, University of California, Berkeley.

WILLIAM J. SABOL is assistant director at the U.S. General Accounting Office.

MICHAEL A. STOLL is associate professor at the School of Public Policy and Social Research, University of California, Los Angeles.

JEREMY TRAVIS is president of John Jay College of Criminal Justice of the City University of New York, former senior fellow of the Urban Institute, and former director of the National Institute of Justice.

CHRISTOPHER UGGEN is professor and chair of the Sociology Department at the University of Minnesota.

JANE WALDFOGEL is professor of social work and public affairs at Columbia University.

Acknowledgments

This volume grew out of the 2001 conference "The Effects of Incarceration on Children and Families," hosted by the Institute for Policy Research (IPR) at Northwestern University. The conference brought together academics, practitioners, and activists to share empirical research, theories, and testimonies on the impact of mass incarceration in the United States. Although only some of the papers presented at the conference are included in this volume, we are grateful to all the participants, discussants, and attendees for helping to frame the scholarly and policy debates on this issue. We would like to thank the conference organizing committee for their work in soliciting and reviewing the conference papers. The committee included Joseph Altonji, Lindsay Chase-Lansdale, Thomas Cook, Greg Duncan, and Dorothy Roberts, who were greatly aided by the creativity and expertise of IPR publications director Audrey Chambers. Fay Lomax Cook, director of IPR, deserves special thanks for financial support and for encouraging this book project. Russell Sage Foundation was a generous financial supporter of the conference and the editing of this volume. The staff at Russell Sage—Lisa Kahraman, Angela Gloria, David Haproff, Genna Patacsil, and especially Suzanne Nichols—have been wonderful to work with at every turn. Finally, we thank the three anonymous reviewers whose critical but supportive comments greatly improved this book.

Bruce Western
Mary Pattillo
David Weiman

1 | Introduction

The growth of the U.S. penal system over the past twenty-five years has significantly altered the role of government in poor and minority communities. Between 1920 and 1975, the state and federal prison population totaled around .10 of 1 percent of the population. After half a century of stability in imprisonment, the incarceration rate increased in every single year from 1975 to 2001. At the beginning of the new millennium, the proportion of the U.S. population in prison had increased four-fold over twenty-five years. If jail inmates are also counted, the U.S. penal system incarcerated a total of .69 of 1 percent of the population in 2001 (Beck, Karberg, and Harrison 2002).

Despite the clear increase in carceral punishment, an incarceration rate of less than 1 percent may not suggest a major expansion of the role of government. Incarceration is highly concentrated, however. Nine out of ten prison inmates are male, most are under the age of forty, African Americans are seven times more likely than whites to be in prison, and nearly all prisoners lack any education beyond high school. Although less than 1 percent of the population was incarcerated in 2001, around 10 percent of black men in their late twenties were in prison. Incredibly, the prison and jail incarceration rate of young black men who have dropped out of high school exceeds 30 percent. Other research indicates that around 10 percent of recent cohorts of white male high school drop-outs and 30 percent of black noncollege men will go to prison at some time in their lives (Western and Pettit 2002).

In this volume we begin to assess the effects of the growth in the penal system. Because prisons now draw so widely from the bottom of the social hierarchy, we are challenged to view its effects quite broadly.

The contributors to this volume add to a burgeoning research agenda that studies the impact of incarceration not on crime but on family, community, and economic life. A focus on these effects places the prison in a wide social context, in which it is an increasingly important part of a uniquely American system of social inequality.

Our focus on the penal system's influences on the life chances of socially marginalized groups departs from previous research on incarceration. Historically, the watchtowers of the American penal system stood at the fringes, separating the most violent and incorrigible offenders from the rest of society. Although young minority men with little schooling had relatively high rates of incarceration, before the 1980s the penal system was not a dominant presence in disadvantaged neighborhoods. Criminal behavior, as officially recognized by the police, was much more unusual than poverty. The utter marginality of prisons and other carceral institutions shaped criminological and penological understanding of punishment.

From the criminological perspective, the penal system was significant chiefly in its connection to crime. Young men who were severely or persistently antisocial but not obviously mentally disordered would find their way into prisons and jails. For the most part, prisons housed extremely violent offenders, hardcore drug addicts, and career criminals—an underground guild of burglars, thieves, and hustlers. The similarly deviant character of crime and incarceration was underscored by the relative infrequency of both experiences.

The link between crime and incarceration was reflected in research and policy analysis. For ethnographers, prisons and juvenile halls were like skid rows and urban street corners in providing the backdrop for those engaged in a life of crime. Prison life was an extension of the criminal subculture that formed the context for crime on the outside (Sykes 1958; Irwin 1970; Cressey 1973). Prisoners inhabited a complex set of social roles that provided institutionalized versions of their social positions as criminal offenders. For the most part, the informal social life of the prisoners offered little hope for rehabilitation. Policy analysts, too, shared an interest in the effects of imprisonment on crime and were similarly pessimistic about former prisoners' chances of reintegration into mainstream society. Studies of prison programming—whether programs were designed to build literacy, teach job skills, or control addiction—focused on the likelihood of rearrest or return to incarceration (Glaser 1964; President's Commission on Law Enforcement and the Administration of Justice 1967). The apotheosis of pessimism in policy analysis was reached in the mid-1970s, when Douglas Lipton, Robert Martinson, and Judith Wilks (1975, 20) reviewed several hundred evaluations of correctional treatment and famously concluded that "rehabilitative efforts that have been reported so far have had no appreciable effects on recidivism."

Not all scholarly research viewed imprisonment as an undiluted consequence of deviant behavior. A sociology of punishment emphasized the state's active role in defining and controlling criminality (Becker 1963). What was deemed criminal and how public authority responded varied across times and places. The formal apparatus of social control, observed some students of punishment, was frequently directed by the powerful toward the weak, who were seen as threatening to the social order (Rusche and Kirchheimer 1939; Melossi and Pavarini 1981). For others, the contemporary organization of punishment was animated by the remedial outlook of a progressive state that combined an expert bureaucracy with democratic institutions. This progressive state aspired to correct social failure and contribute to social improvement (Rothman 1970; Jacobs 1977; Garland 1990). Whether the prison is viewed as an instrument of repression of the marginalized or the product of a progressive impulse, students of punishment see its basic shape as originating in a more fundamental set of social conflicts and institutions (Garland 1991).

Research in the fields of criminology and sociology provide different analyses, but they share a conception of the marginality of institutions of incarceration. In criminology, the prison is colored by many of the characteristics of criminal deviance. In the sociology of punishment, the prison is the product of underlying social structures and political developments.

For most of the twentieth century, this view of prisons as exotic institutions was justified by an incarceration rate that covered a small fraction of the population. The prison boom, however, has overtaken the usual social science analysis. Researchers now observe that incarceration is a pervasive event in the lives of poor and minority men. Punishment has become normalized, affecting large social groups rather than just the behaviorally distinctive deviants in the shadows of social life. Indeed, so great is the reach of the penal system that it is no longer epiphenomenal to some underlying balance of social power. Instead, the criminal justice system has now become a fixture in the passage to adulthood for minority youth with little economic opportunity.

The growth in the penal system thus poses distinctive challenges for criminology and the sociology of punishment. First, imprisonment is no longer a symptom of deviance; its sheer extent challenges us to think about incarceration as an increasingly normal event in the lives of young disadvantaged men. Second, the penal system is not just the product of an underlying balance of social power; its reach is so broad as to be a significant influence on the distribution of social power and large-scale patterns of social inequality. Both these observations inform the research in the following chapters.

The collective significance of the penal system is captured by David Garland's (2001, 2) term "mass imprisonment." In Garland's formulation, the incarceration rate is so high for some groups that its influence is felt not just by individuals but by broad demographic groups as well. A few researchers have connected the polarization of the American labor market to mass imprisonment. In an early statement of the broad influence of the criminal justice system, Richard Freeman (1991, 1) observes that "the magnitudes of incarceration, probation, and parole among black dropouts, in particular, suggest that crime has become an intrinsic part of the youth unemployment and poverty problem, rather than deviant behavior on the margin." Loic Wacquant (2000) argues that the prison, alongside the ghetto, has become a system of forced confinement that marginalizes minority communities from mainstream economic life. The U.S. penal system in the 1980s and 1990s has been described, along similar lines, as a state intervention in the labor market that increases race and class inequalities in earnings and employment (Western and Beckett 1999; Western and Pettit 2000).

The phenomenal growth in the prison system presents us with a novel set of research questions. The prison—and the supporting institutions of jail, probation, and parole—is now a large influence in poor and minority communities. Being poor or black is now more strongly predictive of having a criminal record than in the past. The gap between official crime and poverty has significantly closed. The penal system and criminal justice authorities, more generally, are becoming key points of contact between the government and socially marginal populations. While the government's role in the area of social control is expanding, public assistance and other social services for the poor are contracting. At the same time, income inequality is increasing, so those at the bottom of the social hierarchy are increasingly remote from those at the top. In an era of welfare state retrenchment and rising inequality, what is the effect of the increasing role of government in the lives of socially marginal populations through the criminal justice system?

Early indications are that the effects of increasing incarceration rates on families and communities may not be positive. Former prisoners have extreme difficulty finding stable and well-paying jobs (Western, Kling, and Weiman 2001). They encounter discrimination in labor markets and suffer from restricted eligibility for social services. These and other deficits add to incarceration's disruptive effect on family life, contributing to marital instability and separating parents from their children (Hagan and Dinovitzer 1999). Moreover, because prison and jail inmates tend to be disproportionately drawn from a small number of largely poor and minority communities, the collateral consequences of incarceration are highly spatially concentrated. The spatial concentration of incarceration is disruptive for the social networks of kin and friendship that typically promote economic opportunity and social stability.

Large pools of former inmates with few social supports, family attachments, or economic opportunities may ultimately increase crime rates more than they were lowered by the expansion of the penal system in the first place. At a minimum, a focus on the collateral consequences cautions us not to overstate the gains in public safety obtained from the prison boom. Indeed, if the crime produced by the prison boom in the current and subsequent generations exceeds the reductions in crime achieved through deterrence and incapacitation, the expansion of the penal system may turn out to be a self-defeating strategy for crime control.

TRENDS AND PATTERNS IN INCARCERATION

The novelty of the current period of mass incarceration can be seen in a long historical time series of prison incarceration rates. Figure 1.1 shows the number of state and federal prisoners per 100,000 of the U.S. population between 1925 and 2001. Before 1972, the prison incarceration rate exceeded 130 per 100,000 in just two years at the beginning of World War II. In the thirty years from 1972 to 2001, the prison incarceration rate rose from 93 to 470 per 100,000. In this same period the prison population increased from 196,000 to more than 1.3 million inmates.

Focusing just on the prison population understates the true level of incarceration because imprisonment figures ignore inmates incarcerated in local jails. Whereas state and federal prisons are usually reserved for felony offenders serving a year or more, local jails typically house offenders serving short sentences and defendants awaiting trial. Jail inmates account for about one-third of the total penal population. A long-time series for the jail population is not available, but data from 1980 to 2001 show that during that period the overall U.S. incarceration rate increased from 276 to about 688 per 100,000. By 2001 the American penal system incarcerated about 1.96 million prison and jail inmates.

The risks of incarceration, of course, are not distributed evenly across the population. Although the rate of incarceration among women has grown quickly, about 93 percent of prison and jail inmates are men. There are also large age, racial, and educational disparities in incarceration. This can be seen in table 1.1 which shows two different measures of the risks of incarceration for black and white men. First, we report the prison and jail incarceration rate—the percentage of the population incarcerated on an average day. Second, we report the cumulative risk of imprisonment—the likelihood that an individual was in state or federal

Figure 1.1   *State and Federal Incarceration, from 1925 to 2001*

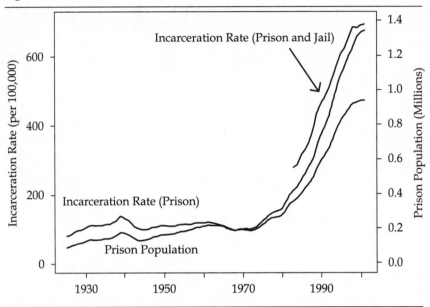

Source: Based on data from Pastore and Maguire (2002).
Note: The figure graphs incarceration rates (per 100,000 U.S. residents) in state and federal prisons from 1926 to 2000, incarceration rates (per 100,000 U.S. residents) in prisons and jails from 1980 to 1999, and the state and federal prison population from 1925 to 2001.

prison, in this case, at the age of thirty to thirty-four. Table 1.1 shows that 7.9 percent of working-age black men were in prison or jail on an average day in 1999 compared with just 1.0 percent of working-age white men. The incarceration rates are higher for younger men, aged twenty-two to thirty, but racial disparity in imprisonment, indicated in the last column, is approximately the same for this group as for working-age men as a whole. Part of the racial disparity in imprisonment derives from race differences in education. Incarceration rates for young high school dropouts shows significantly less disparity than for the population as a whole. Together, race, age, and education generate extremely high incarceration rates for young unskilled black men, more than 30 percent of whom were in prison or jail on an average day in 1999.

The lower panel in table 1.1 expresses the risk of incarceration as the percentage of men born from 1965 to 1969 who by 1999 had ever spent time in state or federal prison. Racial disparities in this cumulative risk of imprisonment are similar to those for prison and jail incarceration.

Table 1.1   *Prison and Jail Incarceration Rates and Cumulative Risks of Imprisonment for Young Men (Percentage)*

	White	Black	Black to White Ratio
In prison or jail			
Adults, aged eighteen to sixty-five	1.0	7.9	7.9
Young adults, aged twenty-two to thirty	1.6	11.6	7.3
Young adult high school dropouts	6.7	32.4	4.8
Risk of imprisonment for young men			
All	2.9	10.6	3.7
With high school diploma or GED	3.6	18.4	5.1
High school dropouts	11.2	58.9	5.3

Source: Percentage in prison or jail is based on Western, Kleykamp, and Rosenfeld (2004); risk of imprisonment is based on Pettit and Western (2004).
Note: "Young men" are defined as those born from 1965 to 1969 and consequently aged thirty to thirty-four in 1999.

Nearly one in five black male high school graduates in their early thirties in 1999 were likely to have a prison record, five times the figure for white men with the same schooling. At the bottom of the education distribution among high school dropouts, one in nine whites and more than half of all blacks have prison records. Prison time has become a modal life experience among young unskilled black men and reasonably common among young unskilled whites.

In sum, the high rates of incarceration currently seen are unprecedented in recent American history. Incarceration is now pervasive among young black men with little schooling. Indeed, because the experience of going to prison or jail is so strongly stratified by education, young white men with little education also face a high risk of early incarceration.

INCARCERATION AND FAMILY LIFE

The effects of incarceration on children and families are potentially far-reaching. The extent of these effects, however, depends on how closely criminal offenders are linked to their spouses and their children. If men are completely absent from the households of their spouses or children, incarceration's effects on family may be negligible. We examine these links by estimating marriage rates among men with children in state prison. The marital status of male state prisoners with children is reported in table 1.2. Among state prisoners, who account for 90 percent of the total prison

Table 1.2   *Marital Status of Fathers in State Prison and the
Noninstitutional Population, 1986 and 1997 (Percentage)*

	1986		1997	
	Prison Population	General Population	Prison Population	General Population
White				
Married	33.3	89.3	25.0	88.5
Divorced	39.1	2.3	39.4	3.5
Never married	17.3	7.5	26.7	6.9
Black				
Married	24.5	76.1	18.7	72.2
Divorced	12.7	2.3	11.4	4.1
Never married	53.4	19.6	62.7	20.1
Hispanic				
Married	40.8	84.9	32.5	79.8
Divorced	21.4	1.9	15.8	1.8
Never married	28.2	12.5	41.0	17.1

Source: Based on data from U.S. Department of Justice (1986, 1997). General population figures for fathers are based on data from the 1986 and 1997 March Current Population Surveys, for fathers aged twenty to forty-five (Freenberg and Roth 2001).

population, fathers have very low marriage rates compared with the general population. In 1986 only a third of white prison inmates with children were married compared with nearly 90 percent of white fathers in the general population. Among the unmarried white fathers in state prison, nearly 40 percent were divorced, about twenty times the percentage divorced in the general population. Among African American fathers, only a quarter of those in state prison were married in 1986, compared with more than three-quarters in the general population. Unlike whites, unmarried blacks were much more likely never to have been married rather than to be divorced. Indeed, more than half of all black fathers in state prison had never been married. Marriage rates are highest for Hispanic fathers in state prison, 40 percent of whom were married in 1986.

By 1997 the family attachments of male prisoners were significantly weaker than they had been in 1986. Marriage rates among fathers had widely fallen. Only a quarter of white fathers in state prison were married. Marriage rates also fell among whites in federal prison, a group for whom marriage rates were relatively high. A similar pattern can be seen for African American men. Fewer than one in five black male prisoners

Table 1.3   *U.S. Children with a Parent in State or Federal Prison, by Race-Ethnicity (Estimate)*

	1986	1991	1997	2000
Total				
Number (thousands)	563	929	1,366	1,526
Percentage of all children	0.9	1.3	2.0	2.2
White				
Number (thousands)	180	264	353	428
Percentage of all white children	0.4	0.6	0.7	1.0
Black				
Number (thousands)	274	456	702	795
Percentage of all black children	2.9	4.4	6.9	7.5
Hispanic				
Number (thousands)	94	185	271	281
Percentage of all Hispanic children	1.4	2.1	2.6	2.3

Source: Based on data from U.S. Department of Justice (1986, 1991, 1997); U.S. Department of Commerce (2001).
Note: The data are for children under the age of eighteen.

with children was married in 1997. Around 60 percent of black fathers in state prison had never been married. Although Hispanics had the highest marriage rates among the three race groups, by 1997 their rates had also decreased: fewer than a third of Hispanic state prisoners who were fathers were married.

The extent of the effects of incarceration on children can be gauged by estimating the number of children with parents in prison. We created these estimates using survey data on correctional facilities in which prison inmates were asked about their children under the age of eighteen. Combining these data with census figures, we estimated the number of children with parents in state or federal prison at four points from 1986 to 2000 (table 1.3). In the mid-1980s, more than half a million children had a parent in prison. By 2000 this number had grown to more than 1.5 million, or 2.2 percent of all children in the United States. Because of the large racial disparity in incarceration rates, parental absence through incarceration is concentrated among African Americans. Our estimates indicate that more than half of all children with imprisoned parents are black, and by 2000 about 7.5 percent of black children had a parent in prison. Rates of parental imprisonment are also relatively high for Hispanics: in 2000 approximately one Hispanic child in forty had a parent serving time in prison.

Table 1.4   *Inmate Fathers Living with Their Children at Time of Father's Admission to State or Federal Prison, by Race-Ethnicity of Father, 1986 and 1997 (Percentage)*

	1986		1997	
	State Prison	Federal Prison	State Prison	Federal Prison
White	51.3	—	44.9	61.5
Black	48.1	—	40.7	46.6
Hispanic	56.5	—	50.0	62.2

Source: Based on data from U.S. Department of Justice (1986, 1991, 1997).
Note: No data available for 1986 federal prison count.

The effect of incarcerating a growing number of parents may be small if criminal offenders are not living with or do not contribute to the well-being of their children. Table 1.4 shows the living arrangements of male prisoners with children at the time of their admission to prison. In 1986 about one-half of all fathers admitted into the state prison system were living with at least one of their children at the time of incarceration. This proportion is roughly the same for all race and ethnic groups, although rates of father residence are a little higher for Hispanics than for blacks or whites. By 1997 the presence of fathers in their children's households at the time of prison admission had fallen. About 45 percent of white and 41 percent of black fathers in state prison in 1997 were living with their children at the time they were incarcerated. This increase in father absence follows the rise in the number of female-headed households observed in the general population over this same twelve-year period (Ellwood and Jencks 2001). Where are the children of incarcerated fathers living? In nine out of ten cases, these children are living with their mothers. This pattern varies little across race or ethnic groups and has changed little over time.

Even though large numbers of children are separated from their incarcerated parents, many retain contact while the parents are in prison (table 1.5). The Surveys of Inmates in State and Federal Correctional Facilities record contact between prisoners and their children through mail, phone calls, and visits (U.S. Department of Justice 1986, 1991, 1997). Nearly half of all incarcerated parents have some kind of regular contact with their children. Most commonly, prisoners receive phone calls or mail. Consistent with other patterns, prisoners in federal facilities, who tend to be older and more educated, have closer links with their children than state prisoners. The surveys also show that only 20 to 25 percent of

Table 1.5   *Monthly Contact Between Fathers in State and Federal Prison and Their Children, by Race-Ethnicity of Father and Type of Contact, 1991 and 1997 (Percentage)*

	1991		1997	
	State Prison	Federal Prison	State Prison	Federal Prison
White				
Receives phone calls	37.5	70.8	36.0	72.9
Receives mail	47.4	68.4	46.9	63.6
Receives visits	21.4	27.2	19.3	26.5
Black				
Receives phone calls	55.4	69.5	50.4	77.3
Receives mail	56.3	66.8	53.2	66.2
Receives visits	26.1	23.5	23.3	25.9
Hispanic				
Receives phone calls	42.7	65.4	33.1	67.0
Receives mail	53.5	71.9	50.3	66.0
Receives visits	19.1	22.3	21.5	20.4

Source: Based on data from U.S. Department of Justice (1991, 1997).

prisoners regularly receive visits from their children while they are in prison. In part this is because many prisons are located in regions remote from the urban centers that supply most of the felony offenders to the penal system.

Many of these introductory descriptive statistics are further probed in later chapters of this book in attempts to uncover causal relationships and to connect incarceration to the institutions of family, community, and the labor market. Yet at this general level, the magnitude of this state intervention and the ramifications for myriad realms of social, economic, and political life are apparent.

PLAN OF THE BOOK

The unifying goal of this volume is to move beyond thinking of incarceration as merely punishment and to place it instead within a larger system of social stratification and institutional relations. Recognizing the simultaneous identities of prisoners (and former prisoners) as fathers and mothers, sons and daughters, spouses, neighborhood residents, workers, and indeed citizens demands an examination of the consequences of the incarceration experience for the fulfillment of those other roles. In addition to studying the effects on individuals, scholarship must interrogate the impact that our mass incarceration policy has on other facets of society, such as citizenship rights or the labor market.

To best achieve these goals we decided that the book must be empirically based, interdisciplinary, and multimethod. First, the concrete exposition of the far-reaching effects of incarceration through the use and analysis of empirical data is crucial to broadening the scholarly and public understanding of contemporary policy decisions. By bringing together leading researchers studying the connections between incarceration and processes such as family formation, unemployment, and community well-being, this volume endeavors to build a foundation of empirical knowledge that will inform public deliberations and generate further questions and debates about approaches to crime and the treatment of marginal groups more broadly. Building such a knowledge base requires input from multiple fields. The contributors to this volume come from economics, criminal justice, psychology, sociology, and social work and hence provide a range of vantage points that require readers (even initiated researchers, practitioners, and advocates) to consider new questions, entertain new hypotheses, and ultimately raise new challenges. Finally, and as a result of this interdisciplinarity, the authors in this volume employ a wide range of methods, spanning the qualitative and quantitative spectrum. They use innovative data sets collected at various levels of generality, from one field site to multiple cities to the nation. Such diversity is necessary for understanding large-scale causal connections as well as particular human stories.

The book is divided into two parts: families and communities. These categories denote the general context within which incarcerees are considered by the contributors, but each of these sections is, in reality, broader than the heading conveys. As the world is not so cleanly organized—families live in communities, and communities are made up of families—and the term "communities" can be used at the neighborhood, city, or even metropolitan level, the authors' analyses and discussions are also not completely constrained by these conceptual divisions. Ultimately, these categories indicate a growing level of specificity from the dyadic spousal-partner relationship to the institutional level of the child welfare system to a more macro-level labor market.

Part I begins with several chapters exploring the effects of incarceration on the ties between parents and between parents and their children. In chapter 2, Bruce Western, Leonard Lopoo, and Sara McLanahan ask the question, "Does incarceration weaken parental bonds?" Using the pioneering Fragile Families and Child Wellbeing Study (McLanahan et al. 2001)—which first interviewed new mothers and fathers at the hospital after the birth of their child and then conducted follow-up interviews twelve months later—the authors find significant and sizable negative effects of incarceration on the probability of marriage and significant but less strong negative effects on the probability of cohabitation. When they estimate the aggregate effects of incarceration on marriage rates in the general population (using Current Population Survey data), they show that the gap in marriage between African American and white men would decline by about 20 percent if the incarceration risk were zero, and by even more for less educated men. The authors are cognizant of the reasons why men who have been incarcerated, along with those who share similar characteristics but have not been incarcerated, may not be attractive marriage partners for women. Yet they also consider the vicious cycle whereby incarceration exacerbates and increases such deficits as antisocial behavior and economic hardship among men, thereby further reducing marriage, which is known to have a deterrent effect on criminal offending.

Deterrence and desistance are the topics of chapter 3 by Kathryn Edin, Timothy Nelson, and Rechelle Paranal, who shift the emphasis from spousal-partner bonds to bonds between fathers and children. Using in-depth life histories of low-skilled, low-income men in Philadelphia, Pennsylvania, and Charleston, South Carolina, the authors explore whether the experience of becoming a father has an impact on men's criminal involvement and whether incarceration has a subsequent impact on fathering behaviors and relationships. With vivid detail and emotion, the men interviewed in this research convey the difficulty in fulfilling their role as father (a role that few take lightly) when they have limited earning potential. The authors describe three pathways taken by such men. For one group, fatherhood is such an intense turning point that it moves them to desist from crime rather than run the risk of imprisonment and ultimate separation from their children. For others who have formed early bonds with their children but do not turn from crime—sometimes because they are supplementing legal employment or because they see crime as their only means of financial maintenance—incarceration is a devastating event, essentially severing paternal bonds and irrevocably souring the relationship between fathers and mothers. Finally, a small group of mainly older fathers, whose relationships with their children had been destroyed before their incarceration, have used the prison experience to reorient their lives and reconnect with their children. Edin, Nelson, and Paranal conclude by emphasizing the thread that runs through these stories: the lack of societal attention to endemic problems (unstable job prospects, substance abuse, and so on) faced by these men and their families.

Continuing the investigation of fatherhood, Anne Nurse focuses in chapter 4 on juvenile offenders and the effect of incarceration on fulfillment of their fathering role. In California, where Nurse conducted her survey, interviews, and observations of paroled juveniles, 25 percent of the state's juvenile wards are fathers. Nurse shows that the quality of the father-child bond is highly determined by the children's mothers, and hence the character of the father-mother relationship is at the center of this chapter. Conflictual relationships between mothers and fathers documented in chapter 3 are equally apparent, and indeed magnified, in the research by Nurse, who documents the volatility of youthful courtship. Such unstable and mistrustful interactions—which moreover include the presence of mothers' new boyfriends and extended family members—exacerbated by an incarceration-related absence all but thwart fathers' attempts to connect with their children. Given the possibility for earlier intervention among this population, Nurse proposes programs that focus on reducing the number of juvenile incarcerees, lessening the length of their absence, and building their capacity for fathering in cooperation with the mother and her family.

Interested in the well-being of families from a social services perspective, Elizabeth Johnson and Jane Waldfogel, in chapter 5, ask the following questions: What risk factors are present in the lives of incarcerated parents and their children? Do these risk factors predict where a child is placed during parental incarceration? Are some living arrangements for children more vulnerable than others? Using data from the 1997 Surveys of Inmates, Johnson and Waldfogel identify eight risk factors that have been shown in previous research to impact child development (for example, low parental education, parental substance abuse, and whether parents' parent had ever been incarcerated). The authors study the impact on children's living arrangements of these risks separately and cumulatively through the use of a multiple risk score. They show that, controlling for demographic characteristics of inmates, the more risks a child has been exposed to, the more likely it is that he or she will be placed in the care of someone other than the other parent (a grandparent, foster care, or other arrangement). Of the eight risk factors, the most consistent predictors of a child's placement with someone other than the other parent, for children of either incarcerated mothers or fathers, is parents' low education, welfare receipt, and, to a lesser extent, parent's having been sexually or physically abused. Regarding gender differences among incarcerated parents, the authors show that children whose mothers go to prison are likely to have more intense service needs than those whose fathers are imprisoned. The authors show empirically that children in foster care face particularly elevated risk and discuss service approaches for this population.

Part II analyzes the impacts of mass incarceration on the organization and functioning of communities. The authors of these chapters conceive of community—that is, the relationships and organizations that structure local social interactions—at two distinct levels. The first level refers to the informal ties and affiliations among neighbors that contribute to social order in communities, sometimes in conjunction with state authorities. The second level corresponds to the political and economic relationships of voting and employment that formally incorporate citizens into the extended collectivities of the labor market and the polity. Communities of neighbors, on the one hand, and workers and voters, on the other, provide the informal social control and stakes in conformity that underlie public safety. To the extent that prisons marginalize rather than reintegrate criminal offenders, the social cohesion and crime-preventive effects of these communities may be weakened.

In chapter 6, James Lynch and William Sabol elaborate and test for the unintended consequences of mass incarceration on the social cohesion of communities and ultimately their levels of public safety. For theoretical inspiration, they draw on the classical sociological literature on social order, especially as it has been updated and revised by Dina Rose and Todd Clear. According to Rose and Clear, high levels of incarceration may ultimately lead to more crime, not less, because of incarceration's "disorganizing" effects. Focusing on Baltimore neighborhoods, Lynch and Sabol assemble a rich data set that includes individual survey evidence tracking, for example, the effect of neighborhood solidarity and interactions and general neighborhood characteristics on arrests, prison admissions, and vacant homes. To test the reciprocal links between incarceration and crime as well as the connections between crime and social order, they estimate increasingly more elaborate statistical models. Using drug arrests to capture the independent influences of higher incarceration rates, for example, they find a negative correlation between crime and imprisonment rates, consistent with the conventional theory of deterrence. At the same time, controlling for neighborhood effects, the authors show that high rates of incarceration may weaken community solidarity, a critical basis of informal social control.

Chapters 7 and 8 move the discussion from the grassroots communities of neighbors to the more formal communities of citizens and workers. Forty-eight of the fifty states bar inmates from voting, thirty-seven bar either parolees or probationers, and thirteen bar various categories of former felons. This totals 4.7 million disfranchised felons and former felons nationally. In chapter 7, Christopher Uggen and Jeff Manza ask the question, what political viewpoints and votes are lost by the exclusion of inmates and some former inmates from this most basic right of citizenship? The authors use a mixed-method design, combining data from a panel survey of youth in St. Paul, Minnesota, and semistructured interviews with more than thirty convicted felons in Minnesota. The quantitative evidence shows that those who have been arrested or incar-

cerated are more distrusting of government, feel less politically effica-
cious, and are less likely to talk with friends, relatives, or spouses about
politics. As expected, having been arrested or incarcerated substantially
suppresses the likelihood of having voted in past elections and having
plans to vote in future elections. The qualitative data allow felons to speak
for themselves on politics, government, and public policy, and the authors
find that being unable to vote is a salient issue for many respondents.
Moreover, despite survey evidence that they discussed politics less frequently, respondents held articulate political views. Uggen and Manza's
conclusion echoes their chapter title: Something is lost when inmates and
former incarcerees are legislated out of the body politic.

In chapter 8, Harry Holzer, Steven Raphael, and Michael Stoll examine the pathways from prison to the labor market from the perspective
of potential employers. The authors observe that employers may be reluctant to hire released prisoners, even those possessing the requisite
skills and experience for the job. To ascertain which types of establishments and jobs are open to those with a prison record, they analyze the
Multi-City survey of firms in the early 1990s and follow-up surveys at
the end of the decade. The surveys offer a unique glimpse into the demand side of local labor markets at both the neighborhood and city levels. From the original surveys the authors detail the characteristics of
establishments that will and will not hire released prisoners in terms of
their size, industrial and spatial location, and hiring practices. From the
follow-up surveys, the authors also gauge whether business cycle conditions significantly altered firms' willingness to hire released prisoners.
As a synthesis of their results, Holzer, Raphael, and Stoll offer an implicit
test of the racial profiling hypothesis and estimate the potential mismatch between the demands for and supplies of released prisoners annually. Their results raise serious concerns about the employability of most
released prisoners, at least in formal labor markets, but also about the
reliability of private sources of information on criminal backgrounds.

The final essay by Jeremy Travis concludes the volume by elaborat-
ing the implications of the preceding chapters for corrections and criminal justice policies more generally. Citing the "iron law of corrections"—
the inexorable connection between admissions to and releases from
prisons—Travis insists that corrections policy must extend beyond prison
walls and encompass the complex, thorny path of prisoners' reentry and
reintegration into their families, communities, and the labor market. This
broader perspective is especially critical under the current criminal justice
regime, not only because of the greater numbers involved but also because
of their spatial concentration in disadvantaged urban neighborhoods,
longer prison spells, and more limited preparation for release. To avoid
the costly vicious cycle of incarceration and recidivism as well as to en-

hance public safety, Travis proposes greater collaboration between prison officials and those in child and family welfare services, educational and job-training programs, and mental and public health agencies. In other words, Travis advocates a new take on corrections policy, which he sees as part and parcel of social policy. In so doing, he affirms our central premise of the ubiquitous impact of prison experience on low-income minority individuals, families, and neighborhoods.

Preparation for this introduction was supported by grants from the Russell Sage Foundation and National Science Foundation grant SES-0004336. Jake Rosenfeld provided invaluable research assistance.

REFERENCES

Beck, Allen J., Jennifer C. Karberg, and Paige M. Harrison. 2002. "Prison and Jail Inmates at Midyear 2001." *Bureau of Justice Statistics Bulletin* (April). NCJ 191702. Washington: U.S. Department of Justice.

Becker, Howard. 1963. *The Outsiders: Studies in the Sociology of Deviance.* London: Free Press of Glencoe.

Cressey, Donald R. 1973. "Adult Felons in Prison." In *Prisoners in America,* edited by Lloyd Ohlin. Englewood Cliffs, N.J.: Prentice-Hall.

Ellwood, David T., and Christopher Jencks. 2001. "The Growing Difference in Family Structure: What Do We Know? Where Do We Look for Answers?" Unpublished paper. Harvard University.

Freeman, Richard. 1991. "Crime and the Employment of Disadvantaged Youths." Working paper 3875. Cambridge, Mass.: National Bureau of Economic Research.

Garland, David. 1990. *Punishment and Modern Society: A Study in Social Theory.* Chicago: University of Chicago Press.

———. 1991. "Sociological Perspectives on Punishment." *Crime and Justice* 14: 115–65.

———, ed. 2001. *Mass Imprisonment: Social Causes and Consequences.* Thousand Oaks, Calif.: Sage.

Glaser, Daniel. 1964. *The Effectiveness of a Prison and Parole System.* Indianapolis, Ind.: Bobbs-Merrill.

Hagan, John, and Ronit Dinovitzer. 1999. "Collateral Consequences of Imprisonment for Children, Communities, and Prisoners." In *Prisons: Crime and Justice,* vol. 26, edited by Michael Tonry and Joan Petersilia. Chicago: University of Chicago Press.

Irwin, John. 1970. *The Felon.* Englewood Cliffs, N.J.: Prentice-Hall.

Jacobs, James B. 1977. *Stateville: The Penitentiary in Mass Society.* Chicago: University of Chicago Press.

Lipton, Douglas, Robert Martinson, and Judith Wilks. 1975. *The Effectiveness of Correctional Treatment: A Survey of Treatment Evaluation Studies.* New York: Praeger.

McLanahan, Sara, Irwin Garfinkel, Nancy E. Reichman, Julien Teitler, Marcia Carlson, and Christina Norland Audigier. 2001. *The Fragile Families and Child Wellbeing Study: National Baseline Report.* Princeton, N.J.: Bendheim Thomas Center for Research on Child Wellbeing.

Melossi, Dario, and Massimo Pavarini. 1981. *The Prison and the Factory: Origins of the Penitentiary System.* Totowa, N.J.: Barnes and Noble Books.

Pastore, Ann L., and Kathleen Maguire, eds. 2002. *Sourcebook of Criminal Justice Statistics, 2001.* Washington: U.S. Department of Justice.

Pettit, Becky, and Bruce Western. 2004. "Mass Imprisonment and the Life Course: Race and Class Inequality in U.S. Incarceration." *American Sociological Review* 69: n.p.

President's Commission on Law Enforcement and the Administration of Justice. 1967. *The Challenge of Crime in a Free Society.* Washington: U.S. Government Printing Office.

Rothman, David J. 1970. *The Discovery of the Asylum: Social Order and Disorder in the New Republic.* Boston: Little, Brown.

Rusche, Georg, and Otto Kirchheimer. 1939. *Punishment and Social Structure.* New York: Russell and Russell.

Sykes, Gresham M. 1958. *The Society of Captives: A Study of a Maximum Security Prison.* Princeton, N.J.: Princeton University Press.

U.S. Department of Commerce, Bureau of the Census. 2001. *Current Population Survey: Merged Outgoing Rotation Group File, 1979–2000* [MRDF]. Cambridge, Mass.: National Bureau of Economic Research.

U.S. Department of Justice, Bureau of Justice Statistics. 1986. *Surveys of Inmates in State and Federal Correctional Facilities* [MRDF]. Ann Arbor, Mich.: Inter-university Consortium for Social and Political Research.

———. 1991. *Surveys of Inmates in State and Federal Correctional Facilities* [MRDF]. Ann Arbor, Mich.: Inter-university Consortium for Social and Political Research.

———. 1997. *Surveys of Inmates in State and Federal Correctional Facilities* [MRDF]. Ann Arbor, Mich.: Inter-university Consortium for Social and Political Research.

Wacquant, Loic. 2000. "The New 'Peculiar Institution': On the Prison as a Surrogate Ghetto." *Theoretical Criminology* 4(3): 377–89.

Western, Bruce, and Katherine Beckett. 1999. "How Unregulated Is the U.S. Labor Market? The Penal System as a Labor Market Institution." *American Journal of Sociology* 104(4): 1030–60.

Western, Bruce, Meredith Kleykamp, and Jake Rosenfeld. 2004. "Crime, Punishment, and American Inequality." In *Social Inequality*, edited by Kathryn Neckerman. New York: Russell Sage Foundation.

Western, Bruce, Jeffrey R. Kling, and David F. Weiman. 2001. "The Labor Market Consequences of Incarceration." *Crime and Delinquency* 47(3): 410–27.

Western, Bruce, and Becky Pettit. 2000. "Incarceration and Racial Inequality in Men's Employment." *Industrial and Labor Relations Review* 54(1): 3–16.

———. 2002. "Beyond Crime and Punishment: Prisons and Inequality." *Contexts* 1(3, September): 37–43.

Western, Bruce, Becky Pettit, and Josh Guetzkow. 2002. "Black Economic Progress in the Era of Mass Imprisonment." In *Collateral Damage: The Social Cost of Mass Incarceration*, edited by Meda Chesney-Lind and Marc Mauer. New York: Free Press.

PART I

Families

Bruce Western
Leonard M. Lopoo
Sara McLanahan

Incarceration and the Bonds Between Parents in Fragile Families

2

The family life of the poor has changed dramatically over the past thirty years. Since 1970, rates of divorce have increased by about one-third (U.S. Department of Commerce 2001, 87) and rates of nonmarital childbearing have roughly doubled (McLanahan and Casper 1995, 11). Consequently, the proportion of single parents in the population increased substantially. Among white women aged twenty-five to thirty-four in the lowest third of the education distribution, about 8 percent were single parents in 1965 as compared with 19 percent in 2000. Race differences are striking. Among black women aged twenty-five to thirty-four with the same level of education, the proportion of single parents increased from 29 to more than 50 percent in the thirty-five years from 1965 to 2000 (Ellwood and Jencks 2001).

Growth in the number of single-parent families was matched by rapid growth in the size of the male penal population. The prison population, numbering 200,000 in 1974, increased to 1.33 million by 2001 (Mauer 1999, 20; Beck, Karberg, and Harrison 2002, 1). Adding jail inmates to these figures yields a total penal population of 1.97 million inmates. These aggregate figures conceal substantial race and class inequality. Incarceration rates for African Americans are about seven times higher than those for whites. Men who have no schooling beyond high school are about six times more likely to be in prison than men who have some college education (Western and Pettit 2002).

Because incarceration is concentrated among young, poorly educated minority men, the growth in the prison population over the past twenty years emerges as a suspect in explaining, at least in part, the growing number of single-parent families in disadvantaged communities. Incarceration is likely to influence the formation of single-parent families directly by separating children from fathers who are serving time in prison or jail. Incarceration also contributes to marital strain and makes male former inmates unattractive partners for unmarried women, weakening bonds among parents after release.

The analysis presented in this chapter uses a unique data source, the Fragile Families and Child Wellbeing Study, to investigate the likelihood that a couple is married or cohabiting twelve months after the birth of their child (McLanahan et al. 2001). As the name of our survey data suggests, we study fragile families—defined as unmarried parents who are planning to raise their child together. Because the study is based on a sample of nonmarital births in urban areas (and a smaller comparison sample of births to married couples), the survey respondents are disproportionately poor, black or Hispanic, and involved in the criminal justice system.

Unusually, the Fragile Families data include information from both the mothers and the fathers in the survey, providing two key advantages for studying the effects of incarceration. First, men with prison or jail records are likely to be underrepresented in social survey analysis, and the Fragile Families design allows us to learn about these men by interviewing the mothers of their children. Second, self-reports of criminal activity and incarceration status may understate respondents' involvement in crime and the criminal justice system. Again, the mothers' reports of fathers' criminal justice status fills an important gap in the survey information about a hard-to-study fraction of the population.

DOES INCARCERATION WEAKEN PARENTAL BONDS?

Little is known about the causal relationship between incarceration and relationships between couples who have had a child together, in part because relatively few studies of prisoners' families have been conducted (Hagan and Dinovitzer 1999; Gabel 1992). Earlier research connecting families and crime focuses on the parental origins of offenders. For example, James Q. Wilson and Richard Herrnstein (1985) have studied the heritability of criminal behavior (see also West and Farrington 1973). John Hagan and Alberto Palloni (1990) examine whether failed parenting causes character problems in children leading to delinquency and crime. Focusing on adult relationships, some researchers find that the social bonds of marriage reduce the risk of crime and incarceration (Horney, Osgood, and Marshall 1995; Laub, Nagin, and Sampson 1998). Common to all this research is the presumption that family life affects criminal offending. Few researchers have examined whether causality flows in the other direction—whether involvement in the criminal justice system affects family relationships.

Research reported in this volume by Kathryn Edin, Timothy Nelson, and Rechelle Paranal (chapter 3) and Anne Nurse (chapter 4) helps fill the gap by reporting on the family relationships of men with incarceration records. Field research by Edin, Nelson, and Paranal on formerly imprisoned, unskilled and semiskilled men in Philadelphia and Charleston investigates the impact of imprisonment on fathers' relationships with their children and with the mothers of their children. Their evidence suggests that incarceration harms these relationships if the father has moderate to strong family ties. Edin and her colleagues report that nearly all of the relationships between the men and the mothers of their children were dissolved over the period of internment.[1] Even among those couples that remained together, missing many of the milestones in the child's life diminished the strength of the couple's bond. Nurse's study of juvenile offenders in California also points to the difficulties faced by an inmate in maintaining partnership with the mother of his children. Nurse finds that long periods of separation allow women to form other romantic attachments that prevent inmate fathers from reuniting with their families after release.

This ethnographic research suggests that the decision of low-income mothers to marry or remarry depends in part on the economic prospects, social respectability, and trustworthiness of their potential partners. Incarceration undermines all these qualities. Labor market research shows that male former inmates earn less and experience more unemployment than comparable men who have not been to prison or jail (Western, Kling, and Weiman 2001). If former inmates are stuck in low-wage or unstable jobs, their opportunities for marriage will most likely be limited. Other ethnographic research finds that the stigma of incarceration makes single mothers reluctant to marry or live with the fathers of their children if those fathers have prison or jail records (Edin 2000; Waller 1996). Ecological analysis yields similar results. William Sabol and James Lynch (1998) report that large numbers of female-headed families are found in counties receiving the most returning prisoners. In short, the stigma and collateral consequences of incarceration shrink the pool of desirable marriage partners.

Incarceration is also destabilizing for intact relationships. The experience of imprisonment can produce strong feelings of shame and anger, both for inmates and their families, providing a source of marital stress after release (Hagan and Dinovitzer 1999, 126–27). The stigma of incarceration may be diminished in communities with high incarceration rates, but prison or jail time is still massively disruptive. Research on veterans finds that long periods of enforced separation during military service significantly raise the risk of divorce (for example, Pavalko and Elder 1990). We expect that prison and jail inmates experience similar effects. Other chapters in this volume also point to the civil disabilities associated with a felony record. Besides facing restricted voting rights, former felons are often barred from public housing and are ineligible for welfare benefits (Hirsch et al. 2002). Bars on public housing and welfare benefits create significant impediments to the formation of stable unions among poor couples. Furthermore, to the extent that incarceration raises involvement in crime or retains former inmates in crime-involved peer networks, marriage and parental relationships will also be strained.

Although theory indicates that incarceration negatively affects family relationships, the marriage prospects of criminal offenders are poor even without imprisonment. Elizabeth Johnson and Jane Waldfogel's report on the status of children of incarcerated parents (chapter 5 in this volume) indicates that the families of prison and jail inmates are under considerable stress. Men who become involved in crime may be egocentric, have little self-control, and have weak social connections to stable family and economic life. All of these characteristics would make a man an unattractive partner for women and undermine a man's commitment to a stable relationship, even in the absence of a prison record. Moreover, crime-involved men may be relatively attractive partners for antisocial women, perhaps increasing the risks of divorce or separation even further (Krueger et al. 1998). In the data analyzed in this chapter, couples are also observed at different stages in their relationships, and the risks of divorce or separation tend to vary with the vintage of the relationship. Unobserved characteristics that are associated with the putative consequences of incarceration provide a key challenge to an assessment of incarceration's effects. If we fail to consider the influence of variables correlated with incarceration and marriage or cohabitation, our estimates of the incarceration effect will be biased. In sum, there are good reasons to think that incarceration erodes marital relationships, but to understand the effects of incarceration we must acknowledge that criminal offenders are relatively unlikely to form stable unions in the first place.

THE FRAGILE FAMILIES DATA

The Fragile Families and Child Wellbeing Study is a nationally representative longitudinal survey of new (mostly unmarried) parents and their children. Data were collected in twenty U.S. cities, stratified by different labor market conditions and varying welfare and child-support policy regimes. Unmarried parents were oversampled by a ratio of about three to one. The total sample size is approximately forty-nine hundred families, comprising thirty-seven hundred unmarried couples and almost twelve hundred married couples. The weighted data are representative of all births to parents residing in cities with populations of more than two hundred thousand. New mothers were first interviewed at the hospital, within forty-eight hours of giving birth. About 60 percent of fathers were also interviewed in the hospital, and another 15 percent were interviewed soon after the child left the hospital.

Baseline data were collected from 1999 to 2001. Response rates were 87 percent for unwed mothers, 82 percent for married mothers, 88 percent for married fathers, and 75 percent for unmarried fathers. We also make use of the first-year follow-up survey, which also had high response rates: among parents who participated in the baseline survey, about 90 percent of unmarried mothers, 92 percent of married mothers, 86 percent of married fathers, and 78 percent of unmarried fathers participated in the follow-up interview.

The design of the Fragile Families Study has several benefits for examining the relationship between fathers' incarceration and family relationships. By following fathers as well as mothers, the capabilities and experiences (including incarceration) of fathers can be studied directly, and relationships between fathers and mothers can be studied from two points of view. In our analysis we study the effects of characteristics of mothers and fathers and the relationship between them.

COHABITATION AND MARRIAGE IN FRAGILE FAMILIES

The Fragile Families survey provides detailed information about the status of new parents' relationships. In addition to marital status, the survey records whether the parents are living together and, if not living together, whether they remain on romantic or friendly terms. This information is recorded at the baseline interview, when the child is born, and again at the follow-up interview twelve months later. Because our interest centers on the stability of parental relationships, we examine patterns of marriage and cohabitation at the follow-up interview, controlling for a couple's relationship status one year earlier.

Table 2.1 reports descriptive statistics on relationship status by the race-ethnicity of the father. The table shows strong race and ethnic differences in marriage rates.[2] Only 19 percent of African American fathers are married at the follow-up interview compared with 33.7 percent of Hispanics and 60.9 percent of whites.[3] African American fathers are also involved in less stable relationships over the twelve months from baseline to follow-up. A third of cohabiting couples with black fathers had dissolved within a year of their child's birth, compared with around 20 percent among other couples. Separation rates for married couples, although low, were also relatively high among black fathers.

INCARCERATION IN FRAGILE FAMILIES

In addition to collecting information about marriage and cohabitation, the Fragile Families survey recorded information on fathers' contacts

Table 2.1   *Relationship Status at Twelve-Month Follow-Up Interview,
by Relationship Status at Baseline Interview and Father's
Race-Ethnicity, 1999 to 2001*

Follow-Up Status	Baseline Status			Total at Follow-Up
	Nonresident	Cohabiting	Married	
African American				
Nonresident (percentage)	74.3	33.4	7.5	50.0
Cohabiting (percentage)	22.4	55.3	.7	31.0
Married (percentage)	3.3	11.3	91.8	19.1
N	912	657	268	1,837
Hispanic				
Nonresident (percentage)	66.9	20.2	2.8	28.1
Cohabiting (percentage)	24.3	62.0	2.8	38.2
Married (percentage)	8.8	17.8	94.4	33.7
N	272	534	251	1,057
White				
Nonresident (percentage)	75.4	22.6	3.0	19.2
Cohabiting (percentage)	18.8	56.9	.4	19.9
Married (percentage)	5.8	20.5	96.6	60.9
N	138	288	537	963

Source: Based on McLanahan et al. (2001).
Note: Cell entries are based on mothers' reports of relationship status in the baseline and follow-up surveys.

with the criminal justice system.[4] In particular, in the follow-up survey fathers were asked whether they had ever served time in a correctional facility and, if so, the date of their most recent release. Interviews completed in prisons or jails were also identified in the survey. Because only a small proportion of interviews was recorded in a correctional facility, most of our information about men's imprisonment status is taken from self-reports. A difficulty with these data is that crime and contact with the criminal justice system may not be completely observed.

Incarceration might be underobserved in two ways. First, some men may be unwilling to record their criminal justice status with the survey interviewer. There is evidence that serious offenses like theft and burglary and minor offenses like disturbing public order tend to be underreported (Babinski, Hartsough, and Lambert 2001; Nagin, Farrington, and Moffitt 1995). Second, criminal offenders are difficult to locate and interview using the standard household-sampling frames of survey research.

Poor, young, and minority men tend to be undercounted by social surveys; the likelihood of undersampling is particularly high among men who are involved in crime (Hagan and McCarthy 1997).

Underreports of crime and undercounting of severe offenders in sample surveys lead to underestimates of the effects of incarceration. With reporting bias, severe offenders who have been incarcerated would be mistakenly included in the comparison group of nonoffenders. As a result, differences between self-reported offenders and nonoffenders would be reduced. Undercounting may also reduce estimated incarceration effects because those at risk of the longest sentences and the most severe incarceration experiences are missing from the survey data.

The design of the Fragile Families survey offers some protection against these problems because information about men's incarceration status is obtained from both male and female respondents in the survey. Data obtained from mothers may improve the measurement of incarceration among the fathers of their children. The mothers were also asked at the follow-up interview whether the fathers had ever been incarcerated. In cases in which men report they have never been incarcerated, their partners agree 76 to 91 percent of the time (table 2.2). Although this pattern is consistent with the underreporting of criminal involvement by men found in other research, we should be careful not simply to treat women's reports as having greater validity. For example, women report no incarceration in about 30 percent of cases in which men acknowledge having been to prison or jail. In these cases, it is unlikely that women's reports are more accurate.[5] Consistent with high levels of criminal involvement among undercounted men, women reported that 34.1 percent (252 of 738) of the men who were not located for a follow-up interview had been incarcerated. This rate was particularly high among African Americans who could not be located, 40 percent of whom had been incarcerated.

The validity of the data deserves close consideration where women report that their children's fathers have been incarcerated but the men deny having ever spent time in prison or jail. In these cases, mothers' accounts of fathers' incarceration may just be flagging bad relationships in which women have little confidence in their partners. We can examine this by studying the reports of incarceration among subsets of fathers who are at risk of crime and involved in bad relationships. We measure a father's risk of criminal behavior with items recording his drug and alcohol abuse and violent behavior. Relationship quality is measured by items indicating fathers who compromise in disagreements and are affectionate and whether they are critical or encouraging of their partners.

Table 2.3 indicates that fathers who abuse drugs or alcohol or are violent are relatively unlikely to agree with their partners that they have

Table 2.2   *Distribution of Agreement of Mothers' and Fathers' Reports of Fathers' Prior Incarceration Status, by Race-Ethnicity, 1999 to 2001*

	Fathers' Reports			
Mothers' Reports	Not Interviewed	No Prison or Jail	Prison or Jail	Total
African American				
Not interviewed (percentage)	0.0	4.8	6.0	3.8
No prison or jail (percentage)	59.7	76.0	31.9	66.5
Prison or jail (percentage)	40.3	19.2	62.1	29.7
N	432	1,170	235	1,837
Hispanic				
Not interviewed (percentage)	0.0	2.1	2.7	1.8
No prison or jail (percentage)	70.6	81.3	27.4	75.7
Prison or jail (percentage)	29.4	16.6	69.9	22.5
N	187	797	73	1,057
White				
Not interviewed (percentage)	0.0	1.2	4.3	1.4
No prison or jail (percentage)	80.7	90.9	28.0	83.6
Prison or jail (percentage)	19.3	7.9	67.7	15.1
N	119	751	93	963

Source: Based on McLanahan et al. (2001).

been to prison or jail. More than 20 percent of fathers at high risk of crime disagree with their partners and deny prior incarceration. The results are strongest for violent fathers. In 22.5 percent of cases, violent fathers report no prior incarceration in contrast to the mother's report that fathers had previously been in prison or jail. Couples in poor relationships are more likely to agree about incarceration status than couples with crime-involved men. For example, men who criticize their partners are no more likely to disagree with their partners about incarceration status than the sample average. The frequency of discrepancies in reported incarceration status is higher in couples in which the men are discouraging, unaffectionate, or uncompromising. For these couples in

Table 2.3 Distribution of Agreement in Mothers' and Fathers' Reports of Fathers' Prior Incarceration Status, by Measures of Criminality and Relationship Quality

Measure	Respondents Agree		Respondents Disagree			Father Missing	
	Mother Yes, Father Yes (Percentage)	Mother No, Father No (Percentage)	Mother Yes, Father No (Percentage)	Mother No, Father Yes (Percentage)	N	Mother Yes (Percentage)	N
Full sample	8.6	73.6	13.8	4.0	3,017	34.1	738
Drug or alcohol abuse							
Yes	16.5	57.1	21.1	5.4	503	53.4	103
No	7.0	77.0	12.2	3.8	2,475	30.6	608
Is violent							
Yes	17.5	57.5	22.5	2.5	80	48.5	80
No	8.6	73.7	13.6	4.1	2,786	33.9	676
Compromises							
Yes	7.7	77.4	11.3	3.6	1,620	26.0	296
No	10.3	67.9	17.1	4.7	1,244	41.3	407
Is affectionate							
Yes	8.4	75.0	12.5	4.1	2,318	29.7	464
No	10.8	65.8	19.6	3.8	546	42.9	240
Is critical							
Yes	8.5	73.7	13.5	4.2	2,784	34.6	29
No	18.8	57.6	23.5	0.0	85	34.5	680
Is encouraging							
Yes	8.2	75.9	12.0	3.9	2,180	29.6	436
No	10.9	65.0	19.6	4.5	688	42.6	272

Source: Based on McLanahan et al. (2001).

poor relationships, however, the frequency of prior incarcerations reported only by mothers remains lower than in couples in which the father is involved in crime. A similar pattern of results is provided by men who were not interviewed at baseline. Among these men, the mothers of their children are more likely to report incarceration for those who are at risk of crime than for those in poor relationships. These results support the idea that in this sample, mothers' reports of fathers' incarceration are more likely to indicate criminal offenders than troubled relationships.

In the data analysis presented here we make extensive use of women's reports on men's prior incarceration status. Men are treated as having been incarcerated if either they themselves report their prior incarceration or the mothers of their children report their prior incarceration. It is hoped that this measurement strategy reduces the error resulting from survey nonresponse and men's reporting bias. Coding prior incarceration status in this way indicates that more than one-quarter (27.7 percent) of the fathers in the Fragile Families Study have spent some time in prison or jail.

METHODS

To study marriage and cohabitation at the follow-up interview, we fit multinomial logistic regressions to a three-category measure of relationship status.[6] The categories are: not living together, living together but not married, and married and living together. Our key predictor is a dummy variable indicating whether the father was previously incarcerated, according to either the mother's or father's reports. The sample data consist of couples in which both parents were interviewed at baseline and the mother was interviewed twelve months later. All variables were measured at baseline, except for incarceration and relationship status at twelve months.

We adopt several strategies to control for selection effects owing to the nonrandom distribution of incarceration. First, in predicting relationship status at the twelve-month interview, we control for relationship status at baseline. This variable will certainly reflect information about the vintage of the relationship and capture other characteristics of offenders that affect their fortunes on the marriage market. The utility of baseline relationship status in helping to identify the causal effect of incarceration is indicated by its large correlation with the dependent variable and the treatment variable, incarceration status. Thus though most of our variables are measured at a single point in time, we use information about relationship status at two time points to help adjust for differences between offenders and nonoffenders.

Second, we control for selection on observed characteristics by adding successive sets of independent variables that are correlated with both relationship status and men's propensity to crime and imprisonment. The first set of controls adjusts for demographic characteristics, through variables for the race, ethnicity, and education of the couple and a dummy variable indicating whether this was the mother's first birth at the initial interview. Because men with weak attachments to regular work are more prone to crime and unattractive marriage partners, we next control for the mother's report of the father's employment in the year preceding the birth. Crime-involved men may also make unsuitable partners because they lack the interpersonal skills necessary to sustain a relationship. Such skills might be undermined by membership in same-sex peer networks (such as gangs) and weak attachments to maternal figures in childhood and adolescence. To capture these relationship skills we measure whether the fathers (as reported by the mothers at baseline) in the survey are open to compromise with the mothers, whether they show affection, and whether they are likely to criticize the mothers or encourage them. Finally, in an effort to tap the aggression or low self-control of crime-involved men, we also control for men's drug and alcohol use and violent behavior in the relationship.[7]

In some ways, our approach leads to a conservative test of the effects of incarceration on marriage and cohabitation. We treat characteristics like employment status and relationship quality as confounding variables that characterize preexisting deficits in former inmates that create obstacles to sustaining family relationships. However, incarceration erodes employment and relationship quality, indirectly contributing to the instability of parental unions. Our data do not let us separate that part of the employment effect, for instance, that derives from incarceration from that part that derives from a preexisting low level of productivity. Instead, we assume that all of a man's employability captured in our data reflects characteristics that predate incarceration. Similarly, we treat relationship status at baseline as a potential source of bias in estimating the impact of incarceration, but if incarceration affects a relationship at follow-up it is also likely to have affected that relationship a year earlier. We will tend to underestimate the effect of incarceration to the extent that relationship status, employment, and relationship quality are themselves influenced by time in prison or jail.

We take this conservative approach because crime-involved men are likely to bring into family relationships significant observed and unobserved deficits that pose a significant threat to causal inference about the effects of incarceration. From our viewpoint, positive evidence from a relatively stringent test is more compelling than similar evidence from a weaker test, even if it leads to an understatement of the impact of incarceration.

An alternative approach to the problem of assessing the causal effect of incarceration on union stability involves restricting the analysis to men who are comparable in all respects except incarceration status. Differences in union stability can then plausibly be related to prior involvement in the criminal justice system and not other variables. If we estimate the propensity of each man in the sample to have been in prison or jail, we can divide the sample into groups of men who share similar a priori risks of incarceration. This analysis, based on propensity scores, can yield consistent estimates of causal effects (Rosenbaum 2002). We estimate the propensity of each man in the sample to have been incarcerated as a function of race and ethnicity, age, education, and city of interview. The resulting propensity score analysis estimates the incarceration effect on union stability for sample stratums that share a similar probability of having been in prison.

Descriptive statistics for the independent variables by incarceration status are reported in table 2.4. Descriptive statistics show that couples with a male former convict are unlikely to be living together at baseline. Of couples in which the male has been to prison or jail, only about 53 percent are living together or married compared with 70 percent of couples in which the father is not a former inmate. Consistent with data on racial disparities in incarceration, most of the former inmates in the survey (59.3 percent) are African American. Men with prison records tend to be slightly younger than the sample average. They also have lower levels of education. The vast majority (81.3 percent) men that have been to prison have no more than a high school education. The economic situation of former inmates also appears to be weaker than the sample average, showing lower levels of employment in the previous year. As we would expect, former inmates also score relatively poorly on variables measuring relationship skills. Whereas, according to reports of the mothers, 57 percent of fathers who have never been incarcerated are willing to compromise, only 44 percent of former inmates demonstrate this trait. Men involved in crime are also relatively more likely to be violent and to insult or criticize their partners. Perhaps most striking of all, men with criminal records are more than twice as likely as nonoffenders to abuse drugs or alcohol.

REGRESSION RESULTS

Regression results for the full sample are reported in table 2.5 for the five different models. The table reports the predicted probability of cohabitation or marriage one year after the birth of their child for a hypothetical couple in which the father has never been incarcerated and was not living with the mother at the time the child was born. The incarcera-

Table 2.4   *Means of Independent Variables for Regression Analysis, by Incarceration Status*

Variable	Full Sample	Ever Incarcerated	
		Yes	No
Married at baseline	.273	.085	.345
Cohabiting at baseline	.382	.441	.360
First birth	.387	.353	.401
Father's characteristics			
Black	.476	.593	.431
Hispanic	.274	.243	.286
White	.206	.133	.234
Other	.044	.031	.049
Age	28.013	26.569	28.567
Less than high school education	.309	.419	.275
High school education	.341	.394	.320
Some college	.235	.174	.258
College graduate	.115	.013	.154
Worked last year	.819	.762	.841
Will compromise	.535	.437	.574
Expresses affection	.778	.716	.803
Insults or criticizes	.032	.045	.027
Encourages	.731	.649	.763
Abuses drugs or alcohol	.166	.267	.127
Violent when angry	.032	.051	.024
Mother's characteristics			
Black	.459	.565	.419
Hispanic	.270	.234	.283
White	.231	.174	.252
Other	.040	.026	.046
Age	25.382	23.613	26.059
Less than high school	.320	.428	.279
High school education	.303	.350	.285
Some college	.256	.201	.277
College graduate	.121	.021	.159
N	3,867	1,070	2,797

Source: Based on McLanahan et al. (2001).

Table 2.5 Estimated Marginal Effects of Incarceration on the Probabilities of Cohabitation and Marriage, Full Sample

Model	Cohabitation		Marriage		
	Predicted Probability	Incarceration Effect	Predicted Probability	Incarceration Effect	N
(1) Relationship at baseline	.247	-.063 (.015)	.059	-.031 (.006)	3,867
(2) Controlling for (1) and race, ethnicity, education, first birth	.254	-.063 (.016)	.070	-.029 (.007)	3,757
(3) Controlling for (1), (2), and father employed last year	.267	-.058 (.017)	.075	-.030 (.008)	3,635
(4) Controlling for (1), (2), (3), and compromises, shows affection, criticizes	.281	-.054 (.018)	.079	-.030 (.009)	3,447
(5) Controlling for (1), (2), (3), (4), and drug or alcohol abuse, violence	.284	-.055 (.019)	.079	-.029 (.009)	3,410

Source: Based on McLanahan et al. (2001).
Note: Predicted probabilities give the probability of cohabitation or marriage versus nonresidence and are calculated for nonresident, never-incarcerated fathers. Standard errors in parentheses.

tion effect gives the change in the predicted probability of cohabitation or marriage associated with having spent time in prison or jail. For example, in the simplest model that controls only for the baseline relationship status, the predicted probability of cohabitation a year after a child's birth is .247 for couples with a nonresident father at baseline. Incarceration is estimated to reduce this probability by .063 to (.184). In short, under the baseline model incarceration is estimated to reduce the likelihood of cohabitation by about 26 percent (.063/.247). Adding demographic characteristics to the baseline specification—race and ethnicity, education, and an indicator for parity—has little impact on the incarceration effect. When father's employment status is added to the model, the incarceration effect declines to −.058, about 22 percent of the predicted probability for couples with a nonincarcerated father. This suggests that at least some of the incarceration effect on cohabitation in the simpler models derives from the relatively low employability of men who have been in prison. Adding measures of relationship quality further reduces the estimated incarceration effect. Under the most complete specification, which includes all covariates including controls for drug and alcohol abuse and partner violence, incarceration is estimated to reduce the probability of cohabitation by about .055, about 19 percent of the probability for a couple with a never-incarcerated father.

The pattern of results for marital stability is slightly different. The baseline model (1) shows that the probability of marriage for a couple that is not living together at baseline is extremely low, just 5.9 percent. Even though marriage is unlikely for such couples, incarceration is still estimated to produce a significant reduction in the likelihood of marriage. Under the simplest model (1), we estimate that incarceration reduces the probability of marriage by .031. That is, incarceration roughly halves the likelihood of marriage (.031/.059). This relative effect of incarceration on marriage becomes smaller when other variables are controlled, but the incarceration effect is always statistically significant. In the full model (5), which includes controls for demographic characteristics, father's employment status, measures of relationship quality, and measures of deviant behavior, incarceration is estimated to reduce the probability of marriage by .029. Under this model, the estimated probability of marriage for a couple with a nonincarcerated father is .079, representing a reduction of about 37 percent (.029/.079).

Have the control variables successfully adjusted for the nonrandom distribution of incarceration across the population? The results for cohabitation and marriage suggest that controlling for observed variables, in addition to relationship status at baseline, adds a little explanatory power and slightly reduces the estimated effect of incarceration. Of course, the estimated incarceration effect may still be confounded with

Table 2.6   *Estimated Marginal Effects of Incarceration on the Probabilities of Cohabitation and Marriage, by Race-Ethnicity*

Race-Ethnicity of Father	Cohabitation		Marriage		
	Predicted Probability	Incarceration Effect	Predicted Probability	Incarceration Effect	N
African American	.258	−.022 (.024)	.043	−.020 (.008)	1,641
White	.206	−.086 (.037)	.145	−.062 (.035)	870
Hispanic	.328	−.085 (.038)	.120	−.023 (.024)	899

Source: Based on McLanahan et al. (2001).
Note: All models control for relationship at baseline, education of couple, first birth, father's employment, relationship skills, drug and alcohol abuse, and violence. Predicted probabilities give the probability of cohabitation or marriage versus nonresidence and are calculated for nonresident, never-incarcerated fathers. Standard errors in parentheses.

unobserved variables, but we are somewhat reassured that the results are robust for different sets of control variables.

We can also check on the robustness of the results by repeating the analysis for different race and ethnic groups (table 2.6). If the results for the full sample are being driven just by African Americans, for example, the disaggregated analysis will indicate nonsignificant results for whites and Hispanics. The effects of incarceration are generally robust across race and ethnic groups. These effects, presented in table 2.6, are substantively large in most cases and statistically insignificant only for blacks in the case of cohabitation and for Hispanics in the case of marriage.

These disaggregated results also suggest some key differences in the effects of incarceration. In couples with black fathers, the estimates indicate that incarceration does not significantly reduce the likelihood of cohabitation. If a black father has been incarcerated, however, we estimate that the probability of his being married twelve months after the birth of his child is reduced by about 47 percent (.02/.043). The absolute magnitude of the effect is quite small because marriage is rare in this group. A different pattern of results can be seen for whites and Hispanics. For white fathers, the effects of incarceration on the probability of cohabitation and marriage are similar. Incarceration is expected to reduce the probability of coresidence in either form by about 42 percent (.086/.206

for cohabitation and .062/.145 for marriage). For Hispanics, the pattern of results is the opposite of that found for blacks. For blacks, our results indicate that incarceration created a bar to marriage but not cohabitation. For Hispanics, incarcerated fathers are relatively unlikely to be cohabiting, but they marry at much the same rate as fathers who have not been incarcerated.

These results imply that the stigmatic effects of incarceration vary across race and ethnic groups. Because incarceration is common in poor African American communities, former-inmate status may provide a much weaker signal of exceptional unreliability. Put differently, if a woman living in a large city strongly desires coresidence with the black father of her child, she may have no choice but to discount his incarceration status. The relatively high marriage rate for Hispanic fathers with prison or jail records is harder to interpret, although pooled analysis shows that the difference between Hispanics and whites is not statistically significant.

A further test of the effects of incarceration is provided by matching individuals with the same likelihood of incarceration, that is, by conducting a propensity score analysis. If this technique correctly separates the sample into men with equal likelihood of having been incarcerated, then the only difference in the relationship outcomes between those who were and were not incarcerated must owe to chance, that is, some had the bad fortune (or good, depending on one's perspective) to be caught. Because one wants to use only predictors of incarceration that occur before incarceration when using the propensity score technique, we used information on the father's race and ethnicity, the city in which he was interviewed, whether he had completed his high school education, and interactions between his dropout status and race and ethnicity.[8]

Benchmark probabilities are similar to those obtained for the full sample (table 2.7). With the exception of the second quintile, the estimates indicate that the probability of cohabitation is reduced among couples in which the father has been incarcerated. The marginal effects are statistically significant at conventional levels for the first, third, and fourth quintiles. For marriage, the marginal effects are statistically significant in all but the first quintile. For the second through fifth quintiles, the marginal effect of incarceration reduces the probability of marriage by approximately one-half.

THE AGGREGATE EFFECT OF INCARCERATION ON MARRIAGE RATES

The Fragile Families data are informative about the effects of incarceration on marriage and cohabitation but relatively uninformative about the aggregate effects of incarceration on marriage rates in the general

Table 2.7   *Marginal Effects of Incarceration on the Probabilities of Cohabitation and Marriage, by Propensity Score Quintile (Estimate)*

Propensity Score Quintile	Cohabitation		Marriage		
	Predicted Probability	Incarceration Effect	Predicted Probability	Incarceration Effect	N
First	.252	−.104 (.045)	.063	−.019 (.020)	768
Second	.212	.001 (.037)	.064	−.035 (.015)	776
Third	.273	−.091 (.034)	.081	−.036 (.016)	758
Fourth	.263	−.088 (.031)	.060	−.027 (.013)	736
Fifth	.234	−.025 (.030)	.030	−.016 (.008)	751

Source: Based on McLanahan et al. (2001).
Note: Predicted probabilities give the probability of cohabitation or marriage versus nonresidence for nonresident, never-incarcerated fathers. Standard errors in parentheses. Couples who were living together at the time of the child's birth (baseline interview) are excluded.

population. This is because the marriage rate in the survey was fixed by the sampling design. To estimate the aggregate effects of incarceration on marriage rates in the general population, we can combine our estimated incarceration effects with population statistics on the risks of incarceration and marriage rates. To tailor our analysis to the Fragile Families sample, we focus on African American and white men, aged thirty to thirty-four, with children, and living in metropolitan areas. Using data from the Current Population Survey, 1999 (Freenberg and Roth 2001), we estimate marriage rates for all these men, those without college education, and high school dropouts. Becky Pettit and Bruce Western (2004) estimate cumulative risks of prison incarceration for this birth cohort at these levels of education. Given data on observed marriage rates, incarceration risks, and the effects of incarceration on marriage, we can calculate the marriage rate we would expect to observe if the risk of incarceration were zero.

This exercise necessarily relies on some strong assumptions. We assume that incarceration risks calculated for the general population are the same as those for men with children. This assumption about incarceration risks is likely to be reasonable because rates of parenthood among inmates are similar to those for the general population at the same levels of age and education. We also assume that the effects of incarceration on marriage, estimated for men with newborn children, are generalizable to men with older children. It is difficult to assess the validity of this assumption, although it seems reasonable to believe that a child's birth temporarily lowers the risk of divorce or separation. If this is true, the incarceration effect estimated for the new parents of the Fragile Families Study might conservatively estimate the incarceration effect on marriage for couples with older children. In any case, our estimates of hypothetical marriage rates at zero incarceration should be interpreted cautiously as a way of quantifying the macro-level implications of our micro-level effects.

The observed and adjusted marriage rates are reported in table 2.8. Given the incarceration effects estimated in the previous section, the overall marriage rate for black urban fathers is estimated to increase by about 13 percent from .400 to .450, in contrast with a 2 percent increase for white fathers, from .584 to .594. The racial disparity in incarceration increases the white-black difference in marriage, and our calculations suggest that the race gap in marriage would decline by about 20 percent if the incarceration risk were zero. Slightly larger aggregate effects of incarceration on marriage rates are obtained if we examine men with no college education. In this case, the white-black difference in marriage rates is calculated to fall by one-quarter, to .151, under a no-incarceration regime. Although these effects are reasonably large, an extremely large influence of incarceration is observed at the bottom of the education distribution, among men who have not finished high school. We calculate that marriage rates would increase by about 45 percent among black male dropouts with children if they faced no risk of incarceration. The white-black difference in marriage rates would be nearly halved were the incarceration rate reduced to zero. We caution, again, that considerable uncertainty accompanies these estimates, but the calculations do suggest potentially large aggregate effects of incarceration on marriage among African American parents with low levels of education in urban areas.

DISCUSSION

As this chapter has demonstrated, men who have been incarcerated are much less likely to be married to or cohabiting with the mother of their children twelve months after the birth of those children than men who

Table 2.8   *Risks of Imprisonment for Young Men, Observed Marriage Rate for Urban Young, Male Parents, and Adjusted Marriage Rate, Assuming Zero Incarceration*

	Cumulative Risk of Imprisonment	Observed Marriage Rate	Adjusted Marriage Rate
All			
Black	.205	.400	.450
White	.029	.584	.594
Difference[a]		.184	.144
Non-college			
Black	.302	.334	.399
White	.053	.534	.550
Difference[a]		.200	.151
High school dropouts			
Black	.589	.296	.434
White	.112	.529	.565
Difference[a]		.233	.131

Source: Based on McLanahan et al. (2001).
Note: To calculate the adjusted marriage rate, race-specific effects of incarceration on marriage were taken from table 2.5. Incarceration was assumed to reduce marriage rates by .46 among blacks and .43 among whites. The adjusted marriage rate is $m/([1 - I] + Ib)$, where m is the observed marriage rate, I is the cumulative risk of imprisonment, and b is the effect of incarceration on marriage.

For purposes of this table, "young men" and "young male parents" are defined as those aged thirty to thirty-four.
[a]White minus black.

have not been incarcerated. Strong associations between incarceration and nonresidence among fathers persist, even after controls are introduced for demographic characteristics, economic variables, relationship skills, and fathers' violence and drug and alcohol abuse. The analysis provides strong evidence that the relative effects of incarceration on marriage and cohabitation are large, on the order of 20 to 40 percent. The relative effects of incarceration tend to be largest for marriage. Although marriage rates in the Fragile Families data are generally quite low, marriage among former inmates is exceedingly rare. This suggests that incarceration creates a much more substantial barrier to marriage than to cohabitation. The results indicate that mothers require more of marriage partners than of cohabitation partners (Gibson, Edin, and McLanahan 2003); the stigmatic effects of incarceration appear to be relatively small in the case of cohabitation. At the aggregate level, our simulation exercise points to the large negative effects of incarceration on aggregate marriage rates of black parents with low levels of education.

The analysis also suggests the utility of survey data for studying the social impacts of crime and punishment. Survey data are often seen as presenting two main problems: self-reports of criminal activity tend to miss more severe offenses, and the household-sampling frames of social surveys tend to undercount young socially marginal men, who are the most likely to be involved in crime. Against these limitations, special features of the Fragile Families survey have been useful for studying the effects of incarceration. In particular, the use of mothers' reports of fathers' incarceration status appears to provide a significantly more complete accounting of the criminal histories of the men in the survey.

More generally, this study points to the disruptive effects of incarceration on the life course, on the partners and children of former inmates, and on the public safety of communities absorbing large numbers of returning prison and jail inmates. The data analysis provides evidence of low rates of marriage and cohabitation among former inmates both at the time of the birth of the child and twelve months following the birth. These results indicate that incarceration is associated with a delayed and disorderly passage through the life course. Marriage and cohabitation apparently occur later, if at all, for former convicts. Stable unions for former convicts with children also appear to be relatively unusual.

Although incarceration is disruptive for family relationships, it is difficult to judge whether mothers and their children are necessarily worse off without male former convicts in the household. Although a substantial body of research finds that father absence is a key cause of child poverty, former convicts may have little to offer their children or the mothers of their children. The data analysis shows that men who have been to prison or jail have lower rates of employment and education, have poor relationship skills, are more likely to abuse drugs or alcohol, and more likely to be violent. Some might argue that such men can provide few of the economic or social supports necessary to improve child well-being.

This argument certainly has merit, but it should be qualified in at least two ways. First, many of the economic and social deficits that we associate with former convicts are partly products of the experience of incarceration. Serving time in prison or jail exacerbates behavioral problems, limits educational opportunities, and raises the risks of unemployment (see, for example, Hagan and Dinovitzer 1999; Western, Kling, and Weiman 2001). Although we treated behavioral characteristics, education, and unemployment as rival sources of variation for the effects of incarceration, the observed deficits of former inmates also reflect the consequences of imprisonment.

Second, marriage itself can contribute substantially to desistance from crime (Laub, Nagin, and Sampson 1998). Strong marital bonds help routinize prosocial behavior and draw men out of the same-sex peer networks that form the social context for criminal offending. A strong marriage thus represents an important step away from a life in crime. Without supports that can compensate for the deficits caused by incarceration and help rebuild marriage markets, poor communities risk being stuck in a high-crime–low-marriage equilibrium. Women in such communities will be understandably averse to marriage because their potential partners bring few social or economic benefits to the relationship. Men who remain unmarried or unattached to stable households are likely to continue their criminal involvement.

In the high-crime–low-marriage equilibrium, incarceration poses a threat to public safety by undermining the crime-preventive effects of marriage. Does the indirect effect of incarceration on crime, through the intervening influence of marriage, outweigh the simple gain in public safety obtained by incapacitating criminals? The answer depends in part on the mix of offenders in any particular community. Research shows that locking up drug offenders does little to reduce crime, although locking up property or violent offenders may produce larger gains in public safety (D'Iulio and Piehl 1995; Zimring and Hawkins 1995). In any event, the pool of released offenders in the community is much larger than the population actually incarcerated. For example, in 1999, the prison incarceration rate among black men with no college education born from 1965 to 1969 was about 17 percent, whereas the pool of men in that age cohort who had ever served time in prison was 30 percent (Pettit and Western 2004). The relatively large pool of former offenders, subject to the postrelease effects of incarceration, may well overshadow the much smaller pool of current prisoners who are prevented from committing crimes by incapacitation. In sum, we cannot quite conclude that incarceration is a self-defeating strategy for public safety; but neither should we think that locking up large numbers of criminal offenders necessarily makes communities safer or socially stable.

Finally, we should also be careful about measuring the effects of the prison boom purely in terms of its ultimate effects on crime. The Fragile Families data provide a clear indication that rising imprisonment rates have reduced marriage rates in communities with large numbers of former inmates. The secondary effects of low marriage rates extend well beyond the province of crime to influence the economic and physical health of mothers and children and the social well-being of subsequent generations. Although we cannot say for sure that the prison boom has improved public safety in high-crime communities, the negative collateral consequences are almost certainly more far-reaching than previously thought.

This research was supported by grants from the Russell Sage Foundation and National Science Foundation grant SES-0004336. We also gratefully acknowledge financial support from the Bendheim-Thoman Center for Research on Child Wellbeing at Princeton University, the National Institute of Child Health and Human Development (grant R01 HD36916), and the Office of Population Research at Princeton University, which is supported by National Institute of Child Health and Human Development grant 5 P30 HD32030.

NOTES

1. Edin, Nelson, and Paranal (chapter 3, this volume) do not discuss the marriage rates of the fathers and mothers but imply that the vast majority of the couples were unwed.
2. Recall that the Fragile Families design oversampled unmarried parents by a factor of three. Thus the percentage of married parents in these data is much lower than in the population as a whole.
3. Throughout this chapter, whites are defined as non–African American, non-Hispanics.
4. All men imprisoned at the time of the twelve-month survey were removed from the analysis as they would obviously be nonresident and have had contact with the criminal justice system. We lose 198 cases (4.9 percent) of the sample owing to this sample selection criterion. We did not use these couples because we could not be certain whether it was their relationship status or their living arrangements to which the mothers were responding when asked about their relationships while the father was imprisoned. For instance, replying that they were separated may have reflected their response to their living arrangements rather than their relationship. Including the addition of these cases actually increases the estimated magnitude of the relationship and improves precision. All families with one deceased parent were removed from the analysis.
5. An independent check on the validity of the incarceration reports might be obtained by a criminal background check on the male survey respondents. Such checks are planned for future research if sufficient consent can be obtained from the respondents.
6. The multinomial logit model assumes that the response categories are conditionally independent (the assumption of the independence of irrelevant alternatives). A Hausman (1978) specification test indicated the data's consistency with this assumption.
7. Fathers were identified as abusing drugs or alcohol if they reported that they

had used drugs in the past three months or if they drank daily. A father was also identified as abusing alcohol if the mother reported that his alcohol or drug use limited his work or friends. A father was identified as violent if the mother reported that he hit or slapped her often or sometimes when he was angry.

8. By using the variable for city of interview we assume that he has never moved, and by using this dropout status we assume that if he was incarcerated, it occurred after the time at which he would have graduated from high school.

REFERENCES

Babinski, Leslie M., Carolyn S. Hartsough, and Nadine M. Lambert. 2001. "A Comparison of Self-Report of Criminal Involvement and Official Arrest Records." *Aggressive Behavior* 27(1): 44–54.

Beck, Allen J., Jennifer C. Karberg, and Paige M. Harrison. 2002. "Prison and Jail Inmates at Midyear 2001." *Bureau of Justice Statistics Bulletin* (April). NCJ 191702. Washington: U.S. Department of Justice.

D'Iulio, John, and Anne Morrison Piehl. 1995. "Does Prison Pay? Revisited: Returning to the Crime Scene." *Brookings Review* 13(1): 30–34.

Edin, Kathryn. 2000. "Few Good Men: Why Poor Mothers Don't Marry or Remarry." *American Prospect* 11(4): 26–31.

Ellwood, David T., and Christopher Jencks. 2001. "The Growing Difference in Family Structure: What Do We Know? Where Do We Look for Answers?" Unpublished paper. Harvard University.

Freenberg, Daniel, and Jean Roth. 2001. *CPS Labor Extracts* [MRDF]. Cambridge, Mass.: National Bureau of Economic Research.

Gabel, Stewart. 1992. "Children of Incarcerated and Criminal Parents: Adjustment, Behavior, and Prognosis." *Bulletin of the American Academy of Psychiatry and the Law* 20(1): 33–45.

Gibson, Christina, Kathryn Edin, and Sara McLanahan. 2003. "High Hopes but Even Higher Expectations: The Retreat from Marriage Among Low-Income Couples." Working paper 03–066-FF. Princeton, N.J.: Bendheim-Thoman Center for Research on Child Wellbeing, Princeton University.

Hagan, John, and Ronit Dinovitzer. 1999. "Collateral Consequences of Imprisonment for Children, Communities, and Prisoners." In *Prisons: Crime and Justice*, vol. 26, edited by Michael Tonry and Joan Petersilia. Chicago: University of Chicago Press.

Hagan, John, and Bill McCarthy. 1997. *Mean Streets: Youth Crime and Homelessness.* New York: Cambridge University Press.

Hagan, John, and Alberto Palloni. 1990. "The Social Reproduction of a Criminal Class in Working-Class London, circa 1950–1980." *American Journal of Sociology* 96(2): 265–99.

Hausman, John. 1978. "Specification Tests in Econometrics." *Econometrica* 46(6, November): 1251–71.

Hirsch, Amy E., Sharon M. Dietrich, Rue Landau, Peter D. Schneider, Irv Ackelsberg, Judith Bernstein-Baker, and Jospeh Hohenstein. 2002. *Every Door Closed: Barriers Facing Parents with Criminal Records.* Washington, D.C.: Center for Law and Social Policy.

Horney, Julie, D. Wayne Osgood, and Ineke Haen Marshall. 1995. "Criminal Careers in the Short-Term: Intra-Individual Variability in Crime and Its Relation to Local Life Circumstances." *American Sociological Review* 60(5, October): 655–73.

Krueger, Robert F., Terrie E. Moffitt, Avshalom Caspi, A. L. Bleske, and P. A. Silva. 1998. "Assortative Mating for Antisocial Behavior: Developmental and Methodological Implications." *Behavior Genetics* 28(3): 173–86.

Laub, John H., Daniel S. Nagin, and Robert J. Sampson. 1998. "Trajectories of Change in Criminal Offending: Good Marriages and the Desistance Process." *American Sociological Review* 63(2, April): 225–38.

Mauer, Marc. 1999. *Race to Incarcerate*. New York: New Press.

McLanahan, Sara, and Lynne Casper. 1995. "Growing Diversity and Inequality in the American Family." In *State of the Union, America in the 1990s: Social Trends*, vol. 2, edited by Reynolds Farley. New York: Russell Sage Foundation.

McLanahan, Sara, Irwin Garfinkel, Nancy E. Reichman, Julien Teitler, Marcia Carlson, and Christina Norland Audigier. 2001. *The Fragile Families and Child Wellbeing Study: National Baseline Report*. Princeton, N.J.: Bendheim-Thoman Center for Research on Child Wellbeing, Princeton University.

Nagin, Daniel S., David P. Farrington, and Terrie E. Moffitt. 1995. "Life-Course Trajectories of Different Types of Offenders." *Criminology* 33(1): 111–39.

Pavalko, Eliza K., and Glen H. Elder. 1990. "World War II and Divorce: A Life-Course Perspective." *American Journal of Sociology* 95(5, March): 1213–34.

Pettit, Becky, and Bruce Western. 2004. "Mass Imprisonment and the Life Course: Race and Class Inequality in U.S. Incarceration." *American Sociological Review* 69(April).

Rosenbaum, Paul R. 2002. *Observational Studies*. 2nd ed. New York: Springer.

Sabol, William J., and James P. Lynch. 1998. "Assessing the Longer-run Consequences of Incarceration: Effects on Families and Employment." Paper presented at the Twentieth Annual Research Conference of the Association for Public Policy Analysis and Management. New York (October 29–31, 1998).

U.S. Department of Commerce, Bureau of the Census. 2001. *Statistical Abstract of the United States*. Washington: U.S. Government Printing Office.

Waller, Maureen R. 1996. "Redefining Fatherhood: Paternal Involvement, Masculinity, and Responsibility in the 'Other America.'" Ph.D. diss., Princeton University.

West, Donald J., and David P. Farrington. 1973. *Who Becomes Delinquent?* London: Heinemann.

Western, Bruce, Jeffrey R. Kling, and David F. Weiman. 2001. "The Labor Market Consequences of Incarceration." *Crime and Delinquency* 47(3): 410–27.

Western, Bruce, and Becky Pettit. 2002. "Beyond Crime and Punishment: Prisons and Inequality." *Contexts* 1(3, September): 37–43.

Wilson, James Q., and Richard J. Herrnstein. 1985. *Crime and Human Nature*. New York: Simon & Schuster.

Zimring, Franklin E., and Gordon Hawkins. 1995. *Incapacitation: Penal Confinement and the Restraint of Crime*. New York: Oxford University Press.

Kathryn Edin
Timothy J. Nelson
Rechelle Paranal

Fatherhood and Incarceration as Potential Turning Points in the Criminal Careers of

3 | **Unskilled Men**

Over the past thirty years, three interrelated trends have profoundly affected the lives of low-income men. First, wages for low-skilled men employed full-time and full-year have declined sharply, as has the proportion of men who do work full-time and full-year. The drop has been substantial for African Americans and Latinos, but especially dramatic for unskilled whites (Bound and Johnson 1992; Katz and Murphy 1992; Lerman 1993), a trend that continued even through the economic expansion of the late 1990s (Holzer and Offner 2001). Second, rates of marriage for low-income and minority men have declined dramatically, driving up the proportion of these men with noncustodial children (Tucker and Mitchell-Kernan 1995). Third, incarceration rates have also increased, especially for low-income and minority men (Federal Bureau of Investigation 1990, 1992).[1]

What does the confluence of these trends mean in the lives of unskilled and semiskilled men? There is substantial evidence that criminal involvement increases when men are unemployed (Farrington et al. 1986), when their wages are low (Doyle, Ahmed, and Horn 1999; Grogger 1998), and when entry-level jobs are scarce (Shihadeh and Ousey 1998). Conversely, offenders tend to desist when they find stable employment and show commitment to their jobs (Shover 1996), especially if this transition occurs when they are older (Bachman and Schulenberg 1993; Hagan and McCarthy 1997; Uggen 2000). Attachment to the military has a similar effect, and timing also matters (after the age of twenty-two, military service tends to disrupt adult bonds to family and work) (Sampson and Laub 1996). Young men also tend to turn from crime when they marry and maintain a stable marital relationship over time (Laub, Nagin, and Sampson 1998; Laub and Sampson 1993; Sampson and Laub 1990, 1993), though the relationship may also be sensitive to age in that a very young marriage can worsen offending behavior (Bachman and Schulenberg 1993). Robert Sampson, John Laub, and others explain these variations in criminal involvement (which persist after controlling for prior delinquent activity) by utilizing aspects of social control theory (Hirschi 1969) and the life-course perspective (Elder 1985; Hagan and Palloni 1988).

Social control theory, which draws from Émile Durkheim's work on anomie (1951), posits that individuals engage in deviant behavior when their bonds to society are weak or disrupted. The life-course perspective examines "pathways through the age differentiated life span," in which age manifests itself through "expectations and options that impinge on decision processes and the course of events that give shape to life stages, transitions, and turning points" (Elder 1985, 17). "Turning points" are key events that occur at a particular stage in an individual's life course (see also Hogan 1980) that may alter his or her trajectory—in this case, a criminal one—by either increasing or decreasing "social bonds to adult institutions of informal social control" (Sampson and Laub 1990, 625) and thus act as either a brake on or a spur to criminal involvement. The life-course perspective recognizes that individuals differ in their adaptations to similar life events and that these responses can lead to different pathways (Elder 1985, 35). The change can lead an offender to desist completely, offend at a lower level, or trade one kind of offense for another (Laub and Sampson 1993).

Turning points may steer a young man away from a criminal path and toward a more normative trajectory (Elder 1985; Warr 1998). However, these need not be unidirectional. In a qualitative reanalysis of data collected on a sample of delinquent and nondelinquent white teenaged males born between 1924 and 1935 (Glueck and Glueck 1950, 1968), Laub and Sampson (1993, 17), analyzing declines in job and marital stability, have found that when these social bonds were disrupted, criminal and deviant behavior increased. In a similar vein, Julie Horney, Wayne Osgood, and Ineke Haen Marshall (1995, 655) consider whether an individual's offending behavior is influenced by "local life circumstances that strengthen or weaken social bonds" over time. They find that men committed more crime during the time periods when they were using drugs and committed less crime during the time periods when they lived with a wife.

GOAL OF THE CHAPTER

Our goal in this chapter is twofold. First, we examine all men in our sample who reported any criminal activity in their past (including those with no imprisonment or incarceration history) and look for any evidence that becoming a father has functioned as a turning point in their criminal trajectories. We do not limit our analysis to the time of the birth of a first child, since we find that it is often a higher-order birth that fathers report as most salient (perhaps because they are older and at a more receptive stage in their lives). In particular, we want to explore whether the event of fatherhood, when combined with fear of being locked up, acts as a deterrent to future criminal activity.

The offending and desistance literature routinely considers men's ties to the institutions of the workplace, school, and marriage as well as their residential mobility or immigration and even exogenous or "chance" events such as being drafted in wartime or being part of a cohort with unique access to a social good like the GI bill. Given this theoretical perspective, we were startled that we could not find a single study that considered the experience of paternity as a potential turning point, despite Sampson and Laub's (1990, 611) observation that "in later adulthood, the dominant institutions are work, marriage, parenthood, and investment in community."[2] This was particularly surprising because many of these studies emphasize the origins or onset not of criminal behavior but of desistance from it (see also Uggen and Piliavin 1998). Our approach in this chapter is entirely consistent with the social control–life-course perspective advanced by Sampson and Laub; it is distinctive in its emphasis on fatherhood as a potential source of adult bonding. Complementary to our investigation here of the effects of fatherhood on somewhat older fathers is Anne Nurse's contribution on juvenile fathers (chapter 4 in this volume). Nurse finds, as do we, a generally strong desire on the part of young fathers to maintain relationships with their children. Yet as she documents, that desire is heavily mediated by the relationship with the child's mother, a factor that is clearly salient in our research as well.

New data drawn from the Fragile Families and Child Wellbeing Study (McLanahan et al. 2001b) show that unmarried fathers often continue to have romantic relationships with the women who bear their noncustodial children, and some say they plan to marry their child's mother. However, an even greater proportion say they intend to stay involved in their children's lives no matter what happens between themselves and their children's mothers. The fact that more than eight in ten unmarried fathers surveyed actually attended the birth of their child or visited the child and mother while they were still in the hospital attests to the importance these men place on their bonds with their children (McLanahan et al. 2001a; also see chapter 2 in this volume for more discussion of the Fragile Families study). For such men, who seldom marry or find stable employment until they are well into their thirties (if at all), paternity is sometimes the only event that has the potential to act as a turning point.

Second, we look at the effect of imprisonment and incarceration on low-income noncustodial fathers' ability to form and maintain social bonds with their children. In this second part of the analysis, we limit our focus to those men in our sample who have been imprisoned or incarcerated since becoming fathers and analyze their life-history narratives to identify the role that incarceration may play in either weakening or strengthening these bonds. If social bonds are important predictors of within-person variations in criminal activity over time—and if the salience of the father-child bond for fathers in this group can be demonstrated—policymakers will have to ask whether incarceration policies inadvertently increase criminal behavior by affecting fathers' ties to their children. On the other hand, we must give equal consideration to the possibility that for some fathers, especially those with particularly high offending rates, incarceration may play a restorative role, allowing bonds that were largely latent to begin to form or re-form.

THE CONTRIBUTION OF QUALITATIVE DATA

Existing data can and have been used to analyze relationships between some of factors outlined here. However, these data have some serious limitations, and our data some distinctive advantages. Most important, noncustodial fathers are seriously underrepresented in large data sets, and this is especially true of low-income, never-married, and minority fathers (Garfinkel, McLanahan, and Hanson 1998). According to estimates made by Irwin Garfinkel, Sara McLanahan, and Thomas Hanson, it is fair to say that, with the exception of the Fragile Families Study (which surveys only new fathers), for low-income and minority noncustodial fathers, the underrepresentation problem in most large surveys is so severe that it constitutes something of a crisis. Although we do have indirect data on these men, drawn from the reports of the women that bear their children and the heads of the households they reside in, little is known about these fathers' own perspectives. We have been able to interview a large number of such men and have enjoyed a high degree of rapport with them in the interviewing process.

In addition, qualitative data such as these can make several unique contributions to the body of research on low-skilled men. First, though the hallmark of quantitative analysis is measuring relationships between variables, the limitations of the data often mean that the processes or mechanisms leading to the outcome of interest remain opaque. Qualitative analysis can help shed light on the processes and mechanisms by which one set of factors leads to another, such as how the event of fatherhood might act as a turning point in some cases but not in others. Second, qualitative data can help reveal actors' motivations for a given course of action. Although we do not always take these accounts at face value, when properly analyzed the data can help to inform theories that make assumptions about such motivations. Third, qualitative methods allow subjects to respond to questions in open-ended narrative form rather than in a fixed-choice manner. The resulting accounts can help to identify important correlates to outcomes of interest that might not otherwise have been considered. Fourth, qualitative interviewers often develop a high degree of rapport with their research subjects and are thus sometimes better able to get accurate measures of sensitive issues (such as criminal activity or family violence).

Hence even in quantitative research using especially thorough survey data, our method makes a significant contribution. For example, in chapter 2 of this volume, Bruce Western, Leonard Lopoo, and Sara McLanahan, using the Fragile Families data, find a statistically significant negative relationship between incarceration and marriage among unwed new fathers and mothers. This chapter (and Anne Nurse's chapter 4) extends those findings to interrogate the tenor, substance, and context of relationships between parents—from the fathers' perspective—that could variably contribute to or deter future criminal behavior.

A chief liability of our approach, though, is that our data are cross-sectional and not longitudinal. Therefore, we rely on retrospective accounts of fathers' experiences and on interpretations that may, in some cases, be no more than post hoc rationalizations of behavior. Given the limitations of our data, we cannot correct for this problem. Thus the results we report here must be interpreted cautiously. Nonetheless, because so little is known about the life experiences and worldviews of low-income noncustodial fathers or how they experience and interpret the world, we believe the following approach is justified and, at the very least, can generate new hypotheses for future scholarship.

RESEARCH METHOD

The data are drawn from verbatim transcripts of repeated in-depth interviews of roughly three hundred unskilled and semiskilled low-income noncustodial fathers living in two U.S. cities (Philadelphia, Pennsylvania, and Charleston, South Carolina) conducted from September 1995 to May 2001. The cities were chosen to reflect variation in economic conditions and policy contexts. Philadelphia and its inner suburb, Camden, New Jersey, both had slack labor markets during the study period, but the Charleston area's was one of the tightest in the nation. Both sites have strict child-support enforcement systems, but Charleston's is especially punitive. The law enforcement regimes of these locales vary as well, though we have not explored these variations in depth. Generally, the primary limitation of qualitative data is that the sample size is small or equivalent data are not collected across all cases. This data set is unique in that we conducted a large number of interviews in a highly systematic manner. Our sample is evenly divided by race-ethnicity (black, white, and Latino in Philadelphia and black and white in Charleston) and by age category (fathers aged thirty and under and fathers over thirty). As a result, we have thirty fathers in each race-age cell in each city and a total sample of three hundred. For this chapter we have analyzed forty-five cases with incarceration histories and an additional forty-five cases with episodes of criminal involvement but no incarceration history. More than one-third of respondents report imprisonment or incarceration (jail, prison, or time served in an alternative institution such as a rehabilitation program or halfway house). Roughly two-thirds reported at least one episode of criminal involvement over their lifetime.[3]

We did not recruit our respondents randomly; rather, we used a targeted neighborhood approach. In each city, we used census data to identify census tract clusters with relatively high levels of poverty, because these were the neighborhoods that also contained the largest number of poor single-parent households. We had to assume that the fathers attached to such families could also be found there. Our initial list of target clusters, or "neighborhoods," contained all those neighborhoods with a poverty rate of at least 20 percent. This relatively low poverty threshold ensured that a sufficient number of white neighborhoods could be identified for the study (typically, the white poor are far more likely than their African American or Puerto Rican counterparts to live in mixed-income neighborhoods). From this list, we selected several target neighborhoods in each city that had demographic characteristics that typified the range of neighborhoods we had identified for each ethnic group. To offer one example, the Philadelphia metropolitan area contains a large number of predominately African American neighborhoods that met our criteria. But because they are concentrated in the cities of Philadelphia and Camden, we chose three Camden neighborhoods and six Philadelphia neighborhoods that roughly represented the range of social conditions (unemployment rates, poverty rates, preponderance of single-parent families) seen in the broader list of predominately African American neighborhoods on our list. Fewer white and Puerto Rican than black neighborhoods ended up fitting our criteria, so we interviewed in all of these communities rather than selecting among them.

Once we had selected our more than two dozen target neighborhoods, we then canvassed each neighborhood on foot, informally interviewing owners of local stores, representatives of local grassroots community groups, clergy, representatives of nonprofit social service agencies, neighborhood employers, and representatives of other social institutions (teachers, social workers, and other government agency representatives). These neighborhood canvasses, along with data on male characteristics from the census, gave us some sense of the range of low-income noncustodial fathers we might find in each neighborhood and how and where we might find them.

We then used referrals from each of these sources and from direct contacts made between fieldworkers and research subjects at bus or train stops, informal day-labor corners, formal-sector places of employment, and other locales where we learned neighborhood males tended to congregate (bars, grocery stores, convenience stores), taking care to try to sample across the range of men we were expecting to find in each neighborhood based on our canvass. Men who were successfully recruited into the study were also asked for referrals to neighborhood men they thought we would be unable to identify through these means. The resulting sample is far from random, but our intent was to maximize heterogeneity to reflect as closely as possible the composition of the population of interest.

According to our sampling strategy, all of our respondents earn less than $8.00 an hour or $16,000 a year from formal-sector employment, and none has a college degree. All have at least one child for whom they are the noncustodial father, most are not married and have never been married, nearly two-thirds are African American or Latino, roughly half report that they use drugs or consume alcohol at levels considered excessive, and most also live in poor urban neighborhoods. Considering the fact that these interviews took place in a period of unprecedented economic growth, our wage restriction alone means that the men in our sample are highly disadvantaged indeed. The fathers in our sample come into contact with the criminal justice system primarily through the drug trade (other common crimes include theft, auto theft, burglary, robbery, and assault, and these are often drug related). Drugs play a large role in the story we tell in this chapter; though not all of the incarceration or imprisonment we observe results from drug involvement, most is at least peripherally related to the use or sale of controlled substances.

This is a new area of interest to us. Our father interviews contain detailed histories of their relationships, both with their children's mothers and with their children, their employment histories (including formal, informal, and criminal employment), a recounting of their experiences with the criminal justice system, and detailed information on their income (from all sources, including informal work and crime) and expenditures. Thus these data are potentially useful for understanding the pathways through which involvement with the criminal justice system may affect a father's bond with his children and whether familial relationships between fathers and children may affect criminal trajectories.

In this research we have used a focused life-history approach that is common to ethnographic studies. Such an approach does have a serious limitation in that it necessarily relies upon retrospective accounts of events that may have happened months or even years before the interview. However, quantitative longitudinal studies of criminal trajectories are rare, and qualitative longitudinal studies even rarer (for exceptions, see MacLeod 1995 and Sullivan 1989). The special advantage of the focused life-history approach to ethnographic interviewing is that it offers the chance for the respondent to give a detailed narrative about important turning points in his life, including his history of criminal offending, his interaction with the criminal justice system, and his formation and maintenance of social bonds.[4]

FINDINGS

The event of fatherhood can sharply alter how men perceive the risks and rewards of criminal activity, particularly because they believe strongly that street crime leads to either victimization (death or debilitation) or eventual incarceration. For those men who choose to activate the fathering role (whether with a first or subsequent birth), this belief is likely to make the risks of crime far less tenable. Additionally, the men we interviewed tend to value the ties to their children above all other social bonds that could potentially link them to institutions of informal social control. As a result, fatherhood in and of itself can prove a powerful turning point that leads men away from crime and toward a more mainstream trajectory.

For offenders who maintained contact with their children (or their children's mother) before their arrest, the event of incarceration has a pronounced negative effect on the bonds with their child and the child's mother. Social control theorists would expect these men to continue their criminal careers after release because of these diminished attachments. For offenders whose lifestyle has created a wedge between them and their families before arrest (usually because of severe drug or alcohol addiction), incarceration itself can be a turning point: an opportunity to take a time-out and reorient one's life. In some cases, fathers in this group use the experience of incarceration to rebuild severed ties with children (though often the romantic tie to the child's mother is not salvageable, a cooperative friendship may sometimes emerge). From the social control perspective, incarceration may have a rehabilitative effect for those men in this group who take advantage of the opportunity to reattach themselves to family.

FATHERHOOD AS A TURNING POINT

One common theme that emerged from our interviews was the dramatic impact that becoming a father often had on men's lifestyles. The stories fathers told us sometimes had the flavor of religious testimonies and were structured into before-and-after accounts. Typically, these fathers had been involved in selling or using drugs, hanging out on the corner, and "messing with" several different women—a lifestyle several respondents referred to as "rippin' and runnin' the streets." However, after their first child was born, many reported a dramatic change in their behavior. Ahmad, a nineteen-year-old African American high school graduate from Camden who works in the formal sector, regularly spends time with his daughter (though he provides only intermittent financial help).[5] Here he describes the impact the birth of his daughter had on his life:

> She changed my life a lot. I was headed down the wrong path. I grew up on the streets, everything from drugs to this and that. I mean, I've been in jail before. But ever since she's been born, I slowed down a lot. You know. . . . 'Cause it's like, before her, I didn't really care too much about anything. I really just lived every day for that day. But as of now, I'm living every day for today and tomorrow.

These sentiments were echoed by "Bucket," a forty-six-year-old African American father of one adult daughter and one twelve-year-old daughter. Bucket has a certificate of general educational development (GED) and does odd jobs (mostly window washing). Though he sees his youngest daughter twice a month, he offers no financial support. "I always wanted to be a father. I always wanted a child. I waited until I was twenty-five years old before I had my first child, but I always wanted to be a father. Before I had her, [I was] in trouble. I was doing wrong things. I was wild, crazy. It always seems as though I was getting in some kind of trouble."

Fathers often enthusiastically embraced the lifestyle changes brought about by their new role and did not merely accept them with reluctance. Robert, a twenty-three-year-old African American college dropout (he dropped out to help support his son) sees his six-month-old son frequently and intermittently contributes a portion of his earnings from his full-time formal-sector job. When we asked him how the pregnancy of his girlfriend and birth of his son had affected him, he told us,

> Yeah, it has definitely changed my day-to-day life because I know that for the whole nine months my girl was pregnant and to this date, I have been like totally with her, if not physically at least like on the phone, [asking] "How is everything?" I don't talk to anybody like my friends and how I used to go to parties and things like that. And it is not because I feel like "Oh darn, I can't go out." I want to be there. I want to be with my son, you know. I would rather know what is going on with

him than be somewhere, because even when I am out, I am like thinking about him. [I have] reoriented [my life].

According to many of these fathers, their child's birth literally "saved" them from the streets. The salvation theme was fairly strong in virtually all of the interviews with fathers who maintained some level of involvement with their children. Even among those fathers whose involvement had lapsed, many still used this salvation motif to describe how their lives had been transformed by a child's birth. For some fathers, the first child was a sufficient impetus to leave the streets. For others, the transformation did not occur until a second or third child was born, when the father was older.

In addition to these retrospective accounts of lifestyle changes, the impact of fatherhood was also apparent from the answers fathers gave when we asked them to imagine what their lives would be like if they had never had children. Some men did tell us that things would be easier for them, that they could have finished school or taken advantage of better employment opportunities. But the overwhelming majority of fathers we interviewed believed strongly (even passionately) that their present situations would be much worse without the presence of children in their lives. The most involved fathers spoke most poignantly to this point, but many less involved fathers (and even some completely uninvolved fathers) said their lives would mean very little if it were not for the fact that they had fathered a child. The following quotes are representative of many others that we could have selected. Kevin, a twenty-one-year-old African American father with a GED, does not work regularly but "babysits" his toddler each day while the child's mother works. Kevin contributes financially when he picks up odd jobs on weekends. "I think [my life] would be a lot different to tell you the truth. Yeah, [I would be] getting into trouble. No, I wouldn't be settled. I'd probably, you know, honestly, I'd probably be in jail or something like that, you know. [Having a kid] calms you down."

Lee, a forty-two-year-old high school graduate, lives with the mother of his youngest child and contributes to the household expenses as well as to the support of his older two children. "Without the kids," he said, "I'd probably be a dog. I hope not with AIDS. . . . I'm more settled now. [Being a father] has stopped me from doing something real stupid." Bucket, whom we described above, told us,

I'd probably still be doing the things I was doing. 'Cause when I did have my first child, it changed me. It stopped me from doing all this stuff I was doing before. So maybe I'd still be doing the things I was doing before if I didn't have her. . . . I was on the weed [and] drinking [a lot]. If I didn't have [my children], I'd still be doing that. . . . Because [of them] I stopped hanging with different people, I stopped going certain places, you know what I mean. And I got an outlook on life that was different.

In particular, some men claimed that their status as fathers was incompatible with selling drugs, an activity that many had engaged in before the birth of their children. Robert, a twenty-three-year-old African American father, asked whether he would consider selling drugs again to clear up his financial problems, replied,

[No], I want to keep it clean, and that is the hardest thing. I could do that and probably make three times over [what I'm making now], and probably get out of all of this [financial mess]. But I don't think that it would make me a better person because it would make me paranoid, and plus I would be bringing an environment around my child that I just do not want. Beeping at twelve o'clock at night and things of that nature—because I used to do that type of thing when I was younger. I experienced it.

SEVERING FRAGILE TIES

The standard perception among scholars is that incarceration has negative effects on the father-child bond. This makes sense, in that jail time necessarily removes the father from his children's lives, in terms of both physical proximity and economic contributions. Fathers in our sample who fell into the severed-ties group had several characteristics in common.

First, the vast majority offended either infrequently or moderately. Second, most had combined their criminal activity with some sort of episodic employment that, though not always formal-sector work, was not illegal in and of itself (that is, "under-the-table" employment). Third, these men generally reported no heavy drug or alcohol use before any particular episode of incarceration. Perhaps for these reasons all the men in this group had established some sort of bond with at least one of their children that involved a pattern of regular visitation or financial support or both. In some cases the bond extended to the child's mother, in others it did not.

For these fathers, the event of incarceration proved devastating to their ties with their children and their children's mothers. Virtually none of the fathers reported that their child's mother had "stayed" with them through the period of incarceration; in virtually every case, the mother broke off the relationship or became involved with another man. Because mothers are generally the conduit through which fathers' communications with children must flow, the severing of the romantic relationship with the child's mother nearly always posed problems for fathers who wanted to maintain a connection to their children.

Second, fathers in this group sometimes claimed that their children's mothers used the fact of incarceration as a justification for prohibiting the father from any subsequent contact with his child or to "talk trash" about the father to the child, thus lessening the child's motivation to remain strongly bonded to the father. Several fathers in this group, for example, found upon release that their children and their children's mothers had moved away or had simply disappeared.

Third, even when mothers attempted to preserve the father-child tie during the period of incarceration, the mere fact of incarceration often means that fathers miss out on those key events that serve to build parental bonds and to signal to the community that they intend to support their children both emotionally and financially. These key events include attending the child's birth or observing developmental milestones such as walking and talking. The father's absence at these crucial moments, we argue, can weaken his commitment to the child and, years later, the child's own sense of commitment to his or her father.

The harmful effects of incarceration can be seen in the case of Mark, a thirty-two-year-old African American in Philadelphia who works under the table as a sandwich maker at a convenience store–delicatessen. Mark has an eleven-year-old daughter whom he sees several times a month and to whose support he contributes intermittently. Mark, one of five children, grew up with his mother and grandmother. His father left the family when he was quite young, and Mark has not seen him since he was seventeen years old. After graduating from high school, Mark went to work as a janitor, and at this time met his daughter's mother, who was still a high school senior. They had been together two years when his daughter was born. When she was five years old, he was arrested for selling drugs.

> It was a situation because why I started selling was because of my daughter. That is an excuse, true, but my daughter didn't have nothing for that Christmas . . . and it sent something inside [of me] and it just totally blew my mind. And I knew friends and family that was [selling drugs] and I always could have got into it but I didn't want to [before]. . . . This was Christmas, and . . . I couldn't get nothing [for her]. And to a dad, I don't care if he is doing drugs or anything, if a dad is out there and he love his child and he love his kids and if he can't get them stuff for that special occasion, it sends something through them.

Mark's plan was to sell drugs for just a short period of time, make a lot of money (he claimed that he made about $700 a day when he sold drugs full-time), and then move back into the legitimate workforce. He thought that his risk of imprisonment was minimal because he had never been convicted of any crime before. "You know what? I thought I could out-slick the system. I said, 'This is my first time. I never did anything [be-fore]. [If I get caught], I am [only] going to get probation and I could walk off that.' [But] it didn't happen that way." Instead, he was arrested only three weeks after he began dealing and was sentenced to one year in prison. "[I was sent to a] prison where it is murderers and rapists and people not coming home for three hundred years, and it totally sent me ballistic. I though I was going to go crazy and I didn't think I was going to make it."

While he was locked up, Mark's girlfriend started seeing another man, and he found out about it through the prison grapevine. Although they got back together when he returned from prison, she was still "creeping" on him, and he decided to move back in with his mother. The girlfriend then married the man she was seeing, and they have re-cently had a son together. Mark feels that his time in prison is to blame for driving a wedge between him and his daughter's mother.

> If I wouldn't have got locked up, I would have still been with her, in the sense that it would have never happened—she would have never met no one else. [But] I can't say that the blame was hers; I can't say that the blame was my daughter's. The blame was [on] me and myself. I put myself in that situation and [now] it is up to me to think with a clear head and take it on another level.

Martinis is a forty-year-old African American father currently serv-ing a sentence for parole violation in a halfway house in Philadelphia. He has a two-year-old son by his current girlfriend and two teenaged children from a previous relationship. Although his eighteen-year-old son is more forgiving of his father's lapses, his seventeen-year-old daughter had become bitter over his going back and forth to prison when she was growing up. Just before we interviewed him, Martinis had made some effort to restore his relationship with his daughter, but he realized that he had a lot of history to overcome.

> In the beginning we were [close]—all the way up until the age of eight or nine were we close. But after me keep getting myself in trouble [go-ing back and forth to prison], I guess she kind of gave up on me. I was never around, and I guess it hurted her. We just recently had a conversation on the phone, and I had to explain to her where I was. Not just where I was literally, but my mindset and why I made the decisions I made, and why I was incarcerated and why I did certain things. It wasn't like I wanted to be away from her. I told her that I loved her dearly, and we had a little rapport. . . . Actually we [hadn't been] speaking to each other. My kids' mother said, "You are the adult.

Go down there and talk to her and get y'all thing together so that y'all can have some kind of rapport." . . . I had to go ahead and do that, and we talked, and she cried and she explained why she feel the way she feel. She feel that she didn't have no dad and it hurted me to hear that, but it was the truth. I don't blame her in a way because I wasn't there.

So now I have been trying to incorporate myself into her life again and in her daughter's life. She is coming around now; she is coming to accept me more. But I don't think she is putting her all in it, because she maybe feels as though she don't know if I am going to disappear again. I used to promise her this and promise her that, and sometimes I didn't come through. I am not a bad dad—they tell me that they love me and everything, but it is just that I am not always there for them when they really need me around.

His latest incarceration is already affecting his relationship with his youngest son, something that disturbs him:

I am not there all the time . . . though I want to be, and it hurts me and it upsets me. . . . I can remember that my dad was never around and I was wondering what it was like to always have your dad around. So I always tell myself that I would want to be around for them and some-times I found myself doing [to them what happened to me], by me being incarcerated and not there in the years when they were growing up and their little personality starting to develop. . . . I know that it upsets the mother. . . . She wants me to be part of his life. [She] calls me now and she says, "Marty, Rahmere doesn't really even know you. . . . " I missed all that time with Rahmere when he was an infant. He was born May of last year and he didn't know who I was. And she was like, "That is your dad." She came twice [to visit me]. . . . But she didn't bring him. I was very disappointed. . . . I seen him through pictures but I didn't really get a chance to see him personally until I came home in May [of this year].

Martinis's daughter was eight and his son was nine when he was first incarcerated for burglary. He thus had some time to establish a close relationship with them before he went to prison. He worries he has lost that opportunity with his younger son.

Donald, a thirty-year-old African American in Charleston, has two children, a teenaged daughter and a younger son, aged six. Donald says that his son does not like him very much because he was born when Donald was locked up—they did not meet until the boy was three years old. Donald's daughter is more forgiving because she had formed an attachment to him before he was incarcerated. She currently spends sum-mers with Donald, and he is negotiating an arrangement with her mother that would allow the daughter to live with him full-time.

Because low-income men tend to become first-time fathers in their late teens and early twenties, at the very same time that they are most likely to be engaged in criminal activity and are at highest risk of incarceration, many of our respondents with incarceration histories report having been incarcerated for the first several years of at least one of their children's lives. As we showed earlier, The Fragile Families and Child Wellbeing Study finds that more than 80 percent of the fathers responsible for these births attended the birth or visited the mother and child in the hospital immediately thereafter. Our data reveal that a father's presence at his child's birth is a key event that signals to the larger community (the father's kin, the mother's kin, and peers) his intention to take some financial responsibility and, more important, to forge a solid emotional bond with that child. Noncustodial fathers who have been present for their children's birth often describe it as one of the most significant events of their lives. On a practical level, many states allow voluntary admissions of paternity in-hospital, and missing this opportunity to form a legal bond to the child means that the father's name is often not on the child's birth certificate and that the mother, the state, or the father can formalize that tie only through more difficult and costly means later on. Fathers who are incarcerated when their children are born miss this crucial opportunity, and we speculate this may have consequences for their financial and emotional investments in their children.

Sometimes the contemporaneous occurrence of childbirth and incarceration plants seeds of doubt as to the child's true paternity. Julio is a thirty-six-year-old African American father living in Charleston, South Carolina. His daughter was born exactly nine months after he was incarcerated, which led him to doubt whether she was really his child. Julio says this doubt "haunts" him, yet he is hesitant to have a blood test, because in his view, the child is already bonded to him, and he is afraid of hurting her.

Donald recounts a similar situation with his son:

> I found out [my son's mother] was pregnant when I was incarcerated . . . and a guy came in that I knew from school, and he said he'd seen Yvette and that she was pregnant. And I was like, "Whatever," you know, I was like, "By who?" So I ended up getting in touch with her and called her mom's house collect and . . . she was like, "Yeah, I pregnant, I'm pregnant from you." . . . I was like, "Whatever, not me. . . . Come on, we dated off and on from seventh grade up until high school and you know we messed around and . . . you never got pregnant [all that time] from me." And she was like, "Yeah, it's from you, and what do you want to do?" and I was like, "I'm not doing nothing. I'm going to be sitting in here for while. I'm locked up." And one night, I was sitting in the cell after a few months and I was like [praying], "God, if its my child, show me it's my child, and just let me know something."

The next day Donald's mother visited him in prison, something she had never done before, and reported that the child had been born. As both events happened only a day after he had prayed, he took them as a "sign" yet told us he had nagging doubts.

Both Donald and Julio were incarcerated for a period of several years. Yet our data show that even quite short periods of incarceration can mean that fathers of very young children regret having missed out on milestones in their child's development. Rick, a young African American father living in Camden, was spending just three months in jail when his son turned a year old. He was quite upset that the time away from his family caused him to miss out on the transition from infant to toddler: "That was last August, and my son had just . . . started walking and talking. And when I went [to jail] they barely let me see him. And when I got out, he was walking and talking. . . . That crushed me. 'Cause, you know, I wanted to see all that, you know. My first son."

Although incarcerated fathers must be separated from their children, one may wonder about the role of visitation in keeping fathers and children connected. In 1999, according to figures from the Bureau of Justice Statistics, 1.5 million children had a mother or father in prison (Mumola 2000). Although about 40 percent of imprisoned fathers reported weekly contact with children by phone, letter, or a visit, nearly 60 percent of incarcerated fathers reported never having seen their children since their admission to prison (Hairston 1998). Although our interviews did not address this question directly, our fathers who had served time seldom reported having received visits from their children, or even their children's mothers, while they were in jail or in prison. For a few, this was largely because they were sent to prison at an institution that was too far away for someone with no access to a car to visit. However, several others told us that serving time was harder if one remained in contact with one's friends and family on the outside. For this reason, they voluntarily cut themselves off from outside relations. Donald, who had been to prison several times, told us, "Normally when I'm locked up I don't accept visits. I don't write if I'm locked up and I don't do any of that, because it makes your time hard, you know, worrying about what's going on out there and thinking about what's going on out there; it makes it hard. You focus on getting this time done and getting this over with."

Mark was one of the few fathers whose child visited him regularly. His daughter was five when he was sent away for one year. Initially, it was her visits that kept him going. Yet toward the end of his sentence, he could not take the strain of constant reminders of home:

And the only thing that kept me going [when I was in prison] was my daughter. . . . [She] came to see me every weekend, every weekend my daughter's mom brought her to see me—every weekend, when I was in the state, when I was still here. And the last three months of my sentence, they sent me all the way up there by the Poconos. . . . [It was too hard for her to] make it, and I didn't want her to make it. She tried a couple of times, and I kept denying it, because the closer you get to [being released] the harder it got when you see people from home. And what you want to do is try to tune them out. [But] I wrote everyday, and she wrote me everyday. Boy, you should see how many letters.

When fathers are incarcerated, they must rely on their children's mothers to be the conduit to their children, though sometimes a kin member (for example, the father's mother) can also play that role. The children's mothers do this either actively by bringing children to visit in prison, or more passively by simply accepting collect phone calls or, more rarely, their letters. Yet as noted earlier, incarceration can sever not only a father's relationship with his children but also his relationship with his children's mother.

Often, a father and his children's mother are still romantically attached when he is initially incarcerated. However, this is a vulnerable time for their relationship, and virtually all of the men in our sample reported that their girlfriends had formed new attachments while they were in prison. Tom, a thirty-year-old white father from Philadelphia, had just been imprisoned for selling drugs when his oldest child (now eleven years old) was born. While in prison and unable to continue a relatively lucrative career selling drugs, he lost his house (bought with drug proceeds) and his girlfriend, who took up with someone else. Although Tom did not return to selling drugs after his release, his child's mother would not let Tom see his son unless he was paying regular child support—something he found hard to do because his prison record locked him out of most conventional employment (see chapter 8 in this volume). At the time of the interview, Tom had not seen his son in five years.

Mark was in prison for less than a year and was planning on getting back together with his daughter's mother when he was released. Yet while he was away, she met a man who drove a bus for the local transit system. When Mark came home and started working for McDonald's, she took him back but still maintained a clandestine relationship with the other man. When Mark found out about it, he broke off the relationship:

We was going to get back together: marriage and everything. But she wasn't totally honest. I had much love for her and she didn't know how much love I had for her. . . . [I didn't really blame her, because] I probably would have [had another relationship] too [if she was serving time]. But she couldn't be person enough to tell me—she kept trying to creep around. . . . I suspected it, and at that time I had people coming to me [and telling me about it]. . . . So I did find out, and she still denied it, and from that point . . . it was just like a thing, "I can't never trust you now." . . . If I wouldn't have got locked up . . . she would have never met no one else.

Mark's statement—that his girlfriend "would never have met no one else" if he had not been incarcerated—raises an interesting point. In fact, despite his belief to the contrary, it is quite likely that Mark and his girlfriend would not have stayed together much longer, even if he had not been incarcerated. Relationships between unmarried parents are extremely fragile (70 percent of poor unmarried parents break up before the child's third birthday), and fathers who engage in criminal activity are particularly likely to alienate their children's mothers (see Edin and Kefalas forthcoming). Seen from this angle, incarceration may not directly cause a breakup but merely provide an additional impetus and opportunity for girlfriends to escape from a relationship a bit earlier than they otherwise might have.

This may partially explain our second finding that when fathers are imprisoned, their children's mothers may use the fact that their child's father has a prison record as a justification to completely cut him out of the child's life, even if they knew full well of his criminal involvement before the incarceration. In low-income communities, particularly African American communities, mothers feel considerable pressure to keep their child's father involved, especially because many of the mothers grew up without a father around and sorely felt the lack. For women who do not want to continue dealing with a father whom they view as a ne'er-do-well, incarceration provides a socially acceptable excuse to deny visitation or even to simply disappear. Rubén, a twenty-year-old Puerto Rican living in Philadelphia, had his only child at the age of sixteen. When he was nineteen, he went to prison on a drug charge and served a one-year sentence. Upon his return to the neighborhood in which he and his child's mother had lived, he could find no trace of either of them. The mother did contact him to let him know that they were okay, but she refused to tell him where she was living or to let him see his son.

If the child's mother is addicted to drugs or otherwise deemed unfit (abusive or neglectful), a criminal record can make a judge unwilling to let the child's father have custody of the child. Thomas, a twenty-eight-year-old white Philadelphia father, has a nine-year-old daughter and a nine-year-old son by different mothers. Thomas was convicted of attempted murder when he was in his early twenties. Subsequently, his son's mother, a drug addict, lost custody of the children to the state. He describes what happened next:

[The state] took [my son] and put him in a foster home. After that happened, I had a court date the next week to see if I could get him. But something happened—I think it was because of my criminal record—they said no and they denied me. And my lawyer said only two things could happen. You have the choice of leaving that child in a foster home or you can sign the rights over to the [maternal] grandmother, just temporarily [until you get yourself together and can convince the judge you can care for the child]. . . . I didn't want him in no foster home so I signed.

When relationships between fathers and their children's mothers break down and become acrimonious, as they often do, men with criminal records may find themselves at a distinct disadvantage. Many fathers report that their former girlfriends use their records of criminal behavior, or simply the fact that they have been in prison or are on parole, as an excuse to "talk trash" about them to their children and to others. Bill, a thirty-one-year-old white father in Philadelphia, claimed that his "ex-wife" (his term for her, though they were never legally married) kept calling his parole officer and "told lies" about him (claiming he had violated his parole in various ways) whenever she wanted something from him and he was hesitant to provide it. He felt powerless in this situation, especially since submitting to her wishes would not guarantee him access to his child.

For those fathers with moderate or strong ties to their children or to their children's mothers, the threat of prison can act as a powerful deterrent to criminal behavior. Rick, a young African American father in Camden who was still together with the mother of his 18-month-old son, exclaimed,

I don't see how those guys want to keep going to jail. That's crazy to me. That's what I be tellin' these guys, man. The most I did was three months in jail. . . . That's a place I don't want to be, I know that. . . . And—I don't see how these guys all just take little times of their life out. You missin' a lot, man. Then they get out, these things have changed. Most of the people I know be doin' two-, three-, four-year [sentences]. Three months, man [was too much for me]. . . . Yeah, it is [a temptation to go back to selling drugs], but see, my son. That's really changed me, and my time that I did in jail . . . that three months.

Kevin's brother Craig has been to prison several times. He now works day labor rather than selling drugs, because he has a child and does not want to be like his father. "[My father] passed away when I was about twenty-three or twenty-four. He was in and out of prison. That is basically why I try to do what I do [work day labor rather than sell drugs], because I do not want to be like that when my children [are] growing up."

Sometimes the threat of prison does not lead fathers who are attached to their children to completely disavow drug sales, but it does slow their rate of offending dramatically. Lee is a forty-two-year-old African American father of three children by three different mothers. He maintains some contact with all three of his children. He has had any number of jobs since graduating from high school (construction, vending, factory work) but now works primarily through formal-sector day-labor agencies. He supplements his day-labor income by doing side jobs for friends and neighbors (yard work, moving) and by selling crack.

Lee sold drugs quite regularly before his son, now aged seventeen, was born. "This was my first [child]. I was nervous. I said, 'What am I going to do? Suppose I get locked up for selling drugs. I'm in jail. I can't provide [for his child's mother and the child].' . . . So I straightened up." Lee is one of many fathers who say they tried to leave their illegal activities behind when they had children. Like these other men, Lee's reasons were threefold: he did not want anything to interfere with his ability to support his child financially, he did not want prison to come between him and his son relationally, and he wanted his son to think of him as an "upstanding" guy rather than as a criminal.

He sees the oldest child, who lives in Colorado, only once a year but is on excellent terms with the child's mother. He corresponds regularly with her and in that way maintains a line of communication to his son. She tells her son that his father is a "good guy," which pleases Lee. He sees his middle child only sporadically (about once a month), whenever "people, places, and things" take him to that part of town and the mother allows the visit. The child does not know that he is her father, and she calls him "Mr. Eddy" rather than "Daddy." He hopes that someday the mother will tell the child that he is her father. This child also gets cash or a bond on her birthday but no other support.

Lee lives with his third child and spends most evenings at home with her and her mother. Lee speaks often about the importance of being honest with his kids and of providing for them. Both, he feels, are compromised by any criminal activity that might end with incarceration.

> What makes a good father is being honest. Being honest and trustworthy in the community and outside the community. Being honest so that people will speak to you. That's the first part. . . . You walk with your kids and people speak to you, they respect you. . . . The second thing is being able to provide for your kids. When you take a walk with them or walk around the neighborhood, they say, "Hey daddy, I want an [Italian] ice or a Popsicle." You can't say "I can't do that right now." . . . [But] the main thing [is] being honest and truthful. Because if you're a liar and a cheat, nothing happens for you, nothing happens for your children because they'll tell them the dirt that you did. [They'll say] "Your father's a rotten motherfucker."

Lee managed to stay pretty clear of the drug trade since his first son was born seventeen years ago, but the birth of each subsequent child has reinvigorated his desire to stay away from the trade and its "fast money." When we asked him what kind of father he wanted to be for his youngest child, he replied, "To be strong. To put a home over her head. And show her that education is the best thing to do, because fast money will get you nowhere."

In his late twenties Lee was arrested twice for possession of marijuana and for shoplifting. Both times, he was released almost immediately, though he is not sure why. Lee considers himself lucky because he has never been arrested for selling drugs and, though he continues to deal on and off, these activities are nothing like those he pursued for about five years in his early twenties. He claims that he now sells drugs only occasionally and then only to "provide" for his family. In the two months preceding our interview, Lee had sold to only three customers, and the month we talked to him he had sold drugs only twice.

REBUILDING SEVERED TIES

It is clear from these cases that incarceration can negatively affect fathers' relationships with their children, either directly or indirectly, by severing ties to their children's mothers or being maligned by the women in front of their children to such an extent that the children want no contact with their fathers. The threat of imprisonment can also deter some of these fathers from criminal behavior altogether, whereas others will reduce their risk of imprisonment by offending only occasionally. However, it is important to keep in mind that for some fathers it is not the time in prison that first drives the wedge between them and their children but rather the criminal behavior that lands them there in the first place.

For fathers hoping to rebuild severed ties, the bond with their children and their children's mothers had generally been destroyed before incarceration. In every case we observed, this resulted from heavy use of either alcohol or illicit drugs. Substance abuse is extremely hard on family ties. First, fathers who engage in heavy substance use often remove themselves from contact with those they care about (even from their own kin) because they are ashamed to be seen so "down and out."

Second, even fathers whose own shame does not cause them to remove themselves often find that the children's mothers shut them out. It is not hard to imagine why mothers do this: Drug addicts tend to steal (even from their own families) to feed their habit. They engage in dangerous behavior that can follow them from the streets into the household. They generally offend at high rates to feed their habits. The debilitating nature of the addiction often makes it difficult for these fathers to combine their criminal activity with other more legitimate (and thus more socially acceptable) economic pursuits. Finally, they generally drink or smoke up all their "profits" from illicit work. None of these tendencies make them good father material in the eyes of their children's mothers. In fact, the involvement of such fathers with their children can be downright dangerous. It is for these reasons that fathers in this group who begin an episode of incarceration often feel they have nowhere to go but up in their relationships with their children.

Of course, not all fathers who had severed their ties with their children before incarceration used the experience to reorient their lives. Our sample, like nationally representative samples, contains a few serious offenders for whom nothing—not fatherhood, incarceration, or any other event—deters them from a criminal trajectory.

We also find that older fathers are more likely than younger fathers to use the event of incarceration to try to repair severed bonds with family. Although it is true that older fathers tend to have older children, making the reconnection potentially more difficult, each child a man fathers, from his first to his last, offers the potential for reconciliation, and these older fathers tend to concentrate their efforts on the youngest child (this is possible because the children often have different mothers).

In addition, we find some evidence in our interviews that fathers are more motivated to reconnect when they are somewhat older because they have learned that crime does not pay and they plan on going straight anyway. That is, the accumulation of experiences with criminal offending tend to change fathers' notions of how well crime—particularly the drug trade—pays in relation to more formal work. When such men transition to mainstream employment, they generally take jobs at the lowest end of local labor markets, as day laborers, factory workers, fast-food workers, and the like. This makes sense in light of the finding in chapter 8 of this volume that only 38 percent of employers in the four cities they studied would accept job applications from former offenders.

When the men we interviewed were younger, they were largely convinced by both street lore and their own early experiences that the drug trade paid better than these legitimate jobs. Over time, they saw that their profits fluctuated wildly, that their business constantly exposed them to long hours out of doors, and that drug dealing carried with it a substantial risk of death or imprisonment (this risk became palpable when they began to see more and more of their own street peers killed or disabled as a result of the trade). Even worse, they noted that because drug dealing often went hand in hand with drug addiction, over time their drug use escalated, and they drank or smoked up their profits, leaving them nothing to show for their efforts. Thus many had adopted the philosophy that "fast money don't get you nowhere" but "slow money is sure money." It is interesting that fathers who had made the decision to pursue "slow money" in "menial jobs" thought they might better be able to forge a reconnection with their children than if they had continued to "live the life" of a street hustler to "get the paper" (the money) to buy things for their children. Provided they could kick their addiction, the very fact that they expressed willingness to engage in menial yet steady employment, some said, was a powerful testimony to the fact that "Daddy got himself together."

Jose, a forty-one-year-old Puerto Rican father from Philadelphia, has a four-year-old son. In his son's infancy, Jose was a heavy drug user. He was arrested for burglary (to feed his habit) when the child was a few months old. After serving his sentence of three years, Jose could not find his former girlfriend or his son. He told our interviewer, "I have not seen [my son], and I don't [know where he is]—I know that I am his father, that is all that I know. . . . He is mine, but I have not been able to be a father to him, [first because of my drug addiction and then because of prison]."

In fact, for fathers whose criminal lifestyle and the drug and alcohol abuse that so often accompanies it has had them "rippin' and runnin' the streets" to such an extent that they had virtually no relationship with their children before incarceration, time spent in jail or prison might actually provide the necessary time-out they need to redirect their lives away from drugs and try to forge a pathway back into their children's lives. To illustrate how a spell of incarceration can serve as a turning point for such fathers, we present the case of Jimmy in some detail.

Jimmy is a forty-year-old African American father residing in Camden, New Jersey. Jimmy's mother died young, and his older sister, who had six children of her own, raised him. He dropped out of high school to work full-time because his sister did not earn enough to provide him with the kind of clothing and shoes he wanted. To relieve some of the pressure on her, and to satisfy his own tastes in clothing, he traded school for a job between ninth and tenth grade. Jimmy works as a landscaper and has held landscaping jobs on and off for nearly two decades, between stints in jail and prison. Most of his employers pay him under the table. Jimmy thinks he would own his own business right now were it not for his ongoing drug addiction and his criminal record.

The mother of Jimmy's children is a woman named Shirley, a fellow drug addict with whom he has had an on-again, off-again relationship. Just after his first child was born, Jimmy went to prison for the first time, for burglary (he has thirty-four burglaries on record, all motivated by his drug habit). When his children were six and seven years old, Jimmy was again imprisoned, and Shirley met and married another drug addict. When Shirley married a second time, her drug habit escalated, and after about a year of heavy using she lost custody of the children. Because he was in prison, Jimmy could not intervene. Currently, both children are in foster care. Jimmy regularly sees his daughter, whom he has taken with him to church on Father's Day, though he has not seen his son since his release three years ago.

Jimmy describes his most recent incarceration (he served an additional fifteen months because of a positive drug test while out on parole) as a "blessing in disguise." He "found God again" in prison and was able to "get himself together." He does not blame the loss of his relationship with his children's mother or his son on his repeated incarceration, because, he says, he was too busy using drugs and burglarizing factories to have much of a relationship with them anyway. Now, for the first time (and thanks to a cooperative foster parent who is a fellow Christian), he has been able to forge a relationship with his daughter. He thinks she loves and respects him now because "Daddy got himself together."

Jimmy's story shows that prison may function as a turning point and an opportunity to redirect one's life for those fathers whose lives have become so out of control (usually because of alcohol or drug addiction) that they need a powerful shock or a highly structured environment, like prison, to break their downward spiral. In Jimmy's case, his criminal lifestyle and the drug addiction that fueled it had already broken his bond with his children. Serving his most recent sentence, and the rekindled religious fervor that resulted, helped him to break the cycle of burglary and drug use and to "keep clean" during the three years since his release. Thus incarceration contributed both directly and indirectly to his rehabilitation as a father.

Jack, a thirty-three-year-old white father from Philadelphia, was convicted of five incidents of driving under the influence (DUI) in a single month after the mother of his children left him. Like Jimmy, serving time gave Jack the necessary perspective on his life and offered him an opportunity to renew a latent religious commitment. During his interview, Jack exclaimed,

> Jail was the best thing that happened to me! I sat down on Christmas Eve in jail. Christmas Day in jail. I reflected on what I'd done. So I did a little soul-searching. I remember I was in maximum security.... Every night my conscience would come to me and beat the hell out of me.... [Before imprisonment], when I was at home watching TV, my conscience would kick in and I'd turn the channel.... This was the first time my conscience actually had me alone so it could work on me, which it did. About four or five nights, whack, whack.... On the fourth night, I said, "Please, help me, God. I'm your son. I want to start again." And I felt forgiven. Well, that happened just before the first of January.

And I've been praying to God ever since. I'm not born again or a Bible-thumper; I just got God back in my life.

Wilbert, a thirty-eight-year-old African American father, tells a similar story. When he was interviewed in 1998, he had been free for just two months after serving a six-month prison sentence for drug dealing. Before he was arrested, he had been an alcoholic, a drug addict, and a full-time drug dealer. In fact, he was so involved in drug trafficking that he used to "stay out in the street all night long for weeks and change clothes right in the middle of the street. The water plugs would be on, and I would wash up in the water plug, get a bar of soap, and change my clothes in the middle of the street, because I was out there on drugs, selling drugs around the block, going in and out of jail."

As Wilbert himself summed it up, "I pretty much didn't give a damn—[I was] running around and I didn't care about anything." While he was incarcerated, he asked the mothers of his thirteen-year-old son and ten-year-old daughter to bring them for a visit, but "they made up excuses: they don't have time, they have [other things to do]—you know how it is," probably because he had not seen either one of them for quite some time before his arrest. Sitting in jail for five months while waiting to be sentenced, Wilbert got a chance to think about his life and how he wanted things to be different.

> I went to prison a couple of times, but this last time really did something to me—it made me find myself. Maybe the first month or so when I was in there, I would say that I wanted a beer, or when I get out I am going to get this weed or this paper (drug money). But I didn't get out in a month, I didn't get out in three or four months. . . . By then I was looking at the right thing to do. I was going to church in there. I was working in an upholstery shop, making something like a dollar something a day, but I learned a lot. It was vocational training, upholstery skills. I could always use it [later].

There are fathers who try but fail to reconnect with their children when they leave prison, either because they cannot locate the child, because their child's mother or guardian is unwilling to facilitate a reconciliation, or because the child does not want a relationship with his or her father. It is also true that the experience of prison does not motivate some fathers to stop offending and reorient their lives. The most "hardened" criminal in our sample was an African American in Philadelphia who calls himself "O." When he was seven years old, O began stealing the money his mother had set aside to pay his tuition at the local Catholic school. In his teens, he would rob anyone he happened to see if he needed money, and he claims the neighbors even started a petition to get him out of the neighborhood. He also broke into local stores and pawned the stolen goods to other stores nearby. By the time he was fourteen he had a crew of seven working alongside him, robbing stores and fencing the items to other local retailers, and reported making about $1,000 a week for the eight of them.

The first time he got caught was when he was twelve. He had stolen a bike that belonged to the son of a police officer who lived in O's neighborhood, and the boy's father made sure that O was put in juvenile detention. Over the next six years, he was in and out of juvenile institutions for various offenses.

When he was eighteen he stopped burglarizing stores and began pimping the woman who would become the mother of his three kids; he later reported having made a good living doing so. When he was nineteen, he pulled a knife on three policemen whom he claims were hassling him. They also found a pound of marijuana on him, for which he served his first sentence as an adult. Although his children's mother is now dead (she was murdered by a client while he was in prison), O occasionally sees his sixteen-year-old daughter, who lives with her mother's mother and now has a child of her own. Regarding his children, O says, "Sometimes I worry about how my children are doing because I'm not in touch with them, and I never really been in touch with them. I see them from time to time, but it really worries me because there is not a bond there." Despite these worries, O's lifestyle has not changed, and he has no connection at all to his two younger children.

CONCLUSION

The first conclusion we draw from these case studies is that for male prisoners with children, the same life event—incarceration—can result in several different pathways, depending on the father's prior situation and his response. For those fathers who have fairly solid ties to family and whose lifestyle before imprisonment had not driven a deep wedge, incarceration disrupts the bonds fathers have to their romantic partners and to their children. Following Sampson and Laub, we expect that such disruption might well have a negative impact on the prospects of the father's rehabilitation and may reinforce his criminal trajectory rather than reverse it. Perhaps lowering some of the barriers to contact with children while imprisoned would mitigate this impact (for a review of these barriers, see Hairston 1998 and Nurse 2000, 2002).

A second conclusion we draw is that for fathers whose lifestyle before incarceration has already driven a wedge between them and their children (and their children's mothers), incarceration offers the opportunity to rebuild severed social ties by curbing the destructive behavior that led to separation in the first place. For these men, the potential of reconnecting with their children may offer a powerful motivation to go straight that is not present for nonfathers. Of course, not all fathers will experience their time in prison as a turning point to desistance, and further research might be able to identify the confluence of factors that allow fathers to effect such a turnaround while incarcerated.

Third, we also find that fear of incarceration, when combined with the event of becoming a father, can act as a powerful deterrent to criminal activity and may reverse a father's career trajectory. For those who reported engagement in offending behavior before having a child but were not incarcerated, criminal behavior suddenly becomes far more "costly" and fraught with risk. Fatherhood, on the other hand, offers powerful perceived rewards to men if they can manage to avoid those things (incarceration or addiction) that might disrupt the father-child bond.

Finally, these qualitative data show that crime can have two different faces. Sometimes low-income men use criminal activity only occasionally to supplement their income from unstable or part-time work in the formal economy, much the same way that low-income mothers rely on kin or off-the-books jobs to supplement their meager incomes from welfare or low-wage work (Edin and Lein 1997). Ironically, the pressure for these men to supply additional income is most acute when they first become fathers and must procure expensive items like strollers, cribs, and playpens. Forays into crime to provide for these family needs or to get by during work slowdowns and layoffs is quite different from the patterns of "real" criminals like O or those fathers who steal or deal to support a drug habit. One possibility is that the courts might try to distinguish between these two different faces of crime, perhaps by taking testimonies from mothers of the father's children into account, and then factor this into the sentencing process. It is also quite apparent that a major culprit in damaging ties between fathers and family is severe drug and alcohol addiction and abuse. Although incarceration may sometimes help these men "dry out" enough to reconnect with children, more emphasis should be put on proactive policies that prevent substance abuse and the crime that almost inevitably follows.

A limitation of the study is that because we cannot assess the representativeness of the sample, we cannot reliably estimate the size of the three groups identified here. Moreover, owing to the qualitative nature of the data we have drawn on, the size of the effects cannot be reliably measured. Knowing the relative size of the groups, as well as the size of the effects of incarceration for each, is vitally important for policy and is thus an important direction for future research.

NOTES

1. A fourth important trend is that the proportion of low-income fathers who are involved in the child-support enforcement system has grown significantly, award amounts have increased, and child-support enforcement policies have become increasingly punitive: many states now routinely garnish wages, seize tax returns, prosecute fathers who flee across state lines to evade a child-support order, revoke driver's and professional licenses, and imprison men for nonpayment of child support (Garfinkel, Meyer, and McLanahan 1998).
2. There are, however, a few excellent studies of incarcerated fathers' bonds with their children, both within prison (Hairston 1998) and after release (Nurse 2000).
3. The median age at first fatherhood is lower for those men who are involved in criminal activity than for the general population (Lerman 1993).
4. Laub and Sampson (1993) advocate a "person-centered" approach to research on criminal careers (Magnusson and Bergman 1988, 1990), which focuses on "persons" rather than "variables" and examines the life histories of persons over time.
5. All names of interviewees and their friends and family are pseudonyms.

REFERENCES

Bachman, Jerald G., and John Schulenberg. 1993. "How Part-Time Work Intensity Relates to Drug Use, Problem Behavior, Time Use, and Satisfaction among High School Seniors: Are these Consequences or Merely Correlates?" *Developmental Psychology* 29(2): 220–35.

Bound, John, and George Johnson. 1992. "Changes in the Structure of Wages in the 1980s: An Evaluation of Alternative Explanations." *American Economic Review* 82(3): 371–92.

Doyle, Joanne M., Ehsan Ahmed, and Robert N. Horn. 1999. "The Effects of Labor Markets and Income Inequality on Crime: Evidence from Panel Data." *Southern Economic Journal* 65(4, April): 717–31.

Durkheim, Émile. 1951. *Suicide.* New York: Free Press.

Edin, Kathryn, and Maria Kefalas. Forthcoming. *Promises I Can Keep: Why Poor Women Put Motherhood Before Marriage.* Berkeley: University of California Press.

Edin, Kathryn, and Laura Lein. 1997. *Making Ends Meet.* New York: Russell Sage Foundation.

Elder, Glen H., Jr. 1985. "Perspectives on the Life Course." In *Life Course Dynamics,* edited by Glen Elder. Ithaca, N.Y.: Cornell University Press.

Farrington, David P., Bernard Gallagher, Lynda Morley, Raymond J. St. Ledger, and Donald J. West. 1986. "Unemployment, School Leaving, and Crime." *British Journal of Criminology* 26(4, October): 335–56.

Federal Bureau of Investigation. 1990. "Age-Specific Arrest Rates and Race-Specific Arrest Rates for Selected Offenses, 1965–1988." Washington: U.S. Government Printing Office.

————. 1992. *Crime in the United States: 1991.* Washington: U.S. Government Printing Office.

Garfinkel, Irwin, Sara S. McLanahan, and Thomas L. Hanson. 1998. "A Patchwork Portrait of Nonresident Fathers." In *Fathers Under Fire,* edited by Irwin Garfinkel, Sara S. McLanahan, Daniel R. Meyer, and Judith A. Seltzer. New York: Russell Sage Foundation.

Garfinkel, Irwin, Daniel R. Meyer, and Sara S. McLanahan. 1998. "A Brief History of Child Support Policies in the United States." In *Fathers Under Fire,* edited by Irwin Garfinkel, Sara S. McLanahan, Daniel R. Meyer, and Judith A. Seltzer. New York: Russell Sage Foundation.

Glueck, Sheldon, and Eleanor Glueck. 1950. *Unraveling Juvenile Delinquency.* New York: Commonwealth Fund.

————. 1968. *Delinquents and Nondelinquents in Perspective.* Cambridge, Mass.: Harvard University Press.

Grogger, Jeff. 1998. "Market Wages and Youth Crime." *Journal of Labor Economics* 16(3): 756–91.

Hagan, John, and Bill McCarthy. 1997. *Mean Streets.* Cambridge, Mass.: Cambridge University Press.

Hagan, John, and Alberto Palloni. 1988. "Crimes as Social Events in the Life Course: Reconceiving a Criminological Controversy." *Criminology* 26(1): 87–100.

Hairston, Creasie F. 1998. "The Forgotten Parent: Understanding the Forces that Influence Incarcerated Fathers' Relationships with their Children." *Child Welfare* 77(5, September–October): 617–39.

Hirschi, Travis. 1969. *Causes of Delinquency.* Berkeley: University of California Press.

Hogan, Dennis P. 1980. "The Transition to Adulthood as a Career Contingency." *American Sociological Review* 45(2, April): 261–76.

Holzer, Harry, and Paul Offner. 2001. "Employment Trends Among Less-Skilled Young Men, 1979–2000." Paper presented at Inequality Summer Institute, Harvard University (June 13–14).

Horney, Julie, D. Wayne Osgood, and Ineke Haen Marshall. 1995. "Variability in Crime and Local Life Circumstances." *American Sociological Review* 60(5, October): 655–73.

Katz, Lawrence F., and Kevin M. Murphy. 1992. "Changes in Relative Wages, 1933–1987: Supply and Demand Factors." *Quarterly Journal of Economics* 107(1, February): 35–78.

Laub, John H., Daniel S. Nagin, and Robert J. Sampson. 1998. "Trajectories of Change in Criminal Offending: Good Marriages and the Desistance Process." *American Sociological Review* 63(2, April): 225–38.

Laub, John H., and Robert J. Sampson. 1993. "Turning Points in the Life Course: Why Change Matters to the Study of Crime." *Criminology* 31(3, August): 301–25.

Lerman, Robert I. 1993. "A National Profile of Young Unwed Fathers." In *Young Unwed Fathers: Changing Roles and Emergent Policies,* edited by Robert I. Lerman and Theodora J. Ooms. Philadelphia, Pa.: Temple University Press.

MacLeod, Jay. 1995. *Ain't No Makin' It.* Boulder, Colo.: Westview Press.

Magnusson, David, and Lars R. Bergman. 1988. "Individual and Variable-Based

Approaches to Longitudinal Research on Early Risk Factors." In *Studies of Psychosocial Risk: The Power of Longitudinal Data*, edited by Michel Rutter. New York: Cambridge University Press.

———. 1990. *Data Quality in Longitudinal Research*. New York: Cambridge University Press.

McLanahan, Sara, Irwin Garfinkel, Nancy E. Reichman, and Julien Teitler. 2001a. "Unwed Parents or Fragile Families?" In *Out of Wedlock: Trends, Causes, and Consequences of Nonmarital Fertility*, edited by Lawrence Wu and Barbara Wolfe. New York: Russell Sage Foundation.

McLanahan, Sara, Irwin Garfinkel, Nancy E. Reichman, Julien Teitler, Marcia Carlson, and Christina Norland Audigier. 2001b. *The Fragile Families and Child Wellbeing Study: National Baseline Report*. Princeton, N.J.: Bendheim-Thoman Center for Research on Child Wellbeing.

Mumola, Christopher J. 2000. *Incarcerated Parents and Their Children*. Washington: U.S. Department of Justice, Bureau of Justice Statistics.

Nurse, Anne M. 2000. "Coming Home: The Transition from Incarcerated to Paroled Young Father." *Families, Crime, and Criminal Justice* 2: 281–308.

———. 2002. *Fatherhood Arrested: Parenting from Within the Juvenile Justice System*. Nashville, Tenn.: Vanderbilt University Press.

Sampson, Robert J., and John H. Laub. 1990. "Crime and Deviance Over the Life Course: The Salience of Adult Social Bonds." *American Sociological Review* 55(5, October): 609–27.

———. 1993. *Crime in the Making: Pathways and Turning Points Through Life*. Cambridge, Mass.: Harvard University Press.

———. 1996. "Socioeconomic Achievement in the Life Course of Disadvantaged Men: Military Service as a Turning Point, Circa 1940–1965." *American Sociological Review* 61(3, June): 347–67.

Shihadeh, Edward S., and Graham C. Ousey. 1998. "Industrial Restructuring and Violence: The Link between Entry-Level Jobs, Economic Deprivation, and Black and White Homicide." *Social Forces* 77(1, September): 185–206

Shover, Neil. 1996. *Great Pretenders: Pursuits and Careers of Persistent Thieves*. Boulder, Colo.: Westview Press.

Sullivan, Mercer L. 1989. *Getting Paid*. Ithaca, N.Y.: Cornell University Press.

Tucker, M. Belinda, and Claudia Mitchell-Kernan. 1995. *The Decline in Marriage Among African Americans*. New York: Russell Sage Foundation.

Uggen, Christopher. 2000. "Work as a Turning Point in the Life Course of Criminals: A Duration Model of Age, Employment, and Recidivism." *American Sociological Review* 65(4, August): 528–47.

Uggen, Christopher, and Irving Piliavin. 1998. "Asymmetrical Causation and Criminal Desistance." *Journal of Criminal Law and Criminology* 88(4, Summer): 1399–1422.

Warr, Mark. 1998. "Life Course Transitions and Desistance from Crime." *Criminology* 36: 183–216.

Anne M. Nurse

| | Returning to Strangers: Newly Paroled Young Fathers and |
| 4 | Their Children |

In recent years, academics have begun to focus more attention on the effects of our nation's high rate of incarceration. One area of concern has been the impact of prison on inmate parents and the other parent of their children (see chapters 2 and 3 in this volume). In general, research and policy efforts have been directed toward adult inmates; little thought has been given to their juvenile counterparts. This lack of attention is surprising in light of estimates suggesting that a large number of imprisoned juveniles are parents. A significant percentage of these are fathers. In California, for example, the state Youth Authority has data suggesting that well over 25 percent of its male juvenile wards are fathers (California Youth Authority 1995). In Ohio, the statistics are similar; a study conducted by the Department of Youth Services estimates that 22.4 percent of its inmates are fathers (Abeyratne, Sowards, and Brewer 1995).

Given these figures, it is important to investigate the social impact of incarcerating juvenile fathers on their families, their communities, and the men themselves. Although it is tempting to extrapolate findings from the adult literature, there are compelling reasons to consider juveniles separately. First, important structural differences exist between the adult and juvenile correctional systems. These differences are particularly striking regarding rules for inmate conduct, outside contact, and sentencing. In many states, for example, the visitation and conduct rules are more stringent for juveniles than for adults (Bortner and Williams 1997). It is likely that the different rule structures uniquely affect the inmates' relationships with their children. A second reason to study juvenile inmates separately from adults is that they are at different points in their life course. Like the analysis by Kathryn Edin, Timothy Nelson, and

Rechelle Paranal in chapter 3 in this volume, the current analysis uses the life-course perspective, which explores the effect of the timing of significant life transitions on other transitions. For example, the age at which a person marries can have long-term repercussions on his or her career, lifestyle, education, and childbearing decisions. The age at which a person is incarcerated is similarly likely to affect postrelease decisions and subsequent life changes.

How does time spent in prison affect a young father's desire and ability to be actively involved with his children? To address this question, I present my findings from participation observation, surveys, and in-depth interviews conducted with young paroled fathers. These data suggest that parolees face especially difficult challenges as they try to integrate themselves into their children's lives. Interestingly, many of these challenges do not directly involve the children but rather stem from a man's relationship with his child's mother, her boyfriend, and her family. These relationships are altered by the experience of incarceration and the role they play in determining father-child involvement. To provide some context, it is important first to look at what we know about juvenile incarceration and its overlap with young fatherhood.

JUVENILE INCARCERATION

The incarceration rate for young men has increased dramatically during the past two decades. The period from 1983 to 1995, for example, saw an increase in juvenile incarceration of almost 50 percent (Sickmund, Snyder, and Poe-Yamagata 1997). In 1995 there were more than eighty-six thousand young men in public and private correctional institutions, camps, and treatment centers nationwide (Sickmund, Snyder, and Poe-Yamagata 1997). Although juvenile arrests for both violent and property crimes have dropped in the past five years, no immediate impact on prison population statistics is expected. During the 1990s, many states passed laws toughening the penalties on juvenile offenders. As a result, more juveniles are going to prison for longer periods of time.

There are several reasons why a significant proportion of the inmates in the juvenile correctional system are fathers. First, both crime and young fathering are concentrated in the same poor and minority communities. Figures from 1999 indicate that whereas 368 of every 100,000 juveniles in the general population are in custody on any given day, the rate among African Americans and Latinos is much higher. For every 100,000 juveniles who are black, 1,018 are incarcerated (U.S. Department of Justice 1999). Latinos also have a high rate of incarceration: for every 100,000 Latino juveniles, 515 are in custody (U.S. Department of Justice 1999). In 1995 minorities made up about 32 percent of the juvenile population but constituted 68 percent of those in secure detention centers (Sickmund, Snyder, and Poe-Yamagata 1997).

Research suggests that the overrepresentation of black and Latino youth in prison derives from several factors. In the United States, race and ethnicity are highly correlated with poverty. Poverty, particularly in combination with unstable family structures or rapid community change, is positively related to both criminal behavior and to the likelihood of arrest (Short 1997). Additionally, some evidence suggests that blacks commit a disproportionate share of some types of violent crimes (Short 1997). Once crimes are committed, race and ethnicity appear to play an important role in decisions made by police, judges, and courts (Bishop and Frazier 1996; Conley 1994; Wordes, Bynum, and Corley 1994). As a result of these decisions, minorities are more likely than whites to have served time in prison, even when the severity of the crime and the defendant's past record are taken into account. Blacks and Latinos also tend to be less able to afford lawyers and alternatives to prison, such as private treatment centers (Bishop and Frazier 1996; Bortner and Williams 1997).

The disproportionate incarceration of young blacks and Latinos ensures that many fathers end up behind bars. Black men from the ages of fifteen to nineteen father children at a rate more than twice that of white men (41.5 births per 1,000 black men per year as compared with 17.5 births per 1,000 white men). The disparity between groups drops only slightly in the twenty- to twenty-four-year-old age category, where the rate is 133.5 per 1,000 black men as compared with 76.8 per 1,000 white men (Ventura et al. 2001, 48). The birth rate for Latinos is comparable to that for blacks (Ventura et al. 2001, 10).

The intersection of race-ethnicity, poverty, and young parenthood leads to an overrepresentation of fathers in the juvenile prison population. This overrepresentation is compounded by the fact that juvenile fathers, regardless of their backgrounds, appear to be more likely than their nonfather counterparts to engage in delinquent behaviors and to go to prison (Christmon and Lucky 1994; Elster, Lamb, and Tavare 1987; Lerman 1993; Thornberry et al. 2000). In a large-scale study of the relationship between delinquency and young fatherhood, Magda Stouthamer-Loeber and Evelyn H. Wei (1998) have found that juvenile fathers are more than twice as likely as juvenile nonfathers to engage in delinquent behaviors. The fathers are also more likely to abuse alcohol and drugs, be disruptive in school, and exhibit aggressive behaviors.

METHODS

My data for the chapter were drawn from three sources: a survey I administered to 258 paroled fathers under the jurisdiction of the California Youth Authority in northern California, in-depth interviews conducted with a subset of twenty of the original survey respondents, and observations from parenting classes offered to Youth Authority parolees. The California Youth Authority is one of the largest juvenile correctional systems in the United States, and it is the last stop for serious juvenile offenders in the state. The northern region extends from Bakersfield to the Oregon border. Youth Authority parolees are inmates who have been released back into the community after serving part of their prison term. They must meet regularly with an agent and abide by a set of restrictions determined by the Board of Parole. These restrictions specify both activities to avoid (drug or alcohol use, associating with gang members) and activities that are required (attending school, seeking work, participating in parenting classes). Any violation of these conditions can result in a parolee's being returned to prison.

The survey of fathers was conducted from October 1996 to October 1997. To compile a list of these men, I requested names from the caseloads of individual parole agents. These agents spent time with the young men, their families, and their girlfriends. For this reason, they were in a unique position to identify fathers. The agent lists were supplemented with California Youth Authority records of prison intake interviews, conducted when the young men first arrived at prison. One of the questions they were asked concerned their fatherhood status. I obtained records of the answer to this question for all men who were on parole during the period of the study. Using the parole-agent lists combined with the intake records, I identified 380 young fathers. I believe this was a fairly complete list of all those who were willing to divulge their fatherhood status to authorities at the Youth Authority. To locate fathers who were not willing to admit to having children, I spent time in the waiting rooms of parole offices talking with parolees. Most parolees are required to report to their agents at least once a month, so I was able to explain the study to a large number of men. In this way I added twenty young fathers who were not on any list.

In total, I identified 400 young fathers on parole in northern California during the period of the study. Of these men, I and a group of interviewers ultimately contacted 275. There were 125 men we were unable to contact. About half of these were absent without leave and could not be located by the parole office; about as many had been returned to prison before we could interview them. There were also seventeen young men whom we contacted but who did not participate in the study. Five refused; the other twelve agreed to be interviewed, but logistical problems made contact impossible. Surveys were administered to the remaining 258 men. The survey covered a large number of topics, including the men's experiences in prison, their experiences after their release from prison, and their current fathering practices.

After performing a preliminary analysis of the survey data, I constructed an in-depth interview schedule. The purpose of the in-depth interviews was to explore areas of interest revealed during the survey stage of the project and to further probe the young men's construction of fatherhood. To select candidates for the in-depth interviews, I used a purposive sampling strategy. First, I stratified the list of fathers by race-ethnicity (among the 258 fathers in the survey, 14 percent were white, 31 percent African American, and 55 percent Latino). I then randomly selected twenty fathers: five whites (25 percent), seven African Americans (35 percent), and eight Latinos (40 percent). I decided to include a disproportionately large number of whites to maximize racial-ethnic variation in the sample. After selecting the respondents, I then checked to make sure that this smaller group was representative of the entire group of survey respondents. Although it was fairly close, I made some minor adjustments to ensure that it was geographically representative and that it contained a representative number of involved and noninvolved fathers. I adjusted the group by adding randomly selected parolees from the underrepresented groups.

The final source of data for this chapter was my observations from parenting classes I observed at the California Youth Authority. These classes were part of an ongoing pilot project to provide parental education and support services to parolees. Class topics included child development, child rearing, discipline, and legal issues associated with fatherhood. The curriculum also contained sections designed specifically for the parolee population; one session, for example, was devoted to a discussion of the young men's transition from prison back into the lives of their children. From January to August 1996, I attended approximately forty parenting class sessions. My presence at the parenting classes was a unique opportunity to collect rich qualitative data about young parolees' concerns, problems, and experiences as fathers. Because most teachers made an effort to focus the classes on topics requested by the young men, I was able to listen as the men discussed the issues they saw as most important in their lives. The classes also provided detailed data about the culture of fatherhood among young male parolees. The frequent group discussions, as well as the less structured interaction of the men in the class, revealed much about their beliefs and feelings regarding fatherhood.

DATA AND ANALYSIS: CHILDREN'S MOTHERS

In both surveys and in-depth interviews, I asked each paroled father to talk about his relationship with his child or children and to describe the factors that determine his level of involvement. The most common response involved the man's relationship with the mother of his child.

About 23 percent of the survey respondents told me that "how well I am getting along with the child's mother" was the primary factor determining their involvement with their children. The in-depth interviews yielded similar findings; men talked at length about how the quality of the relationship with the mother determined how much time they spent with their children.

The qualitative literature on fatherhood suggests two important reasons why mothers play such an important role in determining a young father's contact with his children. First, most mothers live with their children and act as "gatekeeper," controlling any interaction between them and their fathers (Daly 1993). They regulate the time, frequency, and duration of visits (Seltzer and Brandreth 1994). When couples are not getting along, or when a mother feels the father is not living up to his commitments, she is able to restrict his access to the child. In a study of families headed by teenaged mothers, Sheldon Danziger (1987) finds that more than 18 percent of the mothers had, at one time or another, denied visitation to the father of their children. In my own study, slightly more than half of the nonresident fathers said they had been denied visitation.

Frank Furstenberg (1995) identifies a second way in which the relationship between a man and his child's mother affects father-child contact. In his work with young parents, Furstenberg finds that men do not view their relationship with their children as separate from their relationship with the children's mother. Men see mothers and children as a "package deal." When the bond between men and their children's mother weakens, or if it is weak to begin with, the father separates himself from both the mother and the child. Furstenberg points out that weak parental relationships are particularly common among adolescents. Young couples often do not know each other well before they have a child and, in some cases, are virtual strangers. This observation is certainly true for the paroled fathers in my study. Most had known their partners for only a short time—an average of six months—before the woman became pregnant. A quarter of these couples had known each other two months or less when they learned of the pregnancy.

Exacerbating the problems caused by brief courtship, research suggests that teenaged relationships may take place in an atmosphere of hostility and antagonism between the sexes. Elijah Anderson's (1990) work with young African American men in an urban neighborhood, for example, suggests that relationships between men and women can be likened to a game in which each side is trying to achieve its own goal. The game is essentially futile, however, because the teams are striving for different goals: men for sex and women for love, affection, and marriage. Anderson finds that, as a result, relations between the sexes are strained, distrustful, and manipulative. His findings are confirmed by the work of a number of other researchers. William J. Wilson, for example, identifies relationships between African American inner-city men and women as "often fractious and antagonistic" (Wilson 1996, 98).

Like the young African Americans with whom Anderson worked, the paroled fathers in my study perceived deep divisions between themselves and young women. Notably, the mistrust and antagonism Anderson identifies were also present among both rural and urban men of Latino and white backgrounds as well as African Americans. Asked if they agreed with the statement, "Many teenage girls who get pregnant do so to try and trap their boyfriends," about 70 percent of the young men responded in the affirmative, and there were no significant differences by race-ethnicity or community type.

My observations in parenting class suggest that the paroled fathers have something of a "siege mentality" in their dealings with women. In their eyes, women are often out to get them—sometimes for money, other times simply because women take perverse pleasure in causing them trouble. The hostility between young mothers and the fathers in my study seems even sharper than that reported by Edin, Nelson, and Paranal in chapter 3 of this volume. One particularly memorable illustration of this attitude occurred during a discussion in parenting class about domestic violence. The teacher was trying to convince the parolees that they should not hit women. What follows is an excerpt from my field notes. John is the teacher, and Caleb is one of the students:[1]

> John talked at length about how men should not hit women. At some point Caleb brought up abusive women. This really seemed to be a major concern of most of the guys. Caleb wanted to know what to do if a woman was being verbally or emotionally abusive toward him. John first tried to say that this class was about men—the women weren't there—but the students kept pushing him to talk about it. John finally asked how many couples they knew where the woman was abusive to the man. Caleb couldn't think of any, and neither could anyone else offhand, but they all agreed that it was common.

This theme of abusive or manipulative women came up again and again in different ways throughout the parenting classes. Although it is clear that the paroled fathers believe there are deep divisions between them and the women in their lives, one should not take this to mean that parolees are necessarily different from other young, economically disadvantaged men in the general population. Anderson's and Wilson's work suggests that, in terms of antagonism between the sexes, paroled fathers are much like their nonparoled peers. My interactions with the paroled fathers, however, indicate that they face unique pressures in the relationship with the mothers of their children.

One of the first problems newly released men encounter is that their children's mothers are frequently quite different people from the ones they knew before their incarceration. In this study, sentence lengths ranged from a few months to five years, but on average, the men were away for two years. They talked about what it was like to return home and attempt to negotiate child visitation with a woman who had become a stranger. For example, B.J., who had recently been released from prison, told me that he was trying to maintain a good relationship with the mother of his child but that she had changed while he was gone: "Now that I'm home, our relationship is not as good as it was before I went to jail. It's like we are trying to get to know each other again. 'Cause over the years people change, you know. You come home and they are not the same. It's kind of like meeting a new person again. It's hard." When asked how incarceration affected the relationship he had with the mother of his child, Tyrell, after twenty-six months in prison, commented, "It was like we wasn't really close friends anymore. It was like we didn't really know each other 'cause I was gone longer than I was with her, you know, so we had only been together maybe a year and a half, two years, and then I got locked up for over two years."

The literature on spouses of prison inmates suggests that the primary way in which women change during their partner's incarceration is that they become much more independent and self-sufficient. When the men return, the women do not want to go back to the more dependent relationship they had before the man's incarceration. This new independence is hard for many men to accept, especially when they have spent their time in prison imagining how their wife or girlfriend used to act (McCubin et al. 1975; McDermott and King 1992). This theme appeared often in my interviews with the paroled fathers. I asked Ray how the mother of his child had reacted when he was released from prison:

> She was happy at the time, but as the days went by. . . . When I was gone she always used to, you know, party, doing this, going out. While I wanted to be tied down with her and the kids, you know. Get to know each other again. She wasn't, you know, ready for it, I guess, cause she was used to, that whole time that I was away, just partying and doing whatever. You know, she'd do whatever.

As time went by, Ray was unable to reconcile his image of what his child's mother used to be with the person she had become. This situation led to their eventual breakup. Paroled juvenile fathers are not the only men to have difficulty with the transition back into relationships with wives and girlfriends. In a seven-year study of 241 prisoners of war and their families, for example, Edna Hunter (1986) finds that returning prisoners had a higher rate of divorce than did a matched control group of military families (30 percent as compared with 12 percent). Kathleen McDermott and Roy King's (1992) research with newly released adult prisoners in Great Britain indicates that they experience high levels of stress in their relations with wives and children. A primary reason for this is that the children and women have undergone many changes in the men's absence. As a result, the men are no longer able to occupy their former role in the family and find themselves unsure of how to act around their family members.

Another relationship challenge newly released men face is that their parole status gives women more control over them, dramatically altering the balance of power. The mothers are aware that parolees can be returned to the institution for any violation of their parole, and they understand that if they report a violation the young man might be rearrested—or, at the very least, that his parole agent might supervise him more closely. This problem was a topic of discussion in one of the first parenting classes I attended. The theme of the class was domestic violence, and during the break a bright young man named Jacob nervously approached the teacher of the class. He told the teacher that he was trying hard not to hit his girlfriend but felt that she was always provoking him and then threatening to call his parole agent. He said he was at a loss how to handle the situation. Echoing similar sentiments, Charles related an experience to me: "About two years ago, when my daughter was born and we split up, it was hard. We went through a lot because, like after she had the baby, she had an attitude I didn't know she had. So then she started jeopardizing my parole, calling my officer, telling my parole officer lies and stuff, so I had to just cut her off, because my freedom I felt was more important at the time."

The threat of being returned to the institution is obviously serious, and men will go to great lengths to avoid it. Jeremy, a father of two children, told me that he took custody of his oldest son when the child's mother was arrested. He was concerned for the welfare of the child and did not want him to go back to the mother when she was released. "And then she got out," he told me, "probably a week and a half later, and she called my grandma's house . . . talking about bringing my son home. . . . 'If you don't bring my son home, I'm going to call the police on you.' Then my [grandma told me], 'Go ahead and take him home, take him home. You don't need more trouble, you're already on parole, just take him home.'" These experiences indicate that mothers of children can use the parole system to exert power over men and limit the access they have to their children. Compounding the relationship difficulties newly released young men face is the weight of unmet promises many have made to their children's mother from prison. Incarcerated men spend time in prison building up expectations for their own behavior after they are released. Once they develop this set of expectations, they naturally share their hopes with their children and with their children's mother. By the time they are released, the high expectations they have for themselves are also shared by mothers and children. Marco described the promises he made to the mother of his child while he was in the institution: "People always talk, you always write this and that to your girlfriend, 'When I get out it's going to be like this, like that.' This and that, and this and that. And you get out and it's like, 'You wrote it—do it—come on, I'm waiting for it, you know.'"

Many incarcerated men tell their hopes and plans to the mother of their children because they are excited and want to share them with someone. At the same time, some of the men also use their plans to encourage these women to stay in a romantic relationship with them. By making promises about how they will change, they raise the hopes of the mother. Tony described how he had kept his relationship with the mother of his child together by building up her expectations: "I saw a lot [of breakups in prison], but for me, we got closer. The bad part was we got closer because what I was telling her were lies. You know, I was telling her I was going to change when I get out, because I didn't want to be here. And I actually went home, and it was all a bunch of lies." Mothers adopt the expectations the young men create and then begin to embellish them. Fernando told me that he got angry because the mother of his child had such high expectations of him. He commented, "She wanted to see what I was really made of. At times . . . she made me angry . . . 'cause she talked about how good it was going to be and I did too." When young men are finally released they are under great pressure, both self-imposed and from family, to live up to the promises they have made.

As young men fail to live up to the high expectations they have for themselves, they and their children's mother become disillusioned and disappointed. Fernando described what happened with the mother of his child when he was finally released: "When I got my job I was trying real hard to succeed and make everything right, as good as I could, 'cause she was talking about . . . [my] not showing her nothing, I'm still the same person I was before I got locked up. And that kind of like really made me feel bad, you know what I'm saying? It kind of like downgraded me."

Marco, like Fernando, found that he could not live up to his girlfriend's expectations of him. He returned home from prison and was allowed to live with her and his child. Things quickly soured, however, and the girlfriend began complaining that he was a failure. He described what happened: "I got out and I tried, you know. I got a job . . . I was making a little bit of money and I tried. . . . But then after a while I think it just gets back into the same routine. You know, you get tired and you just work your way back into that same old crap." The discouragement caused by a man's failure to fulfill his promises, combined with other relationship difficulties, decreases his desire for any involvement; and since most children live with the mother, many men end up avoiding their children as well.

DATA AND ANALYSIS: NEW BOYFRIENDS FOR A CHILD'S MOTHER

The strains inherent in adolescent relationships, coupled with the unique pressures of parole, ensure that most of the romantic relationships between paroled men and the mothers of their children come to an end. When this happens, both partners are free to date new people. My interviews and surveys with the fathers suggest that when a mother begins to date a new person, it can have serious repercussions for the father's involvement with his children. Specifically, it appears that men tend to decrease their involvement. In the survey, I asked each of the respondents how often he sees his child. I created a six-point scale from this data ranging from no contact to daily contact. The average contact score for men whose children's mother was single was 5.05 (signifying contact at least several times a week) as compared with 3.80 (contact a few times a month) for men whose children's mother had a new boyfriend. This difference remained statistically significant when controlling for the age of the child, race, education, sentence length, and the age of the parents.

The in-depth interviews provided insight into why a mother's acquisition of a new boyfriend might cause men to decrease contact with their children. Jay, a father of a three-year-old son, reported that he did not like going to see his son when the mother's new boyfriend was around. He gave the following reason:

> I don't really be feeling comfortable because, you know, I be feeling like, I can just kind of feel that he doesn't like me—the fact that I come over but he don't come out and say that and then I just be feeling like I know that's really the way he feels but he not saying it so that to me feels funny when I know a person is feeling one way and acting another—that makes me feel uncomfortable. I just don't like to be around a situation like that.

Rodney talked about a similar situation with the new boyfriend of his child's mother:

> Right now, you know, the person that her mom's with, I think he detects that there's still something going on, or that something might hap-

pen between us. I don't understand why he thinks that, but it's wrong.
. . . She's with him, and I'm with who I'm with, and we both getting
on—we living two separate lives. And I don't know why he thinks that
but for one minute I didn't see her for awhile because I had the phone
number and everything and she was staying at one apartment and she
moved and she didn't inform me or nothing about moving, changing
phone numbers—didn't tell me nothing. Really it was because of him,
it wasn't really her—it was him telling her to do that.

A young father's contact with a mother's new boyfriend is often
fraught with the kind of tension and hostility Jay and Rodney described.
This can result in the boyfriend's taking steps to prevent the father from
seeing his child. Alternately, fathers may reduce contact with their own
children to avoid the new boyfriend. Carol B. Stack's (1974) work in a
poor African American community confirms the link between new boyfriends and decreased contact between father and child. Her data indicate that there is often hostility between the father and the new man that
causes the father to withdraw from his children.

Furstenberg's work (1995) suggests two other important reasons why
men may decrease contact with children when their mothers date someone new. First, a mother who begins a serious new relationship often
involves this partner with her children. If the new partner becomes central to the child's life, the father may feel that he has been replaced.
Second, when the mother begins to date someone new the father may
feel ashamed that his level of involvement does not match that of the
new boyfriend. Feelings of guilt, jealousy, and shame may drive men
from active participation with their children.

Like the men Furstenberg studied, the paroled fathers in my study
talked about the guilt and jealousy they felt as a result of the involvement of a mother's new boyfriend with their children. What makes the
parolees unique, however, is the impact of their incarceration experience.
During the in-depth interviews, the men told me that spending time in
prison heightened both their guilt and their desire to be involved with
their children. Men arrived home feeling guilty for their absence and for
failing to provide support for their children. Additionally, many of the
respondents told me that they had spent hours in prison daydreaming
and fantasizing about the activities they would engage in with their children; even more important, they had formed a picture in their minds of
how their children would act. Central to their vision was the idea that
their children would respond to them as "daddy." This meant that the
children would recognize them as their father and treat them with respect. Instead, what many of the men found was that in their absence
other people had come to fill the father role. Jose commented on how
frequently this occurs to parolees:

> When a kid doesn't see their father, original or real father, they tend to latch on to whoever is next to them, you know what I mean? . . . If her mom has a new boyfriend, that's daddy. . . . I mean, I see it everyday. When somebody gets locked up, what we call Sancho—you know, side-kick—that's the next dude in line—takes over and raises the kid with the kid calling him "Dad."

Many of the paroled fathers told me stories of "Sanchos." Robert, for example, reported that while he was incarcerated, his brother became like a father to his child. "My brother, he called my brother Dad, Daddy, one time," he said. "And I was like, man—you know, cause he was there for him as much as possible or whatever." When asked how he had felt when his child called his brother "Daddy," he replied, "I was hurt, bad, bad." Robert went on to say that his disappointment over his son's attachment to his brother caused him to pull away from the child.

Although some parolees, like Robert, return home to find that a brother or a grandmother has taken primary importance in their children's lives, it is far more common for a mother's new boyfriend to be the Sancho. When this occurs, paroled men must face their own failed expectations in addition to jealousy and anger. Marco described what happened when he got out of prison and went to see the mother of his children:

> I got out and I didn't know, just that day I found out she was with somebody else. So I was like, cool, I just want to see my kids. I saw my kids, and told [the new boyfriend], "Hey, whatever, you know, I ain't with her no more, you are. . . . Come here [he gestures like he gestured to the new boyfriend]. Don't ever touch my kids, I'll break your hands, don't ever try to get a hand on 'em, you know those are my kids."

Marco's anger mirrored the reactions of other men whose children's mother had started dating while they were in prison. One of the reasons for their intense anger was that most had received "Dear John" letters while in prison, intended to free the mother to date a new boyfriend. To return home and find this man playing "daddy" to their children was extremely difficult for them to accept. Gerry was one of the men who fit this description. In response to a question about how incarceration had changed his relationship with the mother of his child he told me the following:

> We were together before I went in and were not together when I came out. So, that's how it changed, and then we come apart. I guess it really depends on the relationship also. You know, if they can wait for you or not. But that's pretty rare. . . . [In my case], she met somebody else. Got pregnant with his kid. Had it. . . . She never called me, she just quit

coming to see me. She would make excuses and she wouldn't call me, or she wouldn't be at my grandmother's house when she knew I was gonna call there, cause she didn't have a phone. She didn't write me letters, she just quit coming to see me. No letters, no replies, no nothing. . . . My son told me, and my grandmother told me and my mom. That's how I found out.

Gerry was obviously hurt and angry when his child's mother broke up with him. He told me that he spent the remainder of his prison term thinking about just how upset he was. By the time he was released, his child was living with the mother and her new boyfriend. Gerry focused most of his anger on the boyfriend and refused to have anything to do with him. As a result, he saw little of his child.

DATA AND ANALYSIS: MATERNAL FAMILIES

Most of the children of the paroled fathers live with their mothers. Because many of the mothers are young, they continue to live with their own families. These family members appear to play an important role in determining the men's involvement with their children. During an in-depth interview, Frank told me about the many reasons he sees his son only infrequently. One of the primary explanations he listed was the hostility he encountered from his son's maternal grandmother. Frank talked about the role his son's mother had in promoting the grandmother's negative attitude: "She had her mom thinking I was the bad guy in the whole thing, and I wasn't going to try to be there. This child was going to be born and I couldn't allow myself to, you know, stay in that situation for too long. Something bad would happen."

Like Frank, George also felt disapproval from the parents of his children's mother. Both of her parents took an active role in preventing him from seeing his child. While answering a question about his child's mother, he commented,

I felt weird going to her house 'cause her daddy said all kinds of trash and start cussing me out. I didn't blame her, man, I just felt kind of uncomfortable. And uh, but I wanted to, I wanted to . . . pick [my daughter] up to take her out to go eat, that's the way I wanted it to be, you know I liked it like that. I wanted her to spend days with me but [the mother's] mother wouldn't let me. She said, "I don't trust you." 'Cause she thought I was into all kinds of gangs and stuff.

Furstenberg's work (1995) with fathers in the inner city supports the comments of Frank and George. He finds that the expectations and behavior of the mother's family have a profound impact on the child's father. Families that expect a low level of involvement by the father transmit this feeling and help create a self-fulfilling situation. Young men are quite able to sense hostility from the mother's family; in response, they are less inclined to have contact with that family and, consequently, with their own children. At the same time, families who disapprove of the young father can serve in a gatekeeping capacity to prevent him from seeing his child (Allen and Doherty 1996). Research in the African American community suggests, for example, that maternal grandmothers and other female kin sometimes try to limit an unemployed father's access to his children (Sullivan 1993).

Not surprisingly, it appears that prison places strain on a man's relationship with his child's maternal family. Families who were originally supportive of a young man being romantically involved with their daughter often changed their attitude after the young man's arrest. For families who were not enthusiastic about the young man from the start, his arrest only seemed to strengthen their negative feelings. Samuel told me about how the disapproval of his child's maternal grandfather prevented him from seeing his child while he was in prison and after his release.

> Yeah, her mother wanted to bring [the daughter], but see, the problem was [the mother's] father at first didn't want to let her bring her. My daughter's grandfather didn't want to let his . . . daughter come. If his daughter couldn't come, my daughter couldn't come. . . . He said I was in here for something bad and I was irresponsible. You know, if I was in a place like this obviously I'm no good and have no reason to see her.

Samuel's experience with his child's maternal family is fairly typical. Many of the paroled fathers returned home to find the maternal family less than enthusiastic about their daughter's or grandchild's involvement with them. The men reported many different strategies that they believed families used to discourage their contact with their children. Some strategies, as in Samuel's case, were fairly blatant—families simply forbade the men to come around or denied permission for the mother to see them. Less obvious strategies included making the men uncomfortable when they visited, failing to give phone messages to the mother, or simply being unwilling to help the men set up times to see their children.

CONCLUSION

Men do not father in a vacuum; their involvement with their children is determined, at least in part, by the relationships they have with family. Although families can provide important encouragement for involvement, this study shows some of the ways that they also operate as instruments for social exclusion, helping to estrange men from their children. During in-depth interviews, the men described how the relationships with their child's mother, her boyfriend, and her family created barriers and disincentives for their involvement with their children. They identified incarceration as a major factor creating relationship problems and causing them to decrease contact with their children. These qualitative results help explain the quantitative findings reported by Bruce Western, Leonard Lopoo, and Sara McLanahan, in chapter 2 in this volume, that former offenders face elevated risks of divorce and separation because of the separation entailed by the experience of incarceration. Former offenders' involvement in crime is not the only factor explaining the unstable family relationships of men who are incarcerated.

Although the qualitative data from this project strongly suggest that incarceration has deleterious effects on relationships between former-inmate fathers and their children, a caution should be noted. Elizabeth Johnson and Jane Waldfogel show in chapter 5 in this volume that the children of incarcerated parents are subject to a variety of risk factors, many of which may be in place before a parent enters prison. This suggests that it is possible that the parolees use incarceration as an excuse for problems that actually existed before their arrest. As Furstenberg's (1995) work illustrates, many young fathers who have never been to prison see their children infrequently and have difficulty maintaining healthy relationships with their child's mother, her boyfriend, and her family. To determine incarceration's impact more clearly, it would be useful to conduct a longitudinal study using a comparison group of men with no incarceration history. In lieu of this, however, my survey data allows for a rough gauge of the effects of incarceration through a comparison of two different groups of parolees, the first group made up of survey respondents who had children before their incarceration and the second of respondents whose children were born after they had returned home. This comparison shows that the men who had spent time in prison since the birth of their children scored a 3.67 on the six-point contact scale, signifying that, on average, they have contact with their children between once a month and several times a month. Men who had not spent any time in prison since the birth scored a 4.32—indicating that they saw their children an average of several times a month to once a week. After I controlled for child age, race, education, and age of parents, this difference remained statistically significant at the .05 level. This finding supports the conclusion that a father's absence owing to imprisonment negatively affects his later involvement with his children.

Given the numbers of incarcerated young men and the potential impact of their incarceration on relationships with their children, it is surprising that there are few public policies designed for this population.

Instead, we have one set of policies for young fathers and another for juvenile delinquents. As Jeremy Travis argues in the concluding chapter of this volume, a successful reentry policy must embrace both criminal justice and social service objectives and resolve the perceived conflicts between them. The problem, for incarcerated fathers, is that the two sets of policies currently in force are sometimes in direct conflict with each other. Some states, for example, continue to impose child-support obligations on incarcerated juvenile fathers. By the time they are released, these men are so deeply in debt they can be discouraged from making any payments at all (Nurse 2002). Although both fatherhood policies and juvenile policies emphasize individual responsibility, fatherhood policies are designed to encourage men to take responsibility for their children, whereas juvenile delinquency policies seek to encourage responsible behavior by imposing maximum penalties on offenders. Young criminal fathers are caught in the middle when their lengthy prison terms make it impossible for them to fulfill their parenting duties.

One potential response to the policy contradictions and social problems raised by this situation is to reduce the number of young fathers in prison. There are many policies that might accomplish this aim; I discuss only two of them here. First, in order to provide alternatives to incarceration for young men, education and employment opportunities need to be expanded. William J. Wilson (1996) shows that the flight of unskilled jobs from the inner city has resulted in decreased employment opportunities for young men, particularly for men of color. There is evidence to suggest that juvenile criminal behavior can, in some cases, be reduced by the creation of strong ties to employment and school (Sampson and Laub 1993).

Another strategy for reducing the number of fathers in prison is to reconsider the current guidelines for juvenile sentencing. New and more punitive laws are being enacted that result in longer periods of time spent in prison by juvenile offenders. This trend is seen most dramatically in the application of adult-sentencing laws, such as "three-strikes-and-you're-out," to criminal juveniles. With significant increases in sentence length, potentially productive citizens and fathers are lost to society for a longer period of time. The public needs to assess current sentencing policies with the goal of protecting the public but, at the same time, limiting the amount of time served by juveniles. We should also investigate and employ alternatives to incarceration, including intensive probation, sentencing to halfway houses, and electronic monitoring.

Policies intended to decrease the number of young incarcerated fathers, such as those I have just described, make sense in light of the prohibitive social and financial costs of imprisonment. Unfortunately, current public opinion regarding criminals indicates that such policies will be difficult to implement. Fears about crime, coupled with a desire to punish criminals, have resulted in an environment in which incarceration is seen as the only way to achieve crime prevention. The public seems unwilling to consider the possibility that the long-term costs of imprisonment may outweigh the short-term costs of policies designed to reduce the number of fathers in prison. Given this political reality, it is likely that large numbers of young fathers will continue to enter our correctional system. For this reason, we must develop improved and enlightened policies for dealing with men in our juvenile facilities and on parole. Some of these policies might include parenting and communication classes, extended visitation with children, and relationship counseling.

The implementation of such programs, however, raises a number of difficult questions. One of the most difficult involves the desirability of encouraging criminal men to be involved with their children. Some might argue that these men are unsuitable fathers and should be kept away from their children. High recidivism rates among juveniles indicate that many young men return to criminal behavior after they are released from prison. This is of concern because the criminal activity of fathers can directly endanger the physical safety of children. In addition, children may be emotionally harmed if men return from prison, attempt to reintegrate themselves into their children's lives, and then retreat. As this chapter suggests, there are a host of reasons former inmates might choose to reduce contact with children. These include problems with the mother or her family or with the children themselves, resulting from the men's absence.

These potential risks to children should make us consider our policies carefully. At the same time, it should be noted that most of the newly paroled fathers in this study attempted to be involved with their children—even though few policies were in place to encourage them to do so. This leaves us with a choice. We can continue to allow men to struggle through parenting issues on their own, which often results in problems such as those mentioned, or we can support those men who want to be involved with their children by helping them learn to make better parenting decisions. Part of this training needs to be informing them of the problems they will face upon their release, such as the effects of their absence on their children. In addition, parenting classes can help inmates understand the legitimate fear, anger, and resentment of the mothers of their children.

One group of men raises particular concerns for involvement with children: those who have committed domestic violence or child abuse. These men, however, are a relatively small percentage of the prison population (in my survey, for example, about 3 percent of the men had been convicted of crimes against children), and legal measures such as restraining orders can be employed to keep them away from children. To allow these men to dictate policy for all young incarcerated fathers would be a mistake. The majority of incarcerated young men do not pose a threat to their children, and they have the potential to be active and concerned fathers. For this reason, policies should be developed that give inmates the tools to build strong relationships with their children, with their children's mother, and with her family.

This research was sponsored by the National Science Foundation (Dissertation Improvement Award number SBR-9633153), the U.S. Department of Justice (OJP-97–017-M), and the Ford Foundation (grant 975–1299). Portions of this chapter are excerpted from *Fatherhood Arrested: Parenting from Within the Juvenile Justice System* (Nurse 2002) with permission of Vanderbilt University Press.

NOTES

1.   All names of teachers and parolees are pseudonyms.

REFERENCES

Abeyratne, Senerath, Bruce Sowards, and Laramaria Brewer. 1995. *Youths Incarcerated in ODYS Institutions Who Have Children and Youths Incarcerated in ODYS Institutions Who Are Children of Teenage Parents.* Columbus, Ohio: Ohio Department of Youth Services, Office of Research.

Allen, William D., and William J. Doherty. 1996. "The Responsibilities of Fatherhood as Perceived by African American Teenage Fathers." *Families in Society: The Journal of Contemporary Human Services* 77(3, March): 142–55.

Anderson, Elijah. 1990. *Streetwise: Race, Class, and Change in an Urban Community.* Chicago: University of Chicago Press.

Bishop, Donna M., and Charles E. Frazier. 1996. "Race Effects in Juvenile Justice Decision-Making: Findings of a Statewide Analysis." *Journal of Criminal Law and Criminology* 86(2, Winter): 392–414.

Bortner, M. A., and Linda M. Williams. 1997. *Youth in Prison: We the People of Unit Four.* New York: Routledge.

California Youth Authority. 1995. *Office of Criminal Justice Planning, Juvenile Justice, and Delinquency Prevention Program: Project Summary.* Sacramento: California Youth Authority.

Christmon, Kenneth, and Irene Lucky. 1994. "Is Early Fatherhood Associated with Alcohol and Other Drug Use?" *Journal of Substance Abuse* 6(3): 337–43.

Conley, Darlene J. 1994. "Adding Color to a Black and White Picture: Using

Qualitative Data to Explain Racial Disproportionality in the Juvenile Justice System." *Journal of Research in Crime and Delinquency* 31(2, May): 135–48.

Daly, Kerry. 1993. "Reshaping Fatherhood: Finding the Models." *Journal of Family Issues* 14(4, December): 510–30.

Danziger, Sheldon K. 1987. *Father Involvement in Welfare Families Headed by Adolescent Mothers.* Discussion Paper 856–87. Madison, Wisc.: Institute for Research on Poverty.

Elster, Arthur B., Michael E. Lamb, and Jane Tavare. 1987. "Association Between Behavioral and School Problems and Fatherhood in a National Sample of Adolescent Youths." *Journal of Pediatrics* 111(6, December): 932–36.

Furstenberg, Frank F., Jr. 1995. "Fathering in the Inner City: Paternal Participation and Public Policy." In *Fatherhood: Contemporary Theory, Research, and Social Policy (Research on Men and Masculinities Series,* edited by M. S. Kimmel), vol. 7, edited by William Marsiglio. Thousand Oaks, Calif.: Sage Publications.

Hunter, Edna J. 1986. "Families of Prisoners of War Held in Vietnam: A Seven-Year Study." *Evaluation and Program Planning* 9(3, August): 243–51.

Lerman, Robert I. 1993. "A National Profile of Young Unwed Fathers." In *Young Unwed Fathers: Changing Roles and Emerging Policies,* edited by Robert I. Lerman and Theodora J. Ooms. Philadelphia, Pa.: Temple University Press.

McCubin, Hamilton I., Barbara B. Dahl, Gary R. Lester, and Beverly A. Ross. 1975. "The Returned Prisoner of War: Factors in Family Reintegration." *Journal of Marriage and the Family* 37(3, August): 471–78.

McDermott, Kathleen, and Roy D. King. 1992. "Prison Rule 102: 'Stand By Your Man': The Impact of Penal Policy on the Families of Prisoners." In *Prisoners' Children: What Are the Issues?,* edited by Roger Shaw. London: Routledge.

Nurse, Anne M. 2002. *Fatherhood Arrested: Parenting from Within the Juvenile Justice System.* Nashville, Tenn.: Vanderbilt University Press.

Sampson, Robert, and John Laub. 1993. *Crime in the Making: Pathways and Turning Points through Life.* Cambridge, Mass.: Harvard University Press.

Seltzer, Judith A., and Yvonne Brandreth. 1994. "What Fathers Say About Involvement with Children After Separation." *Journal of Family Issues* 15(1, March): 49–77.

Short, James, Jr. 1997. *Poverty, Ethnicity and Violent Crime.* Boulder, Colo.: Westview Press.

Sickmund, Melissa, Howard N. Snyder, and Eileen Poe-Yamagata. 1997. *Juvenile Offenders and Victims: 1997 Update on Violence.* Washington: U.S. Department of Justice, Office of Juvenile Justice and Delinquency Prevention.

Stack, Carol B. 1974. *All Our Kin: Strategies for Survival in a Black Community.* New York: Harper and Row.

Stouthamer-Loeber, Magda, and Evelyn H. Wei. 1998. "The Precursors of Young Fatherhood and its Effect on Delinquency of Teenage Males." *Journal of Adolescent Health* 22(1, January): 56–65.

Sullivan, Maureen L. 1993. "Young Fathers and Parenting in Two Inner-City Neighborhoods." In *Young Unwed Fathers: Changing Roles and Emerging Policies,* edited by Robert I. Lerman and Theodora J. Ooms. Philadelphia, Pa.: Temple University Press.

Thornberry, Terrence P., Evelyn H. Wei, Magda Stouthamer-Loeber, and Joyce

Van Dyke. 2000. "Teenage Fatherhood and Delinquent Behavior." *Juvenile Justice Bulletin* (January). Washington: U.S. Department of Justice, Office of Juvenile Justice and Delinquency Prevention.

U.S. Department of Justice, Office of Juvenile Justice and Delinquency Prevention. 1999. *OJJDP Statistical Briefing Book.* http://www.ncjrs.org/html/ojjdp/nationalreport99/toc.html (accessed on January 15, 2001).

Ventura, Stephanie J., Joyce A. Martin, Sally C. Curtin, Fay Menacker, and Brady E. Hamilton. 2001. "Births: Final Data for 1999." *National Vital Statistics Reports* 49(1, April). Hyattsville, Md.: National Center for Health Statistics.

Wilson, William Julius. 1996. *When Work Disappears: The World of the New Urban Poor.* New York: Vintage Books.

Wordes, Madeline, Timothy S. Bynum, and Charles J. Corley. 1994. "Locking up Youth: The Impact of Race on Detention Decisions." *Journal of Research in Crime and Delinquency* 31(2, May): 149–65.

Elizabeth I. Johnson
Jane Waldfogel

Children of Incarcerated Parents: Multiple Risks and Children's

5 | **Living Arrangements**

State and federal inmates were parents to more than 1.3 million children in 1997, a near tripling of the 1986 figure (Johnson and Waldfogel 2002). This dramatic increase in the number of parents in prison has prompted concern about the well-being of children whose parents are incarcerated. But parental incarceration is only one of many factors that may influence how these children are faring. We know, for example, that many children whose parents are incarcerated have been exposed to parental (for example, substance abuse, mental health problems) and environmental (for example, poverty) risk factors before their parents' incarceration. Attributes of the particular child, where the child is placed during a parent's incarceration, and the nature of the relationship with the substitute caregiver may also influence how well a child functions in the face of parental incarceration.

Although concern about this population has often been directed at children who enter the child welfare system as a result of parental incarceration, most children of incarcerated parents do not end up in state care. Of the 1.3 million children of state and federal inmates in 1997, an estimated 24,000 were in foster care, and 155,049 were in the care of grandparents (the share of these who are formal kinship foster care providers is unclear) (Johnson and Waldfogel 2002). The remaining children live in a variety of arrangements, including living with the other parent, with other relatives, on their own, or in some other form of care.

Given the probable presence of other preincarceration risk factors, it is likely that children in living arrangements other than foster care have special service needs as well. The primary goals of this chapter are to identify the nature and prevalence of risk factors in the lives of incarcerated parents and their children and to determine whether and how these relate to children's living arrangements. By identifying risk factors facing children in specific living arrangements, we hope to contribute to child welfare and community-based agencies' efforts to tailor and coordinate services to incarcerated parents and their children.

THE EFFECTS OF INCARCERATION ON CHILDREN

The small research literature on children of incarcerated parents suggests that parental incarceration is associated with poorer emotional, behavioral, and psychological development of children (Stanton 1980; Baunach 1985; Bloom and Steinhart 1993). Problems such as aggressive behavior and withdrawal (Baunach 1985), criminal involvement (Johnston 1991, 1992), and depression and concentration problems (Kampfner 1995) have been observed among children whose parents are imprisoned. Existing studies, however, do not allow the effects of incarceration to be teased apart from the effects of other variables such as where the child is placed during the incarceration and the presence of preincarceration risk factors. Parental characteristics, such as substance abuse, mental health problems, and histories of abuse, for example, may already have put the child at risk before the parent went to prison. The child's experiences subsequent to the parental incarceration may also place the child at risk (or may mitigate earlier risks).

ATTACHMENT

Another concern regarding parental incarceration that is often articulated, yet even less well studied in this population, is the issue of parent-child attachment. Attachment is conceived of as "a pattern of organized behavior within a relationship" (Sroufe et al. 1999, 1). Through the relationship with an attachment figure, the child is afforded a secure base from which to explore. This relationship also shapes children's "internal working models," which guide the child's engagement in and interpretation of interactions with others. Internal working models influence not only children's expectations and appraisals of social relationships but also their perceptions of their own capabilities and their ability to self-regulate (Easterbrooks, Davidson, and Chazen 1993), both of which are important developmental tasks.

Since John Bowlby's (1969, 1973, and 1980) attachment trilogy was published, attachment theory has held a prominent place in psychological research. Attachment researchers examining maternal and child characteristics associated with attachment relationships have devoted considerable effort to delineating the short- and long-term consequences of attachment security for child outcomes. Numerous studies suggest that attachment security during infancy has important consequences for later psychosocial functioning. Securely attached infants have been rated as more socially competent with peers (Elicker, Englund, and Sroufe 1992; Erickson, Sroufe, and Egeland 1985; Pastor 1981; Waters, Wippman, and Sroufe 1979) and parents (Pastor 1981; Sroufe 1983), less dependent on teachers (Erickson, Sroufe, and Egeland 1985; Sroufe 1983), and better able to regulate impulses and feelings (Sroufe 1983) than otherwise attached infants.

Although attachment theory has its roots in Bowlby's work with children in institutions, researchers have typically focused on attachment relationships in families in which the mother is present. Attachment theory suggests that changes in family configuration such as divorce, adoption, and foster care may have implications for attachment security, particularly if they occur in infancy or early childhood. Yet little systematic research has been conducted in these areas (Rutter and O'Connor 1999). Thus though there has been some research about the attachment relationships that children living with parents form with other caregivers such as day care providers and teachers (see Howes 1999 for a review), little is known about how children not living with their parents form attachments with full-time substitute caregivers such as foster parents or grandparents.

In a rare study of infants in foster care, Chase Stovall and Mary Dozier (2000) have found that attachment behaviors emerge between infants and foster caregivers within two months of placement. Studies of children adopted from institutions also suggest that, even though these children might theoretically be at risk for attachment disturbances, few children actually exhibit such disturbances, though insecure attachments are more common among previously institutionalized children than children who have never been institutionalized (Zeanah 2000). There is also evidence that such children do form meaningful attachments to grandparents (Myers, Jarvis, and Creasey 1987).

Another issue is whether relationships with surrogate caregivers can mitigate the effects of previous attachment disturbances. At least one study demonstrates that attachment relationships between children and foster caregivers confer benefits similar to those in more traditional samples (Marcus 1991). Specifically, children who have positive emotional ties to foster parents and receive physical affection from them are better adjusted psychologically and academically than other foster children (Marcus 1991). Another study suggests, however, that even though most children adopted from institutions were able to form close and affectionate relationships with their adoptive parents, they exhibited similar levels of social and behavioral problems as children who were returned to their biological families from institutions (Tizard and Hodges 1978).

Although insights from attachment theory may be useful in fleshing out issues of concern when a parent goes to prison, several questions persist. Of particular relevance is how the loss of an attachment figure owing to parental incarceration differs from the loss of a parent because of divorce or parental death. Intuitively, one would expect the impact to depend on the length of time the parent was absent and how far away the parent was (and whether the child could visit). Another question, still relatively unexplored, is the extent to which attachment relationships with alternative or new caregivers can mitigate the negative consequences associated with a disrupted parent-child attachment. Michael Rutter (1990, 8) writes that "it is clear that it is not the [parental] loss per se that creates the risk but rather the inadequate affectional parental care that it may bring about." Thus children's relationships with their substitute caregivers assume particular importance in studying how children fare when a parent goes to prison.

It is also important to be clear that not all parental incarcerations will have the same impact in terms of the disruption of the child's previous relationships. The impact will clearly depend on who the child was living with before the incarceration and who the child is placed with during the incarceration. For instance, consider the situation of a child who has been living with a single mother and then, because of the mother's incarceration, is removed from her home and placed with a foster parent or other substitute caregiver. Consider a second child who has been living with both parents, whose father is incarcerated, and who continues to live with the mother. Consider a third child who had already been removed from her parents' home before the incarceration for reasons of abuse or neglect. Surely the impact of having a parent incarcerated will be different for each of these children.

SUBSTITUTE CARE ARRANGEMENTS AND CHILD OUTCOMES

We know remarkably little about whether children placed into substitute care fare better or worse than similar children remaining with their own parent or parents. Although a substantial literature (beginning with Maas and Engler in 1959; see also Fanshel and Shinn 1978) has established that children in substitute care tend to have poorer outcomes than the general population, most of the studies in this literature have been hampered by the absence of data on the child's functioning before placement and thus cannot determine how many of the children's problems preceded their entry into placement (see Wald, Carlsmith, and Leiderman 1988; Waldfogel 1998, 2000). Moreover, lacking experimental studies that randomly assign children to substitute care or parental care, it is hard to establish what the causal effects of substitute care might be. From a developmental perspective, parental care would generally be viewed as preferable for a child, if all else were equal, because parental care would allow for continuity of relationships, schools, daily routines, and so on. That preference for parental care must be balanced, however, against considerations of the suitability of the parent to care for a child. A parent who is being incarcerated may or may not have been providing adequate care to the child before the incarceration. Thus it is possible that a child might in some ways benefit from the parent's incarceration. Similarly, in thinking about the best substitute care arrangement for a child whose parent is being incarcerated, although parental care would normally be assumed to be preferable, the suitability of the other parent cannot be taken for granted.

Literature that compares the effects of different types of substitute care arrangements on children is also sparse. Many children in the child welfare system are placed with nonrelative foster parents; others are placed with relatives who are paid as foster parents—so-called kinship foster parents; still others are placed in group or institutional settings. Many of the studies that compare substitute care arrangements focus on differences in caregiver characteristics between kinship foster parents and nonrelative foster parents. These studies indicate that kinship foster parents are generally older (Berrick, Barth, and Needell 1994; Gaudin and Sutphen 1993; Gebel 1996; Le Prohn 1994), have lower annual incomes (Berrick, Barth, and Needell 1994; Ehrle and Geen 2002; Gaudin and Sutphen 1993; Gebel 1996; Le Prohn 1994), are less well educated (Berrick, Barth, and Needell 1994; Gebel 1996; Ehrle and Geen 2002), and tend to receive fewer social services than nonrelative foster care parents (Berrick, Barth, and Needell 1994; Gebel 1996).

Although kinship arrangements tend to offer more placement stability (Berrick, Barth, and Needell 1994; Inglehart 1994; Scannapieco, Hegar, and McAlpine 1997) and more regular contact with parents (Benedict, Zuravin, and Stallings 1996; Berrick, Barth, and Needell 1994; Berrick 1997) than nonrelative foster homes, they also have been found to provide a lower level of educational stimulation (Gaudin and Sutphen 1993). Kinship caregivers hold more favorable attitudes toward physical discipline (Gaudin and Sutphen 1993; Gebel 1996) and are less empathic toward children in their care than are nonrelative providers (Gebel 1996).

Studies that compare child outcomes, however, suggest few differences between children in kinship arrangements and those in nonkin arrangements (see, for instance, Benedict, Zuravin, and Stallings 1996, who find no long-term differences in education, employment, or earnings between children who spent time in kinship care and those who spent time in nonrelative foster care). Indeed, some studies find that children in kinship care do marginally better in terms of behavioral and mental health problems than children in nonrelative care (Berrick, Barth, and Needell 1994; Fein et al. 1983; Inglehart 1994).

One set of studies suggests that kinship caregivers face more obstacles to parenting effectively than nonrelative foster care providers (for example, low income, older age, the receipt of fewer services). Another set of studies suggests that children in kinship care fare just as well, or even slightly better, than children in nonkin foster care on certain outcome measures. However, these studies are plagued by the same challenge encountered in most studies of outcomes for children in substitute care—namely, that little is known about the status of the children before their entry into care or about what the children's outcomes would have been had they not been placed in care. Therefore, we do not know whether or how much the differences between children in kinship care and nonrelative care reflect the differential selection of children into those types of care versus an effect of those types of care. Studies that compare children entering kinship care and nonrelative foster care indicate that children enter into each type of care with different problems and for different reasons; for instance, children in kinship care are more often placed for neglect (Inglehart 1994; Landsverk et al. 1996) than for abuse. Moreover, to the extent that there are causal effects of substitute care arrangements, the mechanisms by which those arrangements can exacerbate or ameliorate child functioning and prevent new problems from developing remain unclear (Orme and Buehler 2001). In the absence of studies that establish causal effects of placement and that look specifically at how caregiver characteristics differentially relate to child outcomes in different living arrangements (that is, whether caregiver characteristics operate similarly in different living arrangements), there does not appear to be a clear hierarchy with regard to substitute care arrangements.

RISK AND DEVELOPMENT

The course of child development is determined by a number of factors. Contemporary models of development such as the ecological perspective situate human development within a complex matrix of individual and environmental influences (Brofenbrenner 1979, 1986). The transactional model takes the notion of contextual influence one step further, arguing that development is the product of continuous and dynamic interaction between the child and his or her social context over time (Sameroff and Chandler 1975; Sameroff 1983, 1993). Common to both these frameworks is the idea that a number of individual and environmental factors are important determinants of the course of child development. Personal and environmental factors that adversely affect growth and development are referred to as risk factors; those that facilitate adaptive outcomes in the face of adversity are termed protective factors or mechanisms (see, for example, Rutter 1987; Masten 1994).

There is considerable variability in how researchers have studied the relationship between risk and developmental outcomes. One widely used approach in the psychological literature involves using a multiple risk score that summarizes across risk variables to assess the overall level of adversity. The theory emerging from the multiple risk approach is that it is not just any one risk factor that matters for child outcomes but rather an accumulation of risk factors that can adversely affect the course of child development (Rutter 1979; Sameroff et al. 1998). Thus the greater the number of risk factors in a child's life, the greater the likelihood that he or she will experience difficulty. Several studies have found a relationship between the number of parental and ecological risk factors and outcomes such as cognitive performance (Sameroff et al. 1987a), social competence (Sameroff et al. 1987b; Furstenberg et al. 1999), child psychiatric disorders (Rutter 1979), and behavioral disorders (Williams et al. 1990).

Because it is assumed that it is the quantity not the quality of risk factors that matters, all risk variables are treated equally in the analyses (that is, risk factors are summed). Researchers begin by generating a list of variables that have been shown to adversely affect child development independently (for example, poverty, single parenthood, parental mental health problems) and them summarize them to arrive at an overall indicator of environmental adversity. The number and type of risk variables differ substantially across studies, some studies using as few as four risk variables and others as many as twenty.

Michael Rutter and David Quinton (1977) were among the first to use this methodology. They identify six factors associated with child psychiatric disorder: severe marital discord, low social status, overcrowding or large family size, paternal criminality (maternal criminality was not studied), maternal psychiatric disorder, and admission into the care of local authorities. Analyses of these factors reveals that though the presence of any one risk factor was not associated with increased risk for psychiatric disorders, the presence of two or more stressors was associated with a fourfold increase in risk for psychiatric disorders (Rutter 1979).

A series of studies by Arnold Sameroff and his colleagues yield similar results. The first of these findings derives from the Rochester Longitudinal Study, a study of children followed from the prenatal period through early adolescence. Based on evidence from the literature regarding their potential negative impact on developmental outcomes, a set of ten family risk factors was identified: history of maternal mental illness, high maternal anxiety, rigid beliefs about child development, few positive maternal interactions with the child during infancy, head of household in an unskilled occupation, low educational attainment, minority status, single parenthood, stressful life events, and large family size (Sameroff et al. 1987a).

On a verbal IQ test, children with none of these environmental risks scored more than thirty points higher than children with eight or nine of these risk factors (Sameroff et al. 1987a). When children were split into high- and low-risk groups, similar results were found. Children rated as high risk (four or more risk factors) were more than twenty-four times as likely to have low verbal IQ scores (that is, below 85) than children deemed low risk (zero to one risk factor). Moreover, the multiple risk index accounted for substantially more variance in child outcomes than any single risk factor. In a separate analysis, scores on a measure of social competence decreased linearly as the number of family risk factors increased (Sameroff et al. 1987b). That is, children with a greater number of family risk factors fared worse in terms of socioemotional competence than children with fewer family risk factors.

Similar cumulative effects of risk were found in the Philadelphia Study, a longitudinal study of adolescents in five different Philadelphia neighborhoods (Furstenberg et al. 1999). Families were split into high- and low-risk groups based on the number of risk factors present in the family environment. For mental health and academic performance, the relative risk of a poor outcome increased from 3 percent in the zero-risk group to 50 percent in the high-risk group. For problem behavior, the risk of a poor outcome increased from 3 percent in the zero-risk group to 45 percent in the high-risk group.

In a study of behavioral and emotional disorders in preadolescent children, Sheila Williams and her colleagues (1990) have found similar results regarding multiple risk factors. Although single risk factors did not distinguish children with behavioral disorders from those without behavioral disorders, the number of risk factors did. Specifically, only 7 percent of children with less than two disadvantages (for example, number of changes in residence, single parenthood, low socioeconomic status, parental separation, young motherhood, maternal mental health problems) had behavioral problems, compared with 40 percent of those children with eight or more of these disadvantages. Similarly, Emmy Werner and Ruth Smith (1989) find that children with four or more family risk factors at the age of two fared less well in terms of serious learning and behavioral problems at the age of ten or eighteen than children with fewer than four of these risk factors.

Research indicates that children of incarcerated parents have experienced many of the risk factors delineated in these studies, including low socioeconomic status, single-parent family, and low maternal education. Analyses of national inmate surveys reveal the presence of other parental risk factors, including histories of sexual and physical abuse, mental illness, parental incarceration (U.S. Department of Justice 1993), and poverty (Baunach 1985; Johnston 1995; Kampfner 1995). Substance use is also prevalent among inmates. In one study, nearly 60 percent of women in state prisons reported having used drugs in the month before their offense, approximately 50 percent described themselves as regular substance users, and 65 percent reported a history of prior convictions (Greenfeld and Snell 1999).

The presence of risk factors in the lives of incarcerated parents and their children has increased over time. By several indicators, parents incarcerated during 1997 reported more risk factors than parents incarcerated in 1986 (Johnson and Waldfogel 2002). For example, more of the 1997 parents reported histories of physical or sexual abuse, prior incarceration, incarceration of their own parents, and regular drug use than parents incarcerated during 1986.

Parental incarceration may introduce other risk factors identified in the cumulative risk literature. For example, as reported in chapter 2 in this volume, fathers' incarceration significantly reduces the chances that children's parents will marry, thereby increasing the risk of growing up in a single-parent family. Several of the studies cited here identify placement of a child in the care of local authorities as a risk factor, above and beyond the family and environmental risks that may precede it. Attachment theory might also attribute some risk associated with the placement of a child with someone other than the parent or other familiar caregiver. It may be the case that children who enter substitute care as a result of parental incarceration are high risk to start with and face even higher risks as a result of being in substitute care. Thus foster care may be both an outcome and a risk factor, depending on the circumstances that precede the child's placement and the nature of the relationship with the foster parent.

Given the prevalence of these other risk factors, we briefly consider how each of the factors relates to parenting and child outcomes. Parental history of mental health problems, physical and sexual abuse, substance use, foster care, or parental incarceration may all be relevant. With regard to mental health problems, mothers who are depressed, for example, find parenting more difficult and exhibit less nurturance toward children than less depressed mothers (McLoyd and Wilson 1991). Maternal depression has also been associated with greater social, behavioral, and academic difficulties among children (Downey and Coyne 1990).

A history of childhood physical or sexual abuse may influence parents' disciplinary strategies. Exposure to physical discipline as a child is related to more favorable attitudes toward its use (Rodriquez and Sutherland 1999; Bower-Russa, Knutson, and Winebarger 2001). Endorsement of physical punishment does relate to actual behavior: parents who hold more positive attitudes toward physical discipline are more likely to use physical discipline with their children (Jackson et al. 1999). Although most parents who were abused as children do not go on to abuse their own children, a history of abuse does appear to increase the risk of becoming abusive relative to individuals without an abuse history (Widom 1989; Kaufman and Zigler 1993). Mothers who have been sexually abused themselves exhibit more dependence on their children for emotional caretaking (Burkett 1991), lower levels of maternal involvement (Lyons-Ruth and Block 1996), and more permissive parenting practices (Ruscio 2001) than their nonabused counterparts. Elevated levels of substance abuse have also been observed among women with a history of sexual abuse in clinical (for example, Brown and Anderson 1991; Pribor and Dinwiddie 1992) as well as in community (Wilsnack et al. 1997) samples.

Substance abuse is often implicated in cases of child abuse and neglect, an estimated 40 to 80 percent of families involved with the child welfare system having alcohol or drug use problems (Child Welfare League of America 2001). Moreover, children whose parents abuse substances are three to four times more likely to be abused than children whose parents do not abuse substances (Child Welfare League of America 2001). Much of what we know about the correlation between parental substance use and adolescent substance use is based on studies of children of alcoholics, which indicate a strong link between parental alcohol use and adolescent alcohol use (Colder et al. 1997; Chassin, Rogosch, and Barrera 1991; Pandina and Johnson 1989; Finn et al. 1997). Parental substance abuse has also been associated with low parental monitoring, which, in turn, may heighten risk for adolescent substance use (Chassin et al. 1993, 1996). Infants who have been prenatally exposed to maternal substance use weigh less at birth (Chouteau, Namerow, and Leppert 1988), exhibit more behavioral problems (McNichol and Tash 2001), and have more special health and caregiving needs relative to their nonexposed counterparts (McNichol 1999); they may also have more chaotic home environments in early childhood (Berger and Waldfogel 2000).

Two other factors that may be relevant for thinking about this population of parents and children are whether the parent ever lived in foster care and whether the parent's own parent was ever incarcerated. One important way in which parental incarceration might affect the next generation's parenting is through diminished social and economic resources. Growing up in foster care may have similar effects on parents' access to resources and supports. However, we are aware of no studies that have looked at specific parenting outcomes in adults who lived in foster care while growing up or whose parents were incarcerated during their childhood.

To summarize, studies of cumulative risk suggest that parental and environmental risk factors that were present in children's lives before the parent went to prison may continue to influence how well they function during a parent's incarceration. However, it is important to point out that not all children will respond similarly in the face of parental and environmental risk. This is precisely the point made by more transactional models of development, which posit dynamic interactions between characteristics of individuals and the social context over time (Sameroff and Chandler 1975) and is implicit in research on resilience, which examines differential outcomes in the face of adversity (for example, Rutter 1987, 1993). Nonetheless, examining the presence of multiple risk factors in the lives of incarcerated parents and their children and considering how these relate to children's living arrangements provides us with a better understanding of children of incarcerated parents and the problems they may face as they grow into adolescence and young adulthood.

DATA, METHODS, AND RESULTS

We analyze children's living arrangements using the 1997 Survey of Inmates in State and Federal Correctional Facilities (U.S. Department of Justice 2000). The U.S. Census Bureau has conducted national inmate surveys every five years since 1974. Based on personal interviews with inmates, the data set yields detailed information on inmates' criminal history, drug and alcohol use, prison activities, conditions of confinement, family background, demographic characteristics, and a number of other variables. Parents were selected for analysis if they had at least one child under the age of eighteen. Cases with missing data were dropped from all analyses, producing a final sample of 6,870 fathers and 2,047 mothers who were incarcerated in state or federal prison in 1997. Descriptive statistics for all variables used in the analyses for mothers and fathers are displayed in table 5.1.

Three questions drive our analyses. First, what risk factors are present in the lives of incarcerated parents and their children, and how prevalent are they? Second, do we see higher levels of parental and environmental risk factors in certain living arrangements than in others? Third,

Table 5.1   *Sample Means for Variables Used in Analyses*

Risk Variable	Mothers (n = 2,047)	Fathers (n = 6,870)
White	.327 (.469)	.289 (.453)
African American	.480 (.499)	.507 (.499)
Other race	.037 (.188)	.033 (.179)
Hispanic	.155 (.362)	.170 (.376)
U.S. citizen	.942 (.233)	.924 (.265)
Age	33.4 (6.58)	33.8 (8.19)
Unmarried	.770 (.420)	.738 (.439)
Number of preschool-aged children	.408 (.677)	.460 (.738)
Number of school-aged children	1.93 (1.25)	1.66 (1.29)
Lived with child before incarceration	.697 (.459)	.468 (.499)
Less than twelfth-grade education	.562 (.496)	.572 (.494)
Own parent was incarcerated	.201 (.401)	.173 (.378)
Ever in foster care	.106 (.308)	.101 (.301)
Previously incarcerated	.358 (.479)	.545 (.497)
Ever used heroin, crack, or cocaine	.429 (.495)	.263 (.440)
Ever physically or sexually abused	.541 (.498)	.131 (.337)
Mental or emotional problem	.131 (.337)	.068 (.252)
Received public assistance before arrest	.345 (.475)	.065 (.248)
Total number of risk factors	3.42 (1.70)	2.65 (1.43)

Source: Authors' compilation from U.S. Department of Justice (2000).
Note: Standard deviations in parentheses.

controlling for other characteristics, do these risk factors predict where a child is living during the parent's incarceration? We use two different strategies to examine the relationship between risk factors and children's living arrangements. We estimate one set of models using a multiple risk score that summarizes across variables and one set of models in which each risk variable is entered separately.

Given our interest in multiple parental and environmental risk factors, we begin by creating a multiple risk score. Nine indicators of risk were selected based on their importance for child outcomes or their predictive utility in previous studies of cumulative risk. Although myriad other parental and environmental factors matter for child development, our analyses were constrained by variables available in the data. The risk factors we selected are low parental education (that is, less than a twelfth-grade education); parental substance use (that is, parent reported ever having used heroin, crack, or cocaine regularly); parental mental or emotional problem (that is, parent reported ever having had a mental or emotional problem); low socioeconomic status (that is, parent received

Table 5.2   *Prevalence of Risk Factors Among Incarcerated Parents, by Sex of Parent (Percentage)*

Number of Risk Factors	Mothers	Fathers
0	3.3	5.1
1	10.8	17.0
2	16.0	25.5
3	22.5	25.9
4	19.7	16.4
5	15.2	6.8
6	8.6	2.7
7 or more	4.0	0.6

Source: Authors' compilation from U.S. Department of Justice (2000).

public assistance before incarceration); parental history of physical or sexual abuse; history of prior incarceration; parent ever lived in foster care while growing up; parent's own parent had ever been incarcerated; and parent is unmarried.

Risk variables were dummy coded and then summed to arrive at a multiple risk score. Risk scores ranged from zero to nine, with a mean risk score of 3.4 for mothers and 2.7 for fathers (see table 5.1).

We present the frequency distribution for the multiple risk score in table 5.2. Because few parents had more than seven risk factors, we collapsed those with seven or more risk factors into a single category. Altogether, about 48 percent of the women surveyed had four or more risk factors, as compared with 27 percent of the men. More than two-thirds (70 percent) of the women had three or more risk factors, compared with just over half (52 percent) of the men.

Next, we examine how these multiple risk scores are distributed across children's living arrangements. We coded children as living in one of four main types of arrangement: with the other parent, with a grandparent or other relative, in foster or agency care, or other. Children in the first category lived exclusively with the other parent during a parent's incarceration. Children in the second category lived with a grandparent or other relative or lived with more than one family member, such as a grandparent, the other parent, or some other relative. Children in the third category lived exclusively in foster or agency care or had living arrangements involving foster or agency care and some other type of care. Children in the fourth category lived on their own, in an-

Figure 5.1   *Children's Living Arrangements During Parents' Incarceration*

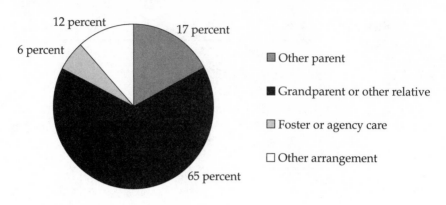

Children of Incarcerated Mothers

12 percent
6 percent
17 percent
65 percent

■ Other parent

■ Grandparent or other relative

□ Foster or agency care

□ Other arrangement

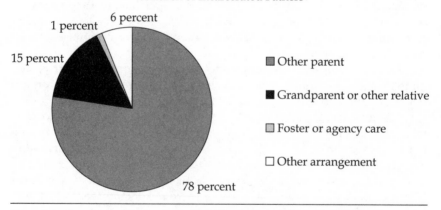

Children of Incarcerated Fathers

1 percent
6 percent
15 percent
78 percent

■ Other parent

■ Grandparent or other relative

□ Foster or agency care

□ Other arrangement

Source: Authors' compilation from U.S. Department of Justice (2000).

other type of care, or in multiple arrangements that included living on their own or in another type of care.

We show the distribution of children by living arrangements in figure 5.1. As shown in this figure, children's living arrangements during their parent's incarceration vary considerably by parent gender. Children of incarcerated fathers were most likely to be living with a parent (the mother), while children of incarcerated mothers were most likely to be living with a grandparent or other relative. Only about 1 percent of incarcerated fathers' children were in foster care, as compared with nearly

6 percent of incarcerated mothers' children. It should be noted here that the number of children in foster care may be understated in the survey. Parents did not have the option in the survey of identifying "kinship care," that is, care with a relative that is paid as foster care. Thus it is likely that children in kinship foster care are counted here as children living with a grandparent or other relative, not as children in foster care. In the results that follow, cross-tabulations of these four categories of living arrangements are presented by multiple risk score.

We estimate a series of multinomial logit models, which examine the effects of the multiple risk score and specific risk factors on the likelihood that a child lives in a given arrangement during a parent's incarceration, as compared with living with the other parent. Multinomial logit models are used because there are several categories of living arrangements that cannot be placed in any particular order. As the review of the literature on substitute care arrangements suggests, there is no clear hierarchy with regard to children's living arrangements; whereas children living with kin may fare better on some outcomes, on other outcomes there is no difference between children raised by relatives and those raised by nonrelative foster parents. Moreover, extant literature does not permit ranking all possible living arrangements (parent, grandparent, relative, agency, institution, alone, other) with confidence. We can, however, assume that in terms of continuity of care, prior relationships, residence, school, and so on, living with a parent will usually be the least disruptive arrangement for a child whose other parent has been incarcerated.

Based on previous studies suggesting that living arrangements differ for children depending on the gender of the parent who is incarcerated (Johnston 1991; Mumola 2000; Johnson and Waldfogel 2002), we estimate separate models for mothers and fathers. For both mothers and fathers, we estimate two sets of models, one using the multiple risk score and one using the individual indicators of risk. Our control variables include an extensive set of parent and family characteristics, including whether the parent is African American, Hispanic, or of other race or ethnicity (non-Hispanic white is the omitted category), whether the parent is a noncitizen, the parent's age, and the number of preschool-aged and school-aged children the parent has. Although some of these factors (for example, minority status, family size) are sometimes included as risk factors, we prefer to treat them as controls, on the assumption that they are not risks in and of themselves but rather may be associated with elevated risk through their association with other risk factors.

We also control for whether the parent and child lived together before the parent's incarceration. As indicated in table 5.1, about 70 percent of mothers and 47 percent of fathers were living with their children be-

Table 5.3   *Children's Living Arrangements During Parent's Incarceration,
by Number of Risk Factors*

Living Arrangement	0	1	2	3	4	5	6	7 or More
Children of incarcerated mothers								
With other parent	55.2	28.5	16.0	18.0	13.0	14.0	9.7	7.4
With grandparent or relative	41.8	64.7	65.0	65.2	69.0	66.0	64.2	73.0
In foster or agency care	0.0	0.5	4.9	5.6	5.0	8.7	10.2	11.0
In other arrangement	3.0	6.3	14.0	11.3	13.0	12.0	15.9	8.6
Children of incarcerated fathers								
With other parent	83.0	78.2	79.3	76.0	74.0	79.2	69.4	65.1
With grandparent or relative	11.0	15.4	13.4	15.8	18.0	12.9	18.3	23.3
In foster or agency care	0.6	0.9	0.5	1.7	2.2	2.1	1.6	4.7
In other arrangement	5.5	5.5	6.8	6.5	6.0	5.8	10.8	7.0

Source: Authors' compilation from U.S. Department of Justice (2000).

fore incarceration (in the remaining families, the children were already living elsewhere, although we do not know from our data where those children were living, just that they were not living with the parent). To understand more specifically the situation of children who were living with their parents before this incarceration, we conduct supplemental analyses for this subset of families.

Multiple Risk Scores and Children's Living Arrangements

Table 5.3 shows the distribution of children's living arrangements by risk score. The top panel presents data on risk scores of mothers, the bottom panel shows risks scores of fathers. Reading across rows, the table indicates what share of children within each risk-score group lived in a particular type of arrangement during a parent's incarceration. For instance, reading across the first row, "With other parent" for mothers, we can see that 55 percent of children with no risk factors were residing with a parent, compared with only 7 percent of children with seven or more risk factors. Thus, at least in the raw data, the chance of residing with a parent declines as the number of risk factors increases. In contrast, the share of children living in foster care increases as the number of risk factors increases, rising from 0 percent for children of mothers with no risk factors to 11 percent for children of mothers with seven or more risk factors. The share of children living with grandparents or other relatives increases with the presence of one risk factor and remains fairly stable across other risk-score groups, rising steeply only for children of mothers with seven or more risk factors. The pattern for the share of children in other living arrangements is less clear; it rises from one and two risk factors, dips at three factors, increases again from four to six risk factors, and then declines at seven or more risk factors.

The patterns for children of incarcerated fathers are fairly similar. The overall share of children living with a parent is much higher, but as in the results for mothers, the share of children living with a parent declines as the number of risk factors increases (from 83 percent of children with no risk factors to 65 percent of children with seven or more risk factors), while in general the share of children living in foster care increases with the number of risk factors (rising from less than 1 percent for children of fathers with no risk factors to almost 5 percent for children of fathers with seven or more risk factors). Again, the share of children living with grandparents or other relatives increases in the presence of one risk factor, stays relatively constant across risk score groups, and then rises steeply with seven risk factors. The share of children living in some other nonparental arrangement peaks at around six risk factors.

Thus the raw data indicate that children who face more risks are less likely to be living with a parent and more likely to be living in foster care. This is the case for children of incarcerated mothers and fathers alike. There is also a tendency for higher-risk children to be living with a grandparent or other relative or in another form of care. We cannot tell from the raw data, however, whether these relationships will hold when we control for other characteristics of these families. Therefore, we turn now to the multivariate results.

Impact of Risk Factors on Children's Living Arrangements

We estimated multinomial logit models to learn what effects the multiple risk score and individual risk factors had on children's living arrangements during a parent's incarceration, holding other family characteristics constant. In each model, the reference category is living with the other parent, so we are estimating the effect of the risk score or risk factors on the likelihood that a child is living in one of the other types of arrangements rather than with the other parent. We show the results (odds ratios and p values) for the multiple risk score in table 5.4 and for individual risk factors in table 5.5. In each table, the top panel presents

Table 5.4   *The Effect of Multiple Risks on Children's Living Arrangements During Parent's Incarceration*

Parent Characteristic	Grandparent or Relative	Foster or Agency Care	Other Arrangement
Incarcerated mother			
Multiple risk score	1.279**	1.651**	1.485**
	(.000)	(.000)	(.000)
Age	.971**	1.042**	1.103**
	(.006)	(.037)	(.000)
Number of preschool-aged	1.212*	2.836**	1.150
children	(.090)	(.000)	(.408)
Number of school-aged	1.052	1.271**	1.011
children	(.351)	(.006)	(.885)
African American	2.377**	2.147**	1.588**
	(.000)	(.003)	(.019)
Other race	1.762	2.943**	1.808
	(.093)	(.041)	(.184)
Hispanic	1.681**	1.263	1.263
	(.007)	(.521)	(.421)
Noncitizen	1.431	1.202	1.395
	(.211)	(.763)	(.398)
Lived with child before	1.120	.412**	1.074
incarceration	(.417)	(.000)	(.709)
R-squared = .169			
N = 2,047			
Incarcerated father			
Multiple risk score	1.099**	1.462**	1.202**
	(.000)	(.000)	(.000)
Age	.995	1.067**	1.139**
	(.338)	(.000)	(.000)
Number of preschool-aged	.927	1.173	.856
children	(.148)	(.340)	(.153)
Number of school-aged	.982	1.152*	.865**
children	(.527)	(.085)	(.003)
African American	1.144	.675	.808
	(.102)	(.113)	(.074)
Other race	1.067	.780	1.037
	(.742)	(.685)	(.896)
Hispanic	.931	1.020	.694
	(.553)	(.952)	(.051)
Noncitizen	1.125	1.095	.902
	(.432)	(.843)	(.683)

Table 5.4   *Continued*

Parent Characteristic	Grandparent or Relative	Foster or Agency Care	Other Arrangement
Lived with child before incarceration	1.519**	1.170	1.020
	(.000)	(.476)	(.859)
R-squared = .087			
N = 6,870			

Source: Authors' compilation from U.S. Department of Justice (2000).
Note: Living with other parent is the reference category. P-values are in parentheses. The odds ratios and p values are derived from multinomial logit models.
*p < .10 **p <.05

Figure 5.2   *Multiple Risks and Children's Living Arrangements*

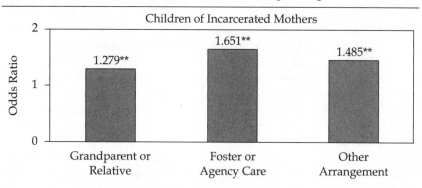

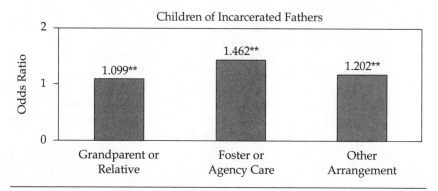

Source: Authors' compilation from U.S. Department of Justice (2000).
**p < .05

results for mothers, and the bottom panel results for fathers. The results for the multiple risk scores are also displayed graphically in figure 5.2. Looking first at the results for children of incarcerated mothers in the top panel of table 5.4 (and figure 5.2), it is clear that the higher the multiple risk score, the greater the odds that a child is living with someone other than the other parent during the mother's incarceration. Each additional risk raises the child's odds of living with a grandparent or other relative by 28 percent, the odds of residing in foster or agency care by 65 percent, and the odds of living in some other arrangement by 49 percent. These effects are above and beyond those of other family characteristics, which also matter in predicting children's living arrangements. For instance, family size matters: families with more children are more likely to have children living somewhere other than with the other parent and are particularly likely to have children living in foster or agency care. This finding is consistent with the child welfare literature, which typically finds larger family size correlated with higher rates of out-of-home placement (see, for instance, Berger 2002). Race also matters. African American children are more likely than non-Hispanic white children (the reference category) to reside in any of the nonparental living arrangements. Given that our models control for a number of other characteristics of the child's mother, the higher risk for African American children to be living with someone other than the father may reflect the poorer living circumstances (for example, lower employment and earnings, higher rates of incarceration, poorer community environments) of these fathers.

The general pattern of results is fairly similar for children of incarcerated fathers (see the bottom panel of table 5.4 and figure 5.2). As with the results for mothers, higher multiple risk scores predict a greater likelihood that the child is residing in a nonparental care arrangement. For children of incarcerated fathers, each additional risk raises the odds that a child resides with a grandparent or other relative by 10 percent, the odds of residing in foster or agency care by 46 percent, and the odds of residing in some other arrangement by 20 percent. Although the overall pattern is similar to that for children of incarcerated mothers (that is, the effects are strongest for foster care, weakest for grandparents), the effects of multiple risks and the effects of other family characteristics are considerably smaller and weaker than they were in the mothers' model. The overall weakness of the model, and its poor explanatory power (the R-squared here is only .087, compared with .169 in the mothers' model) may reflect the fact that fewer than half of these fathers were living with their children before incarceration (see table 5.1). Fathers' characteristics may be poor predictors of living arrangements of children who were not living with them to start with. We examine this in more detail later in

Table 5.5   *Effect of Specific Parent's Risk Factors on Children's Living Arrangements During Parent's Incarceration*

Risk Factor	Grandparent or Relative	Foster or Agency Care	Other Arrangement
Incarcerated mother			
Unmarried	2.811**	2.670**	2.876**
	(.000)	(.000)	(.000)
Ever used heroin, crack,	1.344**	1.293	1.224
or cocaine regularly	(.040)	(.290)	(.302)
Ever physically or sexually	.936	2.385**	1.574**
abused	(.633)	(.001)	(.020)
Own parent was incarcerated	.853	.901	.889
	(.354)	(.714)	(.625)
Ever in foster care	1.464*	2.039**	1.337
	(.095)	(.034)	(.349)
Previously incarcerated	1.179	1.077	1.067
	(.257)	(.760)	(.752)
Less than twelfth-grade	.962	2.327**	1.954**
education	(.774)	(.001)	(.000)
Mental or emotional health	1.200	1.425	1.345
problem	(.378)	(.233)	(.260)
Received public assistance	1.940**	1.788**	1.866**
before arrest	(.000)	(.024)	(.002)
R-squared = .204			
N = 2,047			
Incarcerated father			
Unmarried	1.311**	1.363	1.310**
	(.000)	(.225)	(.029)
Ever used heroin, crack, or	1.019	1.648**	1.173
cocaine regularly	(8.13)	(.028)	(.182)
Ever physically or sexually	1.159	2.168**	1.135
abused	(.153)	(.003)	(.419)
Own parent was incarcerated	1.014	1.318	1.289
	(.881)	(.318)	(.102)
Ever in foster care	.843	.804	.786
	(.154)	(.542)	(.219)
Previously incarcerated	1.000	1.000	1.350**
	(1.00)	(.999)	(.009)
Less than twelfth-grade	1.128*	1.813**	1.172
education	(.091)	(.012)	(.146)
Mental or emotional health	1.191	1.131	1.231
problem	(.184)	(.729)	(.257)

(*Table continues on p. 118.*)

Table 5.5   *Continued*

Risk Factor	Grandparent or Relative	Foster or Agency Care	Other Arrangement
Received public assistance	1.254*	2.627**	1.390*
before arrest	(.087)	(.001)	(.080)
R-squared = .086			
N = 6,870			

Source: Authors' compilation from U.S. Department of Justice (2000).
Note: Model includes all controls from table 5.4 except the multiple risk score. Living with the other parent is the reference category. Odds ratios and p values are derived from multinomial logit models.
*p < .10 **p < .05

this chapter, when we conduct separate analyses for the subset of families in which children were living with the parent before incarceration.

Nevertheless, the results for mothers and fathers are consistent in pointing to a pattern of higher-risk children being more likely to be residing in foster or agency care and, to a lesser extent, in other care or grandparent or relative care. Thus it is fair to conclude that, all else being equal, children of incarcerated parents who reside in foster or agency care are a particularly high-risk group but children in other nonparental care arrangements are at elevated risk as well.

To learn what specific risks might be driving these results, we reestimated our models for mothers and fathers, replacing the multiple risk score with dummy variables for the nine individual risk factors (and controlling for all the other covariates included in the prior model). We show the results (odds ratios and p values) for the individual risk factors in table 5.5, again with results for mothers in the top panel and results for fathers in the bottom panel.

For mothers, being unmarried almost triples the odds that children are residing in any of the three types of nonparental care (grandparent or other relative, foster or agency care, or some other arrangement) during her incarceration. We also see that drug use is associated with higher rates of nonparental living arrangements, although this effect is statistically significant only for grandparent or other relative care. The mother's having ever been abused herself, and the mother's not having completed twelve years of school, are strongly associated with children's residing in foster or agency care or other care. The mother's having lived in foster care herself doubles the risk that her children are in foster or agency care while she is incarcerated and increases the odds that her children are in the care of a grandparent or relative by nearly 50 percent. The mother's having received public assistance before incarceration nearly doubles her children's risk of being in any of the three types of nonparental care during her incarceration. The parent's own parent having been incarcerated, having had a prior period of incarceration, and having had a mental or emotional health problem were not significantly related to children's living arrangements.

The pattern of results for children of incarcerated fathers is again similar but generally weaker than that for children of incarcerated mothers. For fathers, being unmarried increases the odds that their children are residing in some form of nonparental care by only about 30 percent (being unmarried nearly tripled the odds for incarcerated mothers' children). Drug use is strongly linked to higher rates of foster or agency care for children of fathers who are incarcerated, as is the father's having ever been physically or sexually abused himself. The father's having less than twelve years of schooling raises the odds of all three types of nonparental living arrangement, with a particularly large effect on foster or agency care. Having received public assistance before the arrest raises the odds of foster or agency care for children more than twofold, the odds that the child is living with a grandparent or other relative by about 25 percent, and the odds that the child is in other care by 40 percent. In contrast to the results for mothers, the father's having a parent who was incarcerated or having had a prior incarceration himself significantly raises the odds that his child is in other living arrangement. There are no significant effects of the father's having been in foster care himself or having had a mental or emotional health problem.

Parents Who Lived with Children Before Incarceration

In supplemental analyses (not shown but available on request), we reestimated our models limiting the sample to parents who lived with the children before incarceration (this represents 70 percent of mothers [n = 1,427] and 47 percent of fathers [n = 3,218]). The rationale here is that parental characteristics or family background variables may have a different effect on living arrangements for children who were living with the parent before the incarceration (different, that is, from the effect for the overall sample, which also includes some children who were already living elsewhere at the time of the incarceration). Moreover, separate analyses for these subgroups may help us identify more specifically which factors are related to changes in living arrangements that occur in conjunction with incarceration.

In the raw data for the subgroups of mothers and fathers who were living with their children before this incarceration, the overall pattern of children's living arrangements is the same as for the overall sample: the majority of incarcerated fathers' children live with the other parent (75 percent), whereas the majority of incarcerated mothers' children live with a grandparent (67 percent). The share of incarcerated mothers' children who are in foster care is slightly lower than for the overall sample of mothers (4 versus 6 percent), whereas this percentage is basically the same for fathers who lived with children before incarceration (1.3 percent) as it is in the overall sample of fathers (1.4 percent).

In the regression models, the effect of the multiple risk score on nonparental care arrangements is almost identical to the effects found in the overall sample, for both mothers and fathers, although the effects of demographic characteristics on living arrangements do change in some cases. For instance, being African American increases the odds that children of incarcerated fathers are living in foster or agency care, but only for men who lived with their children before incarceration. At the same time, among mothers, being African American, Hispanic, or other race or ethnicity does not predict a child's being in foster care among children who lived with their mothers before incarceration, although it did in the overall sample of children of incarcerated mothers.

When we reestimated the models with the individual risk factors for the restricted sample of families in which parents lived with their children before incarceration, again few differences emerged. The effect of a parent's being unmarried on the likelihood that the child is living with someone other than a parent was larger across all the placement types for mothers who lived with children before incarceration than it was for the overall sample of mothers. Overall, fewer risk factors were significant for models using the restricted sample of mothers than in the full sample. For instance, the effect of the incarcerated parent's own history of foster care on relative or agency placements and the effect of the parent's substance use on placement with grandparents were statistically significant in the overall sample but not in the restricted sample of mothers. However, these differences were slight and may derive from the smaller sample size in the restricted sample. Overall, the risks and other factors that are associated with a child's not living with the other parent during a parent's incarceration seem to be similar across children who were living with the parent before the incarceration and the full sample of children of incarcerated parents (some of whom were not living with the parent before incarceration).

DISCUSSION AND CONCLUSION

One consequence of the dramatic increase of incarceration during the late 1980s and early 1990s has been a sharp increase in the number of children whose parents are incarcerated. Our data confirm earlier work (for example, McGowan and Blumenthal 1978) indicating the presence of many risk factors in the lives of incarcerated parents and their children. Previous studies have defined high-risk families as those with four or more risk factors (Sameroff et al. 1987a; Sameroff et al. 1987b), a categorization that has proved useful in distinguishing children on important psychosocial outcomes. A substantial share of incarcerated parents—48 percent of women and 27 percent of men—meet this definition of high risk, and more than two-thirds of women (70 percent) and just over half of the surveyed men (52 percent) have three or more risk factors. Moreover, our data suggest that it is not only children living in foster care (and other child welfare institutions) who have been exposed to parental and environmental risk factors before the parent's imprisonment but also children living with grandparents or other relatives and in other settings.

The raw data indicate that as the number of risk factors rises, children are increasingly likely to be residing with someone other than a parent and are particularly likely to be living in foster or agency care. Our multivariate results confirm that these relationships hold even after controlling for other child and family characteristics such as race or ethnicity, age, family size, and so on. The highest-risk children of incarcerated mothers and fathers are residing in foster or agency care, but those residing with grandparents or other relatives and in other arrangements also enter those homes with more risks than those residing with parents. Moreover, given that placement into nonparental care could be considered an additional risk factor in its own right, it must be assumed that relative to children living with a parent, children who do not live with a parent are at even higher risk than we are estimating here.

We also learned something about the specific risk factors that seem to be most strongly associated with children's living in nonparental care during a parent's incarceration. For both mothers and fathers, several risk factors were significantly associated with the child's being in foster care or placed with an agency, although the specifics differed slightly by gender. A parent's history of physical or sexual abuse, less than a twelfth-grade education, and benefit receipt increased the odds that both mothers' and fathers' children would be living in foster care. For mothers, being unmarried or ever having lived in foster care while growing up also increased the risk that their children were in foster care, whereas for fathers, a history of regular heroin or crack cocaine use raised the chances that their children were in foster care.

Regular substance use was an important risk factor for a child's living with someone other than a parent. As well as predicting foster care for children of incarcerated fathers, it also predicted living with a grandparent or other relative for children of incarcerated mothers. These results make sense given that substance use is often a factor in child placement into foster care or kinship care (Child Welfare League of America 2001).

A history of mental health problems was not significantly related to children's living arrangements for incarcerated parents, perhaps because self-reported history of mental or emotional problems is a poor indicator of actual mental health. Parents' prior history of incarceration was also a weak indicator of children's living arrangements when considered independently. Among mothers, prior sentence to incarceration was not significantly related to children's living arrangements, and for fathers, prior sentence only increased the odds that a child was in the "other arrangement" category. Working out the mechanisms by which parental and environmental characteristics directly and indirectly influence children's living arrangements, and their eventual outcomes, and identifying other risk factors that we could not measure in our data are important challenges for further research.

Our results speak to the need for a broader service response that reaches out to all nonparental caregivers of incarcerated children, not just to those who are formal foster or agency care providers. Children who are residing with relatives, or in other settings outside the formal child welfare system, are a higher-risk group than children who live with another parent during their parent's incarceration and are thus more likely to be in need of services. At the same time, children in foster or agency care do warrant special attention. Our results confirm that they are the highest-risk group of children of incarcerated parents, as evidenced by their significantly higher multiple risk scores (and higher odds of having specific risk factors).

Given their incarceration, parents whose children are in foster care may face special challenges in meeting the mandates of child welfare agencies. Legal trends and institutional policies may inhibit the maintenance of relationships between incarcerated parents and their children. Indeed, few child welfare agencies have specific policies and procedures to address the situation of children of incarcerated parents (Johnson and Waldfogel 2002). In the absence of such policies, these children's needs may go unmet. It is particularly important that permanency planning for such children be specialized to take account of the challenges faced by parents who are incarcerated as well as the problematic family histories that many of these children have.

Policies for children of incarcerated parents must also take account of their diversity. As we have seen, living arrangements for these children differ by a number of parental demographic characteristics, including gender and race. Such demographic factors are consistently associated with type of living arrangement and with risk factors for children. Children whose mothers are incarcerated are much more likely to end up in nonparental care than children of incarcerated fathers. There are also notable gender differences in the mean number of risk factors (3.4 for children of incarcerated mothers versus 2.7 for children of incarcerated fathers). Thus children whose mothers go to prison are likely to have different, and more intensive, service needs than children whose fathers go to prison. Because many of these risk factors (for example, drug abuse) can be directly harmful to children's well-being, removal of the child may be in the child's best interest. However, given the research on attachment reviewed earlier in this chapter, such a course seems plausible only if supportive and rehabilitative services are in place that facilitate family reunification.

Another demographic factor that has a consistent influence on children's living arrangements is race. Given past research that suggests that children's living arrangements during a parent's incarceration vary by race (Baunach 1985; Snell 1994), this is not particularly surprising. What is striking, however, is that the children of incarcerated African American mothers are at increased risk of residing in some form of nonparental care arrangement (grandparent, relative, or foster care), even after controlling for other factors such as the mother's marital status, education, and so on. This pattern of results might reflect the fact that the fathers of African American women's children are relatively more disadvantaged in terms of their employment, earnings, and own incarceration (compared with other fathers) and thus may be less able to care for their children when the mother is incarcerated.

Although our data suggest that children of incarcerated parents in all types of nonparental living arrangements may be at elevated risk by virtue of certain parental and environmental characteristics that they were exposed to before the parent's incarceration, it is important to remember that not all children will respond similarly to such environmental risk. As noted earlier, this is the point made by more transactional models of development, which posit dynamic interactions between characteristics of individuals and their social context over time (Sameroff and Chandler 1975) and is implicit in research on resilience, which examines differential outcomes in the face of adversity (for example, Rutter 1987, 1993). Again, some children may benefit from a parent's incarceration— if, for example, the parent was abusive or neglectful and if the child can be cared for in an alternative setting that better meets his or her needs. The circumstances under which parental incarceration harms or benefits children is an important empirical issue that has yet to be addressed.

We are unable to explore the impact of incarceration and alternative living arrangements during incarceration on children's development because we do not have data on child outcomes. Although the presence of several parental and environmental risk factors may increase the odds of adverse outcomes, this is probabilistic, not deterministic—especially since how well a child functions depends on many other factors. Longitudinal outcome studies that examine the role of preincarceration risk factors, children's living arrangements, relationships with their parents, and relationships with substitute caregivers in children's functioning are sorely needed. Examining the extent to which children's living arrangements mediate the effect of parental incarceration on child outcomes is an important avenue for future research. For some children, being removed from a "risky" environment and placed with a relative or in a foster home may be beneficial. Although developmental research has examined attachment relationships between children and other caregivers (for example, teachers, daycare providers), we know less about attachment relationships with alternative caregivers, an issue of obvious relevance for some children whose parents go to prison. The extent to which these relationships may serve a compensatory function in the parent's absence is still unexplored, despite its importance for thinking about intervention. As Ross Thompson (1999) points out, attachment relationships with different caregivers may serve different functions for children and influence different outcomes. Thus looking at the impact of relationships with surrogate caregivers as well as with the imprisoned parent may be useful.

In general, there is a need for more methodologically rigorous research. Much of the existing literature on children whose parents are incarcerated is descriptive or anecdotal in nature, and the few studies that do exist fail to specify methods and measures in a manner that allows for replication. Moreover, data on children are typically collected through interviews with parents, which provide a limited view of children's behaviors. This may be of particular concern when a parent is incarcerated, as he or she does not have daily contact with the child. Some mothers do not know basic information about their children, including developmental milestones and the names of children's teachers (Johnston 2001). Studies that utilize multiple informants of child behavior and control for preincarceration risk factors and children's living arrangements will make it possible to determine the impact of parental incarceration on families and children. Understanding whether and how parental absence owing to incarceration differs from other forms of parental separation (for example, through death or divorce) will also be useful in designing interventions for families with an incarcerated parent.

A few other limitations are noteworthy. First, as mentioned earlier, the survey data do not allow us to identify children in "kinship care" separately from children living in informal care with grandparents or other relatives. We do not know what share of children living with grandparents may be connected with the child welfare system. Thus our count of children in foster care may be too low. Second, if children were not living with the responding parent before the incarceration, the survey data do not allow us to identify children's living arrangements before the parent's incarceration (other than that they were not living with the parent). Our data indicate that many children, especially those whose fathers are in prison, did not reside with the incarcerated parent before the incarceration. Given the prevalence of drug use histories and prior incarcerations, it would be useful to know more about children's placement histories before this incarceration. Moreover, the amount of variance explained by our models is relatively low across models, although higher for mothers. Thus many factors other than those we consider here may influence where a child resides during a parent's incarceration.

Following studies suggesting that it is not any one risk factor that may negatively influence child development but rather an accumulation of such risk factors (for example, Rutter 1979; Sameroff et al. 1998), we utilized a multiple risk model in these analyses. Because this approach indexes the overall level of ecological adversity, it is useful in identifying high-risk groups. Our results suggest that children whose parents are in prison are a high-risk group, with 70 percent of all incarcerated mothers and 52 percent of all incarcerated fathers reporting three or more risk factors. Our results also indicate that among this high-risk group, the children who have experienced the highest number of risk factors tend to be those who are not living with a parent, particularly children living in foster or agency care. Gaining more knowledge about the risks these children face, and the impact of incarceration and alternative living arrangements on their developmental outcomes, is an important priority for further research.

REFERENCES

Baunach, Phyllis J. 1985. *Mothers in Prison.* New Brunswick, N.J.: Transaction Books.

Benedict, Mary I., Susan Zuravin, and Rebecca Y. Stallings. 1996. "Adult Functioning of Children Who Lived in Kin Versus Nonrelative Family Foster Homes." *Child Welfare* 75(5): 529–49.

Berger, Lawrence. 2002. "Children Living Out-of-Home: Effects of Family and Environmental Characteristics." Mimeo: Columbia University.

Berger, Lawrence, and Jane Waldfogel. 2000. "Prenatal Cocaine Exposure: Long-Run Effects and Policy Implications." *Social Service Review* 74(1): 28–54.

Berrick, Jill Duerr. 1997. "Assessing Quality of Care in Kinship and Foster Family Care." *Family Relations* 46(3): 273–80.

Berrick, Jill Duerr, Richard P. Barth, and Barbara Needell. 1994. "A Comparison of Kinship Foster Homes and Foster Family Homes: Implications for Kinship Care as Preservation." *Children and Youth Services Review* 16(1): 33–63.

Bloom, Barbara, and David Steinhart. 1993. *Why Punish the Children? A Reappraisal of the Children of Incarcerated Mothers in America.* San Francisco: National Council on Crime and Delinquency.

Bower-Russa, Mary E., John F. Knutson, and Allen Winebarger. 2001. "Disciplinary History, Adult Disciplinary Attitudes, and Risk for Abusive Parenting." *Journal of Community Psychology* 29(3): 219–40.

Bowlby, John. 1969. *Attachment and Loss.* Vol. 1, *Attachment.* New York: Basic Books.

———. 1973. *Attachment and Loss.* Vol. 2, *Separation: Anxiety and Anger.* London: Hogarth Press.

———. 1980. *Attachment and Loss.* Vol. 3, *Loss: Sadness and Depression.* London: Hogarth Press.

Brofenbrenner, Urie. 1979. *The Ecology of Human Development.* Cambridge, Mass.: Harvard University Press.

———. 1986. "Ecology of the Family as a Context for Human Development: Research Perspective." *Developmental Psychology* 22: 723–42.

Brown, George R., and Bradley Anderson. 1991. "Psychiatric Morbidity in Adult Inpatients with Childhood Histories of Sexual and Physical Abuse." *American Journal of Psychiatry* 148(1): 55–61.

Burkett, Linda Padou. 1991. "Parenting Behaviors of Women Who Were Sexually Abused as Children in Their Families of Origin." *Family Process* 30(4): 421–34.

Chassin, Laurie, Patrick J. Curran, Andrea M. Hussong, and Craig R. Colder. 1996. "The Relation of Parent Alcoholism to Adolescent Substance Use: A Longitudinal Follow-up." *Journal of Abnormal Psychology* 105(1): 70–80.

Chassin, Laurie, David R. Pillow, Patrick J. Curran, Brooke S. Molina, and Manuel Barrera, Jr. 1993. "Relation of Parental Alcoholism to Early Adolescent Substance Use: A Test of Three Mediating Mechanisms." *Journal of Abnormal Psychology* 102(1): 3–19.

Chassin, Laurie, Fred Rogosch, and Manual Barrera, Jr. 1991. "Substance Use Escalation and Substance Use Restraint among Adolescent Children of Alcoholics." *Psychology of Addictive Behaviors* 7(1): 3–20.

Child Welfare League of America. 2001. *Alcohol, Other Drugs, and Child Welfare.* Washington, D.C.: Child Welfare League of America.

Chouteau, Michelle, Pearila Brickner Namerow, and Phyllis Leppert. 1988. "The Effect of Cocaine Abuse on Birth Weight and Gestational Age." *Obstetrics and Gynecology* 72(3): 351–54.

Colder, Craig R., Laurie Chassin, Eric M. Stice, and Patrick J. Curran. 1997. "Alcohol Expectancies as Potential Mediators of Parent Alcoholism Effect on the Development of Adolescent Heavy Drinking." *Journal of Research on Adolescence* 7(4): 349–74.

Downey, Geraldine, and James C. Coyne. 1990. "Children of Depressed Parents: An Integrative Review." *Psychological Bulletin* 108(1): 50–76.

Easterbrooks, M. Ann, Cherilyn E. Davidson, and Rachel Chazen. 1993. "Psychosocial Risk, Attachment, and Behavior Problems among School-aged Children." *Development and Psychopathology* 5(3): 389–402.

Ehrle, Jennifer, and Rob Geen. 2002. "Kin and Non-Kin Foster Care—Findings from a National Survey." *Children and Youth Services Review* 24(1–2): 15–35.

Elicker, James, Michelle Englund, and L. Alan Sroufe. 1992. "Predicting Peer Competence and Peer Relationships in Children from Early Parent-Child Relationships." In *Family-Peer Relationships: Modes of Linkage,* edited by Ross D. Parke and Gary W. Ladd. Hillsdale, N.J.: Lawrence Erlbaum.

Erickson, Martha Farrell, L. Alan Sroufe, and Byron Egeland. 1985. "The Relationship Between Quality of Attachment and Behavior Problems in a High-Risk Sample." *Monographs of the Society for Research in Child Development* 50(1–2): 147–66.

Fanshel, David, and Eugene B. Shinn. 1978. *Children in Foster Care: A Longitudinal Investigation.* New York: Columbia University Press.

Fein, Edith, Anthony N. Malucco, V. Jane Hamilton, and Darryl E. Ward. 1983. "After Foster Care: Outcomes of Permanency Planning for Children." *Child Welfare* 62(6): 485–558.

Finn, Peter R., Erica J. Sharkansky, Richard Viken, Tara L. West, Jamie Sandy, and Gary M. Bufferd. 1997. "Heterogeneity in the Families of Sons of Alcoholics: The Impact of Familial Vulnerability Type on Offspring Characteristics." *Journal of Abnormal Psychology* 106(1): 26–36.

Furstenberg, Frank, Jr., Thomas D. Cook, Jacquelynne Eccles, Glen H. Elder Jr., and Arnold Sameroff. 1999. *Managing to Make It: Urban Families and Adolescent Success.* Chicago: University of Chicago Press.

Gaudin, James M., and Richard Sutphen. 1993. "Foster Care vs. Extended Family Care for Children of Incarcerated Mothers." *Journal of Offender Rehabilitation* 19(3–4): 129–47.

Gebel, Timothy J. 1996. "Kinship Care and Nonrelative Family Foster Care: A Comparison of Caregiver Attributes and Attitudes." *Child Welfare* 75(1): 5–18.

Greenfeld, Lawrence A., and Tracy L. Snell. 1999. *Women Offenders.* NCJ-175688. Washington: U.S. Department of Justice, Bureau of Justice Statistics.

Howes, Carollee. 1999. "Attachment Relationships in the Context of Multiple Caregivers." In *Handbook of Attachment: Theory, Research, and Clinical Applications.* New York: Guilford.

Inglehart, Alfreda P. 1994. "Kinship Foster Care: Placement, Service, and Outcome Issues." *Children and Youth Services Review* 16(1–2): 107–22.

Jackson, Shelly, Ross A. Thompson, Elaine H. Christiansen, Rebecca A. Coleman, Jennifer Wyatt, Chad W. Buckendahl, Brian L. Wilcox, and Reece Peterson. 1999. "Predicting Abuse-Prone Parental Attitudes and Discipline Practices in a Nationally Representative Sample." *Child Abuse and Neglect* 23(1): 15–29.

Johnson, Elizabeth I., and Jane Waldfogel. 2002. "Trends in Parental Incarceration: Implications for Child Welfare." *Social Service Review* 76(3): 460–79.

Johnston, Denise. 1991. *Jailed Mothers.* Pasadena, Calif.: Pacific Oaks Center for Children of Incarcerated Parents.

———. 1992. *Children of Offenders.* Pasadena, Calif.: Pacific Oaks Center for Children of Incarcerated Parents.

———. 1995. "Effects of Parental Incarceration." In *Children of Incarcerated Parents,* edited by Katherine Gabel and Denise Johnston. New York: Lexington Books.

———. 2001. "Incarceration of Women and Effects on Parenting." Paper presented to the Institute for Policy Research, Conference on the Effects of Incarceration for Children and Families. Chicago: Institute for Policy Research, Northwestern University (May 5, 2001).

Kampfner, Christina J. 1995. "Post-traumatic Stress Reactions in Children of Imprisoned Mothers." In *Children of Incarcerated Parents,* edited by Katherine Gabel and Denise Johnston. New York: Lexington Books.

Kaufman, Joan, and Edward Zigler. 1993. "The Intergenerational Transmission of Abuse Is Overstated." In *Current Controversies on Family Violence,* edited by Richard J. Gelles and Donileen R. Loseke. Newbury Park, Calif.: Sage Publications.

Landsverk, John, Inger Davis, William Ganger, Rae Newton, and Ivory Johnson. 1996. "Impact of Psychological Functioning on Reunification from Out-of-Home Placement." *Children and Youth Services Review* 18(4–5): 447–62.

Le Prohn, Nicole S. 1994. "The Role of the Kinship Foster Parent: A Comparison of the Role Conceptions of Relative and Non-Relative Foster Parents." *Children and Youth Services Review* 16(1–2): 65–84.

Lyons-Ruth, Karlen, and Deborah Block. 1996. "The Disturbed Caregiving System: Relations Among Childhood Trauma, Maternal Caregiving, and Infant Affect and Attachment." *Infant Mental Health Journal* 17(3): 257–75.

Maas, Henry S., and Richard E. Engler. 1959. *Children in Need of Parents.* New York: Columbia University Press.

Marcus, Robert F. 1991. "The Attachments of Children in Foster Care." *Genetic, Social, and General Psychology Monographs* 117(14): 336–94.

Masten, Ann S. 1994. "Resilience in Individual Development: Successful Adaptation Despite Risk and Adversity." In *Educational Resilience in Inner-City America: Challenges and Prospects,* edited by Margaret C. Wang and Edmund W. Gordon. Hillsdale, N.J.: Lawrence Erlbaum.

McGowan, Brenda G., and Karen L. Blumenthal. 1978. *Why Punish the Children: A Study of Children of Women Prisoners.* Hackensack, N.J.: National Council on Crime and Delinquency.

McLoyd, Vonnie C., and Leon Wilson. 1991. "The Strain of Living Poor: Parenting, Social Support, and Child Mental Health." In *Children in Poverty: Child Development and Public Policy,* edited by A. C. Huston. New York: Cambridge University Press.

McNichol, Theresa. 1999. "The Impact of Drug-Exposed Children on Family Foster Care." *Child Welfare* 78(1): 184–96.

McNichol, Theresa, and Constance Tash. 2001. "Parental Substance Abuse and the Development of Children in Family Foster Care." *Child Welfare* 80(2): 239–56.

Mumola, Christopher. 2000. *Incarcerated Parents and Their Children.* NCJ-182335. Washington: U.S. Department of Justice, Bureau of Justice Statistics.

Myers, Barbara J., Patricia A. Jarvis, and Gary L. Creasey. 1987. "Infants' Behaviors with Their Mothers and Grandmothers." *Infant Behavior and Development* 10(3): 245–59.

Orme, John G., and Cheryl Buehler. 2001. "Foster Family Characteristics and Behavioral and Emotional Problems of Foster Children: A Narrative Review." *Family Relations* 50(1): 3–15.

Pandina, Robert J., and Valerie L. Johnson. 1989. "Familial Drinking History as a Predictor of Alcohol and Drug Consumption among Adolescent Children." *Journal of Studies on Alcohol* 50(3): 245–53.

Pastor, Donald L. 1981. "The Quality of Mother-Infant Attachment and Its Relationship to Initial Sociability with Peers." *Developmental Psychology* 17(3): 326–35.

Pribor, Elizabeth F., and Stephen H. Dinwiddie. 1992. "Psychiatric Correlates of Incest in Childhood." *American Journal of Psychiatry* 149(1): 52–56.

Rodriquez, Christina M., and Dougal Sutherland. 1999. "Predictors of Parents' Physical Disciplinary Practices." *Child Abuse and Neglect* 23(7): 651–57.

Ruscio, Ayelet Meron. 2001. "Predicting the Child-Rearing Practices of Mothers Sexually Abused in Childhood." *Child Abuse and Neglect* 25(3): 369–87.

Rutter, Michael. 1979. "Protective Factors in Children's Responses to Stress and Disadvantage." In *Primary Prevention of Psychopathology*, vol. 3, *Social Competence in Children*, edited by Martha W. Kent and Jon E. Rolf. Hanover, N.H.: University Press of New England.

———. 1987. "Psychosocial Resilience and Protective Mechanisms." *American Journal of Orthopsychiatry* 57(3): 316–31.

———. 1990. "Maternal Deprivation." In *Handbook of Parenting*, vol. 4, *Applied and Practical Parenting*, edited by Marc H. Bornstein. Hillsdale, N.J.: Lawrence Erlbaum.

———. 1993. "Resilience: Some Conceptual Considerations." *Journal of Adolescent Health* 14(8): 626–31.

Rutter, Michael, and Thomas G. O'Connor. 1999. "Implications of Attachment Theory for Child Care Policies." In *Handbook of Attachment: Theory, Research, and Clinical Applications*, edited by Jude Cassidy and Phillip R. Shaver. New York: Guilford.

Rutter, Michael, and David Quinton. 1977. "Psychiatric Disorder: Ecological Factors and Concepts of Causation." In *Ecological Factors in Human Development*, edited by Harry McGurk. Amsterdam: North-Holland.

Sameroff, Arnold J. 1983. "Developmental Systems: Contexts and Evolution." In *Handbook of Child Psychology*, edited by Paul H. Mussen, vol. 1, *History, Theories and Methods*, edited by William Kessen. New York: Wiley.

———. 1993. "Models of Development and Developmental Risk. In *Handbook of Infant Mental Health*, edited by Charles H. Zeenah. New York: Guilford.

Sameroff, Arnold J., W. Todd Bartko, Alfred Baldwin, Claire Baldwin, and Ronald Seifer. 1998. "Family and Social Influences on the Development of Child Competence." In *Families, Risk, and Competence*, edited by Michael Lewis and Candace Feiring. Mahwah, N.J.: Lawrence Erlbaum.

Sameroff, Arnold J., and Michael J. Chandler. 1975. "Reproductive Risk and the Continuum of Caretaking Casualty." In *Review of Child Development Research*, edited by Francis D. Horowitz, vol. 4. Chicago: University of Chicago Press.

Sameroff, Arnold, J., Ronald Seifer, Ralph Barocas, Melvin Zax, and Stanley Greenspan. 1987a. "Intelligence Quotient Scores of 4-Year-Old Children: Social Environmental Risk Factors." *Pediatrics* 79(3): 343–50.

Sameroff, Arnold, J., Ronald Seifer, Melvin Zax, and Ralph Barocas. 1987b. "Early Indicators of Developmental Risk: The Rochester Longitudinal Study." *Schizophrenia Bulletin* 13(3): 383–93.

Scannapieco, Maria, Rebecaa L. Hegar, and Catherine McAlpine. 1997. "Kinship Care and Foster Care: A Comparison of Characteristics and Outcomes." *Families in Society* 78(5): 480–88.

Snell, Tracy L. 1994. *Women in Prison: Survey of State Prison Inmates, 1991.* Washington: U.S. Department of Justice, Bureau of Justice Statistics.

Sroufe, L. Alan. 1983. "Infant-Caregiver Attachment and Patterns of Adaptation in Preschool: The Roots of Maladaptation and Competence." In *Minnesota Symposium in Child Psychology* 16, edited by Marion Perlmutter. Hillsdale, N.J.: Lawrence Erlbaum.

Sroufe, L. Alan, Elizabeth A. Carlson, Alissa K. Levy, and Byron Egeland. 1999. "Implications of Attachment Theory for Developmental Psychopathology." *Development and Psychopathology* 11(1): 1–13.

Stanton, Ann M. 1980. *When Mothers Go to Jail.* Lexington, Mass.: Lexington Books.

Stovall, K. Chase, and Mary Dozier. 2000. "The Development of Attachment in New Relationships: Single Subject Analyses for 10 Foster Infants." *Development and Psychopathology* 12(2): 133–56.

Thompson, Ross A. 1999. "Early Attachment and Later Development." In *Handbook of Attachment: Theory, Research and Clinical Applications,* edited by Jude Cassidy and Phillip R. Shaver. New York: Guilford.

Tizard, Barbara, and Jill Hodges. 1978. "The Effect of Early Institutional Rearing on the Development of Eight-Year-Old Children." *Journal of Child Psychology and Psychiatry* 19(2): 99–118.

U.S. Department of Justice, Bureau of Justice Statistics. 1993. *Survey of State Prison Inmates, 1991.* NCJ-136949. Washington: U.S. Department of Justice, Bureau of Justice Statistics.

———. 2000. *Survey of Inmates in State and Federal Correctional Facilities, 1997.* Computer file compiled by the U.S. Department of Commerce, Bureau of the Census. Ann Arbor, Mich.: Inter-university Consortium for Political and Social Research.

Wald, Michael, J. Merrill Carlsmith, and P. Herbert Leiderman. 1988. *Protecting Abused and Neglected Children.* Stanford, Calif.: Stanford University Press.

Waldfogel, Jane. 1998. *The Future of Child Protection: Breaking the Cycle of Child Abuse and Neglect.* Cambridge, Mass.: Harvard University Press.

———. 2000. "Child Welfare Research: How Adequate Are the Data?" *Children and Youth Services Review* 22(9–10): 705–41.

Waters, Everett, Judith Wippman, and L. Alan Sroufe. 1979. "Attachment, Positive Affect and Competence in the Peer Group: Two Studies in Construct Validation." *Child Development* 50(3): 821–29.

Werner, Emmy E., and Ruth S. Smith. 1989. *Vulnerable but Invincible: A Longitudinal Study of Resilient Children and Youth.* New York: McGraw-Hill.

Widom, Cathy Spatz. (1989). "Does Violence Beget Violence? A Critical Examination of the Literature." *Psychological Bulletin* 106(1): 3–28.

Williams, Sheila, Jessie Anderson, Rob McGee, and Phil A. Silva. 1990. "Risk Factors for Behavioral and Emotional Disorder in Preadolescent Children."

Journal of the American Academy of Child and Adolescent Psychiatry 29(3): 413–19.

Wilsnack, Sharon C., Nancy D. Vogeltanz, Albert D. Klassen, and Robert T. Harris. 1997. "Childhood Sexual Abuse and Women's Substance Abuse: National Survey Findings." *Journal of Studies on Alcohol* 58(3): 264–71.

Zeanah, Charles H. 2000. "Disturbances of Attachment in Young Children Adopted from Institutions." *Developmental and Behavioral Pediatrics* 21(3): 230–36.

PART II

Communities

James P. Lynch
William J. Sabol

Effects of Incarceration on Informal Social Control in Communities

6

Over the past twenty years, the United States has experienced a massive increase in imprisonment (Lynch and Sabol 1997; Blumstein and Beck 1999). From 1980 and 2002, U.S. prison populations increased from about 330,000 persons (Gilliard and Beck 1996) to more than 2 million (Harrison and Beck 2003). The estimated number of persons who had ever been incarcerated in state or federal prisons increased from 1.8 million in 1974 to more than 5.6 million in 2001 (Bonczar 2003). It is generally conceded that this increase in incarceration was driven primarily by shifts in policy toward more punitive treatment of drug, habitual, and violent offenders (Blumstein and Beck 1999; Western, Kling, and Weiman 2001).

The unprecedented increase in the use of incarceration has raised questions about its impacts on crime and has also led to speculations about its possible unintended negative consequences for individuals, families, and communities. Evaluations of the crime control impacts of incarceration suggest that it has contributed to reductions in violent crime by incapacitating offenders (Cohen and Canela-Cacho 1994); that increases in time served arising from administrative decisions (for example, parole release) deter the commission of index crimes (Levitt 1996; Nagin 1998); and that increases in incarceration for drug offenders may have contributed to reductions in property and violent crimes (Kuziemko and Levitt 2001). On the other hand, the increased incarceration of drug offenders has not generated deterrent or incapacitation effects on drug offenders, largely because incarcerated drug offenders were replaced by younger offenders who, during the 1980s and early 1990s, were also more prone to use violence to resolve disputes (Caulkins et al. 1997; Blumstein 1995). In general, however, the evidence seems to suggest that while aggregate crime rates have declined in response to expanding prison capacity and that further expansions of capacity are likely to result in further reductions in crime, not enough is known about the magnitude of the relationship between increases in incarceration and reductions in crime to determine whether additional expansion of prison capacity is warranted (Spelman 2000).

The unprecedented increase in incarceration has also led to theorizing that both its increase and its clustering in certain areas or among certain subpopulations can have unintended negative consequences for individuals, families, and communities (Lynch and Sabol 1992; Rose and Clear 1998a, 1998b; Clear 1996; Moore 1996; Nightingale and Watts 1996). Research on the impact of prison terms on the economic consequences for individuals shows time in prison produces large and persistent effects on employment and earnings (Grogger 1995; Kling 1999). Bruce Western (2002) estimates that the earnings loss associated with incarceration ranges from 10 to 30 percent and finds that serving time in prison is also associated with decreased earnings growth. When findings such as these are combined with data (discussed later in this chapter) indicating that in a given year more than 10 percent of young African American men in some neighborhoods enter prison, it becomes clear that prison terms, although not necessarily the cause of economic disadvantage, are not likely to enhance the economic position of potentially large portions of (particularly male) residents of disadvantaged neighborhoods (see chapter 8 in this volume).

Incarceration may also have consequences for family structure. William Darity and Samuel Myers (Darity and Myers 1989, 1994; Myers 2000) argue that incarceration contributes to the prevalence of black families headed by single women. In previous work (Sabol and Lynch 2003) we have estimated that increases in incarceration of black men were associated with about 20 percent of the increase in the number of black families headed by single women during the 1980s. Bruce Western, Leonard Lopoo, and Sara McLanahan (chapter 2 in this volume) also find that incarceration significantly reduces the likelihood of marriage among new parents, and Anne Nurse's ethnography of juvenile fathers (chapter 4 in this volume) presents some of the beliefs, behaviors, and interactions that underlie this decreased likelihood of marriage. The effects of incarceration on family structure are hypothesized to occur through its effects on the supply of men whom William Julius Wilson (1987) and others term "marriageable," that is, men who are sufficiently integrated into labor markets, education institutions, and other formal institutions to be able to contribute to the support of families. By decreasing the supply of these men, incarceration increases, in turn, the number of female-headed households. Furthermore, Robert Sampson (1987) argues that a high prevalence of families headed by single females also contributes to high neighborhood crime rates, in part because of the absence of supervision for young males in these areas.

More recently, Dina Rose and Todd Clear (1998a) theorize that incarceration may have unintended negative consequences for the organization of communities; they introduce the concept of "coercive mobility" (that is, mobility induced by removal to and return from prison) and posit that it can undermine the less coercive institutions of social control—such as families, community associations, and a community's capacity to enforce norms—that are the first line of defense against crime. Severe disruption of these institutions, Rose and Clear argue, can mean that the long-term consequence of the massive increases in incarceration will be increases, and not continued decreases, in crime.

In this chapter we explore hypotheses about the impact of incarceration on community processes and ultimately on crime. Using survey data from individuals in thirty Baltimore neighborhoods collected by Ralph Taylor (2001) to measure community processes (such as neighboring, involvement in voluntary associations, shared values, and willingness of residents to engage in social control), and adding to these data neighborhood-level data on community structure, crimes, arrests, and incarcerations, we describe relationships between incarceration and community processes. We estimate several models of these relationships. We examine direct and indirect effects of incarceration on the capacity of communities to implement informal social control, or what is popularly called "collective efficacy." We find mixed support for our hypothesis that incarceration lessens the capacity of communities to engage in social control, but we also find (consistent with the literature on the crime-reducing effects of incarceration) that higher incarceration rates are associated with lower crime rates.

HOW INCARCERATION CAN CONTRIBUTE TO DECREASES IN SOCIAL CONTROL

Research on the relationship between community social organization and crime has long stressed that the patterns of residents' relationships among themselves and with their local institutions contribute to the strength of shared values within communities and to the capacity of communities to maintain effective social controls over residents (Bursik 1988; Kasarda and Janowitz 1974). In contemporary criminological research, these basic concepts have been expressed in terms of "social capital" (Putnam 1993) or "collective efficacy" (Sampson, Morenhoff, and Earls 1999). However, as Taylor (2002) points out, these new concepts essentially describe the same patterns of relationships among community residents that lead to shared capacity and willingness to enforce social control that community researchers dating back to Clifford Shaw and Henry McKay (1942) have explored.

Within this social organization framework, Robert Bursik and Harold Grasmick's (1993) general systems model (GSM) describes how community disorganization leads to crime. The principal exogenous variables in the model are heterogeneity, mobility, and socioeconomic status. These variables can facilitate or inhibit interaction in communities that allow residents to set and achieve collective goals. They can enhance private control that takes place in intimate groups as well as "parochial" control that takes place outside of intimate groups but in the neighborhood. Parochial control would include control in the context of neighboring and in voluntary associations. Heterogeneity, mobility, and socioeconomic status can also affect the amount of public control that occurs in a community by influencing its residents' ability to negotiate service with municipal bureaucracies, including the criminal justice system. In this model, the level of private, parochial, and public control in a community determines the crime rate. Communities that are stable and homogeneous will have high levels of private and parochial control as well as optimum levels of public control, with the result that levels of crime will be low relative to other areas.

Working within this framework, Rose and Clear (1998a) describe an elaborate set of processes through which incarceration can affect less coercive institutions of social control. They hypothesize that incarceration introduces mobility and heterogeneity into communities, thereby abetting the process of disorganization. They focus specifically on certain institutional arrangements, how excessive amounts of incarceration can weaken them, and how this weakness, in turn, reduces private, parochial, and public control in these communities. According to Rose and Clear, incarceration can weaken families by removing men from families and by reducing the supply of marriageable men; this makes families less effective as socializing agents and less able to supervise teenaged children. Removal through incarceration can also affect community economic institutions by removing people who bring money to families and the community. Many of the men Kathryn Edin, Timothy Nelson, and Rechelle Paranal interviewed (for chapter 3 in this volume) combined legal and illegal work, and they did so to contribute to household expenses. Political institutions may be affected by the removal of people from networks that mobilize the community in response to external threats. As Christopher Uggen and Jeff Manza find (chapter 7 in this volume), incarcerees hold strong and informed political views that ultimately have no outlet because former felons are stripped of their rights to participate in the political system in many states. Moreover, removing persons from the area reduces the amount of time available to those who take up their tasks to become involved in neighborhood mobilization processes. Rose and Clear (1998a) also hypothesize that massive use of incarceration in communities will lessen the stigma (and hence the effectiveness) of this type of public control for community residents.

This perspective on how incarceration affects communities has not been fully tested empirically. Rose, Clear, and Elin Waring (2003) examine the relationship between incarceration rates and crime at the neighborhood level.[1] Their work, however, does not take account of simultaneous equation bias in estimating the effects of incarceration on crime, nor does it assess the impact of incarceration on community organization per se. Rather, they examine only the effects of the geographical concentration of incarceration on perceptions of the legitimacy of the criminal justice system and on crime. Community, in their study, is the context for vicarious experiences with incarceration, not the entity that is being affected by incarceration. Residence in a neighborhood with high incarceration rates means that one's vicarious experience with incarceration or the collateral effects of incarceration will be high.

EXAMINING A MODEL OF THE EFFECTS OF INCARCERATION ON COMMUNITY ORGANIZATION AND INFORMAL SOCIAL CONTROL

We attempt to build upon this framework of social disorganization by addressing the question of how incarceration affects community organization and ultimately the willingness of area residents to engage in informal social control. We also examine the effects of incarceration on the patterns of interaction that underlie the social organization of neighborhoods. These patterns of interaction are, according to the social disorganization framework, believed to be prerequisites to informal social control.

We posit a model that describes the effects of incarceration practices on community organization and ultimately on an individual's decision to engage in informal social control. The model suggests that the willingness of community residents to engage in informal social control is driven by the amount of interaction in which they engage with their neighbors (neighboring) and the extent to which they have positive attitudes toward and feel as if they belong to the neighborhood (community solidarity). High levels of interaction among neighbors in the daily activity of the area lay the foundation for the more specific mobilization of these networks for activities such as informal social control.

For example, neighbors who interact in voluntary associations (for example, advisory neighborhood councils) would also find it easier to cooperate on other community activities, such as the local school funding drive. Residents who borrow and lend tools are better equipped to cooperate with one another on other endeavors. They have established precedent for interacting, and if prior interactions have been mutually beneficial, additional future interactions are likely to follow. These types of positive interactions lead to understandings of and positive attitudes toward neighbors and the neighborhood and a sense of solidarity within the community. This understanding and trust also encourage neighbors to engage in informal social control (Hackler, Ho, and Urquhart-Ross 1974). Expressions of willingness to engage in informal social control in communities include intervening in minor disorders. This willingness stems from shared beliefs about appropriate behavior. If residents have expectations that norms will be observed, invoking the norms in the context of implementing informal social control is likely to bring about compliance because the belief is shared (and both parties know that) or because there are others in the area who will support the enforcement of the norms.

Without the foundation of persistent patterns of interaction and shared beliefs about norms (or community solidarity), invoking norms can be unproductive and even dangerous. Residents who are not sure that others in the neighborhood will agree and acquiesce to the norms or lend support in the request made of others will be much less likely to enforce norms.

At the neighborhood level, the stability of the area, the extent of crime, and the amount of coercion on the part of criminal justice agencies sets the context for informal social control. Stable neighborhoods offer the continuity necessary for interaction between residents. Stability refers to the low rates of residential mobility as well as constancy in the economic status of the neighborhood population. This permanence encourages and provides the opportunity for interactions among neighborhood residents that result in shared norms of appropriate behavior and a willingness to enforce these norms through informal social control. Crime in the neighborhood inhibits interaction and weakens solidarity. The actual risk of crime or the fear of being victimized by crime reduces levels of interaction among neighbors and thereby reduces levels of solidarity and the willingness to engage in informal social control. High levels of incarceration are expected to reduce crime and thereby encourage the interaction among neighbors that builds shared norms of appropriate behavior and solidarity and encourages informal social control. Rose and Clear, on the other hand, speculate that coercive mobility through incarceration could disrupt social networks, thereby inhibiting informal social control.

THE DATA USED TO EXAMINE THIS MODEL

We used four data sources to examine these complex sets of relationships between formal social control (incarceration) and informal social control; these include data previously collected by Taylor (2001), Baltimore City

Police Department data on crimes and arrests, data on admissions into Maryland state prisons, and census data on neighborhood social indicators. The Taylor data were collected in 1982 and 1994 for his study of Baltimore neighborhoods to examine the relationship between crime and social organization in communities. The data include aggregate community-level measures of the demographic and socioeconomic attributes of neighborhoods, along with their crime rates, and interviews of residents within each community about community attachment, cohesiveness, participation, satisfaction, and experiences with crime and self-protection. Resident surveys were conducted in 66 and 30 of the 277 named neighborhoods in Baltimore City in 1982 and 1994, respectively. For our exploration of the effects of incarceration on informal social control, we used the data collected from the thirty neighborhoods in 1994, for which the number of surveys per neighborhood ranged from eighteen to twenty-four, with an average of twenty-three respondents. However, in our descriptive analysis, we report data on incarceration concentrations for the 277 neighborhoods. We supplement the Taylor data with our fourth source—census data—which provide social and economic characteristics of the census tracts that make up the Taylor neighborhoods.

The second data source, Baltimore City police data, describes both offenses recorded by the police and arrests made by the police in 1987 and 1992. The offense data include the type of offense and the address where it occurred. The arrest data include the type of charge and the street address where the arrest was made. For this study, we grouped offenses and charges into four categories—drugs, violence, property, and public order violations. Street addresses were geo-coded into longitude and latitude coordinates; using these coordinates, crime and arrest events were aggregated up to the neighborhood level (neighborhood boundaries were also defined by named communities) to produce counts of events occurring within neighborhoods.

The Maryland Department of Public Safety and Corrections provided the third set of data (Gowen 2000). These data include all of the admissions to and releases from prison in neighborhoods in Baltimore City and Baltimore County for the years 1982 to 2000. Each record gives the admission date, the release date, the charges for which the person was incarcerated, and the address of the person's residence at the time of admission or release. As with the police data, these addresses were geo-coded and associated with the appropriate neighborhood in Baltimore City.

Not every crime that occurs is reported to the police, and the police may also fail to record an incident or may deal with it by means other than arrest; hence the police reports we used understate the true level of crime.[2] Moreover, the incarceration data understate the true level of prison admissions, owing to missing address information. By comparing the Maryland Department of Public Safety and Corrections data to Bureau of Justice Statistics data on county-level prison admissions (in the National Corrections Reporting Program) for the six-year period 1993 through 1998, we found that on average the data from the Maryland Department of Public Safety and Corrections represented 67 percent of the admissions recorded in the National Corrections Reporting Program from Baltimore County. This coverage rate peaked at 87 percent in 1993, suggesting that the admissions data used here underestimate prison admissions in the neighborhoods by about one-third. The offense distributions of the National Corrections Reporting Program data and the Maryland Department of Public Safety and Corrections data were comparable, lending some support to the notion that the missing address data do not vary systematically by neighborhood. Consequently, we believe that the relative position of neighborhoods with regard to admissions into prison should be unaffected by this underestimation of the volume of incarceration.

Measures for testing the model were derived from community-level census data, police data, and information reported in the residential survey. Census data for 1980 and 1990 were used to develop measures of residential tenure, poverty, and other structural features of communities. Police data were used to measure crime. Prison admission rates were used to measure incarceration. Measures of neighboring, participation in voluntary associations, community solidarity, and informal social control were all developed using Taylor's individual-level survey data. A more detailed description of how these variables were measured is provided in table 6.1.

We used prison admissions rates to measure coercion. We define prison admissions rates per 1,000 population as the number of persons admitted from a specific neighborhood divided by the at-risk population in the neighborhood multiplied by 1,000, where the at-risk population equals the number of persons aged eighteen to thirty-four. In most of the regressions reported later in this chapter, we use changes in prison admissions rates to represent the effect of incarceration on community processes. We computed this change measure by taking the difference between the 1992 and 1987 prison admissions rates.

We used the restricted denominator because it is a reasonable approximation of the at-risk population, given that the vast majority of admissions into prison are of younger persons. Using the total population would have included very young and very old populations that had little or no risk of incarceration. It may have been better to further restrict the denominator to males, but data on the gender of inmates was not available, and the gender distribution in population aggregates is not nearly as variable as the age distribution.

Table 6.1   *Description of Key Individual- and Community-Level*
             Variables Used in the Analysis of Informal Social Control

Variable	Description	Mean
Community level		
Crime	Change in police-reported crime rate in communities from 1987 to 1992	49.96 (31.86)
Incarceration	Change in the rate of admissions to Department of Corrections annually between 1987 and 1992. The rate is the number of admissions over the number of persons aged eighteen to thirty-four in the neighborhood	18.20 (114.93)
Poverty	Sum of the percentage change in vacant homes and the percentage change in households below the poverty level from 1980 to 1990	117.65 (191.29)
Tenure	Average number of years that residents resided in the neighborhood	18.92 (5.41)
Individual level		
Informal social control	A five-point scale of informal social control constructed from items asking about neighbors' help in stopping crime and neighbors' help in stopping disorderly teenagers. Specific items in the appendix to this chapter	2.01 (1.41)
Community solidarity	A sixteen-point scale of community solidarity constructed from four questions asking about feelings of attachment to the community, neighborhood, and block. Specific items listed in the appendix to this chapter	9.08 (2.13)
Neighboring	An eight-point scale of interaction with neighbors constructed from items asking about visiting, running errands, borrowing tools, working together to improve the block, watching one another's home, taking in mail, and exchanging keys. Specific items listed in the appendix to this chapter	4.49 (1.92)
Voluntary associations	The number of organizations (0 to 9) in which an individual claimed membership, including neighborhood associations, church, Parent Teacher Association, youth group, recreation center, political club, block club, social club, or other type of community organization	.90 (1.19)

Source: Authors' compilation.
Note: Standard deviations in parentheses.

In addition to the variables described in table 6.1, a number of individual-level control variables were included in the model to take account of other factors that could affect community organization and informal social control. Individual controls include gender, race, educational level, whether or not the respondent had children, home ownership, tenure in the area, and marital status. These variables were included in the analysis because theory and prior empirical research indicate that these attributes are related to people's participation in the community and especially their involvement in informal social control (Sampson, Raudenbush, and Earls 1997).

PATTERNS OF INCARCERATION USE AND COMMUNITY WELL-BEING

While we argue that incarceration can have negative unintended effects on communities, our theory is not strong enough to predict how much incarceration is required to produce these consequences. On the one hand, it is plausible that relatively small levels of incarceration occurring in relatively stable communities could be sufficient to disrupt patterns of interaction that contribute to social order, enforcement of norms, and informal social control. On the other hand, in disadvantaged communities that have experienced high levels of poverty, crime, and instability for long periods of time, comparatively high levels of incarceration might not contribute further to disorder. These are empirical issues that we attempt to assess by means of our models.

However, before reporting the results of our empirical models, we observe several outcomes. The first is the concentration of prison admissions within the 277 named neighborhoods in Baltimore City for 1987, 1992, and 1994 (figure 6.1). The x-axis shows the percentage of communities, and the y-axis shows the percentage of prison admissions accounted for by these communities. Note that the general pattern of concentration did not change much over these years. Note also, however, that there are fairly extreme concentrations of prison admissions, as 60 percent of all admissions (in any or all years) occurred in about 17 percent of all neighborhoods. In other words, of the roughly four thousand prison admissions in each of the three years, about twenty-four hundred came from forty-five neighborhoods. Conversely, at the low end of incarceration, 110 (or about 40 percent) of the 277 Baltimore neighborhoods contributed, collectively, about 5 percent (or two hundred per year) of all prison admissions in any (and all) of the three years. In sum, during the period from 1987 through 1994, prison admissions from Baltimore City tended to be concentrated in comparatively few communities.

Concomitant with the variation in the volume of prison admissions

Figure 6.1   *Neighborhood Concentration of Prison Admissions*

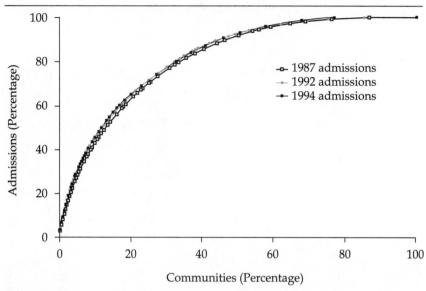

Source: Authors' analysis of Maryland Department of Corrections data on persons admitted to state prison.

across neighborhoods, the prison admissions rates for males aged eighteen to thirty-four also varied widely. These rates averaged about 35 admissions per 1,000 across the neighborhoods, but they ranged from 0 per 1,000 to 276 per 1,000 (or 27.6 percent of the at-risk population). Nine neighborhoods had admissions rates of 10 percent or more of the at-risk population; 38 neighborhoods had admissions rates of zero.

High rates of concentration in communities in and of themselves do not indicate whether incarceration has disruptive or stabilizing effects on community processes. Figures 6.2 and 6.3 illustrate the relationships between prison admissions and selected measures of community well-being. The selected indicators include median housing value, percentage of housing units that were vacant, percentage of the population living below the poverty level, percentage of high school dropouts, percentage of housing units that were renter occupied, and percentage of the population consisting of young children (aged six to thirteen). In both of these figures, the values of these indicators of community well-being are plotted against the deciles of the prison admissions distribution within which they fall.

In general, we expect to find the communities that fall within the

Figure 6.2   *Housing and Poverty Indicators of Community Well-Being,*
               by Deciles of the 1987 Prison Admissions Distribution, 1990

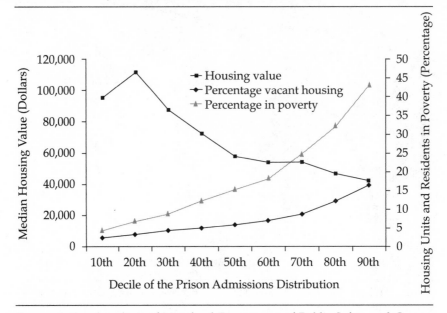

Source: Authors' analysis of Maryland Department of Public Safety and Corrections data on persons admitted into Maryland state prisons and U.S. Bureau of Census data from Taylor (2001).

upper deciles of the prison admissions distribution to rank higher or lower in terms of the social indicators that we measured, depending upon whether the indicator reflects weaker or stronger community structure or organization. For example, communities falling in the upper ends of the prison admissions distribution would be expected to have lower housing values, higher poverty rates, higher percentages of vacant housing units, higher high school dropout rates, and higher percentages of renter-occupied housing units.

The data in figures 6.2 and 6.3 are generally consistent with our expectations of the relationship between high levels of incarceration and measures of social disorder. For example, in figure 6.2, median housing values decline rapidly over the twentieth percentile of the prison admissions distribution through the fiftieth percentile and continue to decline thereafter through the ninetieth percentile. Poverty rates increase with the higher deciles of the prison admissions distribution; however, above the sixtieth percentile, the rate of increase in poverty rates rises. Vacant

Figure 6.3   *Educational, Housing, and Family Size Indicators of Community Well-Being, by Decile of the 1987 Prison Admissions Distribution, 1990*

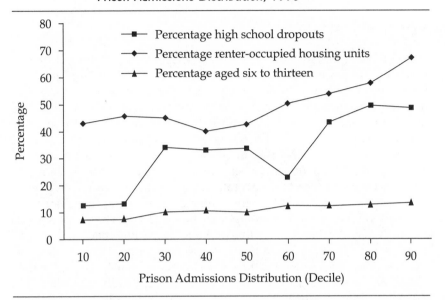

Legend:
- ■— Percentage high school dropouts
- ◆— Percentage renter-occupied housing units
- ▲— Percentage aged six to thirteen

Y-axis: Percentage
X-axis: Prison Admissions Distribution (Decile)

Source: Authors' analysis of Maryland Department of Public Safety and Corrections data on persons admitted into Maryland state prisons; and U.S. Bureau of Census data from Taylor (2001).

housing also increases at an accelerated rate, but not until the seventieth percentile of the prison admissions distribution.

These relationships are suggestive of jointly high levels of concentrations of incarceration and measures of social disorder for the neighborhoods that fall into the upper ends of the distribution of prison admissions. Of course, whether incarceration is the cause or consequence of these high levels of disorder is the subject of the modeling that follows.

Figure 6.3 shows the relationships between incarceration and three indicators of community well-being: high school dropout rates, rates of renter occupancy, and presence of young children in the population. For dropout and renter occupancy rates, the general pattern is one of increase as one moves up the deciles of the prison admissions distribution. Above the sixtieth percentile, the rate of increase in the high school dropout rate increases; beyond the sixtieth percentile, the rate of increase in renter occupancy increases up to the ninetieth percentile. Thus while the patterns of increasing rates of change in dropout rates and renter occupancy are not as sharp as those for poverty and vacant housing, they are similar. These bivariate patterns demonstrate the high degree of association between high rates of prison admissions and high rates of indicators of social disorder.

MODEL SPECIFICATION

We approach estimating the conceptual model of the effects of incarceration on community organization and informal social control by taking into account several substantive and technical matters. First, incarceration can affect informal social control and community organization in both direct and indirect ways (through other variables in the model). Second, the model is not recursive—that is, at any given point in the model, not every variable is a function of other variables at prior points in the model. The relationship between crime and coercion is obviously reciprocal—crime affects incarceration and incarceration affects crime.[3] This reciprocal effect will bias the coefficient describing the effect of incarceration on crime. Instrumental variables and two-stage least squares are methods of accounting for this problem, providing that useful instruments can be found. We use the "discretionary portion" of the drug arrest rate as an instrument for the prison admissions rate.[4] Third, the data are nested in that they include information on the individuals living in a neighborhood as well as information on the neighborhoods themselves. Prior research has shown that using ordinary least squares regression or the general linear model with nested data violates some of the assumptions of these techniques and can produce biased estimates of the effects of neighborhood and individual-level variables in the model (Bryk and Raudenbush 1992; Taylor 1997).

In light of these complexities, we estimate three different types of models. The first is a single-equation ordinary least squares model testing the direct effects of community-level incarceration rates on informal social control while holding other variables in the model constant. The second set of models employs instrumental variables and two-stage least squares procedures to estimate the full model. This model permits estimating the sum of direct and indirect effects of variables in the model on community organization and informal social control. The final set of models is estimated using hierarchical linear models.

TESTING THE MODEL OF THE EFFECTS OF INCARCERATION ON COMMUNITY ORGANIZATION AND INFORMAL SOCIAL CONTROL

Our first set of results addresses the question whether incarceration has direct effects on community social organization. Table 6.2 presents re-

Table 6.2   *Standardized Ordinary Least Squares Coefficients: Direct-Effects Models of Incarceration on Informal Social Control*

Variable	Beta	T	Significance
Community			
Incarceration[a]	.052	1.070	.279
Crime[a]	.031	.708	.479
Poverty[a]	.027	.603	.547
Individual			
Solidarity	.140	2.990	.003**
Neighboring	.187	3.940	.000***
Voluntary associations	−.016	−.368	.713
Controls			
Gender	−.052	−1.290	.199
Race	.009	.179	.858
Education	.065	1.500	.133
Married	.040	.946	.344
Children	−.450	−1.022	.307
Home owner	−.057	−1.270	.203
Residential tenure	−.038	−.811	.418
Average income	−.015	.708	.479
R-squared	.091		

Source: Authors' compilation.
[a]These three variables—crime, poverty scale, and incarceration—were measured by the change in rates. For incarceration and crime, the change was from 1987 to 1992; for poverty, the change was from 1980 to 1990.
**$p < .01$ ***$p < .001$

sults of an ordinary least squares regression of informal social control on the change in the prison admissions rate (1992 admissions rate minus 1987 admissions rate), controlling for other individual- and community-level variables described in table 6.1. Only two variables—residents' feelings of community solidarity and the extent to which they engage in neighboring—have positive and significant effects on the willingness to engage in informal social control.[5] The effect of the change in the prison admissions rate on an individual's decision to engage in informal social control is not significant.

These findings are consistent with the general theories about the effects of community organization on informal social control. Communities in which residents have high levels of interaction and high levels of solidarity are areas in which residents will engage in informal social control. These results do not suggest that removing residents through incarceration is related to greater willingness to engage in informal social control.

This simple direct-effects model is flawed, however, as it does not test the effects of coercion on communities in a manner consistent with the model. The effects of incarceration may operate indirectly, by encouraging interaction among residents, rather than directly, by encouraging residents to engage in informal social control. These indirect effects are better measured in a structural-equation model in which both direct and indirect effects of incarceration can be assessed. Moreover, the reciprocal relationship between crime and incarceration may bias the coefficient describing the relationship between incarceration and informal social control. Instrumental variables should be used to take account of the simultaneity of changes in crime and changes in incarceration. For these reasons we estimate structural-equation models using instrumental variables and two-stage least squares.

Conceptually, the instrumental variable used in this analysis is the discretionary portion of drug arrests. We used this variable because of the strong correlation between drug arrests and prison admissions and because drug arrests, unlike index arrests, occur primarily as the result of law enforcement targeting decisions rather than a victim's report of a crime. During the 1980s and 1990s, drug law violations became a priority for prosecution and sentencing, as reflected in the sentencing reforms (such as mandatory minimum sentences) that were implemented to increase the severity of punishment for these crimes. Thus drug arrest rates should be positively correlated with prison admissions rates. At the same time, the discretionary nature of drug enforcement could make drug arrests independent of the portion of the crime rate that was not associated with the drug offenses.

We computed the instrument by first taking the residual from a regression of the change in drug arrest rates between 1987 and 1992 on the change in the index crime rate over the same period and then regressing the change in the prison admissions rate on this residual. This instrument satisfies the conceptual and empirical requisites for an instrument: it was correlated with the incarceration rate and independent of the crime rate. As table 6.3 illustrates, the instrument is independent of the crime rate. The correlation of the instrumental variables with changes in the incarceration rate is relatively strong ($r = .50$) and statistically significant, while the correlation with change in the crime rate is zero.

We used this instrument in helping to estimate the structural-equation model. This model results in six equations, as identified in the columns in table 6.4. The dependent variables in these equations are the prison admissions rate, the index crime rate, patterns of voluntary association among neighborhood residents, neighboring activities, community

Table 6.3   *Correlation Matrix for Crime Rate, Change in Admissions Rate, and the Instrumental Variable for the Ratio of Drug Arrests to Total Arrests*

Variable	Change in Admissions from 1987 to 1992	Crime Rate Change from 1987 to 1992	Ratio of Drug Arrests to Total Arrests, 1992
Change in admissions from 1987 to 1992	1.00	−.33**	.50**
Crime rate change from 1987 to 1992		1.00	.00
Ratio of drug arrests to total arrests, 1992			1.00

Source: Authors' compilation.
**p < .01

solidarity (or shared norms), and participation in informal social control. Moving from left to right across the columns, each dependent variable that measures community processes (beginning with voluntary associations) includes the prior dependent variable.

For the crime equation in table 6.4, we used two-stage least squares regression and the instrumental variable, along with the other exogenous variables in the model, to predict the change in the rate of admissions from 1987 to 1992. This predicted change in the incarceration rate was employed as a measure of incarceration in estimating all of the other equations in the model, including the crime equation. Consequently, the estimate of the relationship between incarceration and crime should be reasonably free of simultaneity bias. The coefficients obtained in the various equations are presented in table 6.4.

The direct effects of incarceration on informal social control and on aspects of community organization in the structural-equation model are consistent with those from the single-equation model in which simultaneity bias was ignored. Change in the level of incarceration has no direct, statistically significant effect on participation in informal social control in the structural equation model. Increases in incarceration are also associated with decreases in aspects of community organization that encourage informal social control—specifically, community solidarity.

Changes in prison admissions rates have a negative relationship with changes in crime rates (the second column of table 6.4), but the effect is not statistically significant. We considered whether the insignifi-

Table 6.4 Coefficients of Simultaneous Equations for the Effects of Incarceration on Community Organization and Collective Efficacy, Using Two-Stage Least Squares Regression

	Dependent Variables					
Predictors	Incarceration	Crime	Voluntary Association	Neighboring	Community Solidarity	Informal Social Control
Area attribute						
Poverty[a]	-.568***	.372***	.146**	-.090*	.038	.034
Tenure	.072**	.093**	.048	.065	.021	-.005
Crime[a]	-.023	—	-.021	.064	.119***	.027
Incarceration[a]	—	-.031	-.001	.004	-.107**	.085
Individual attribute						
Community solidarity			—	—	—	.149***
Neighboring			—	—	.419***	.170***
Voluntary association			—	.156***	.204***	-.024
Control						
Gender			.054	-.002	.069*	-.035
Race			.048	-.142***	.177***	-.012
Education			.154	.189***	-.100**	.071
Married			.083*	.066	-.075*	.043
Children			.138***	.088*	-.046	-.011
Home owner			.134***	.173***	.082*	-.029
R-squared	.353***	.148***	.099***	.164***	.314***	.083***

Source: Authors' compilation.

[a]These three variables—crime, poverty scale, and incarceration—were measured by the change in rates. For incarceration and crime, the change was from 1987 to 1992; for poverty, the change was from 1980 to 1990.

*p < .05 **p < .01 ***p < .001

cant sign on the change in prison admissions rates in the crime equation arose from the relatively small case base (that is, thirty neighborhoods). To increase the case base in examining the impacts of prison admissions on crime, we estimated the relationship between prison admissions and crime rates in the thirty Baltimore neighborhoods in our study for the two time periods, 1987 and 1992. We pooled the data over the two periods so that we were dealing with sixty cases rather than thirty. We estimated fixed-effects models with and without instrumental variables for the relationship between crime and incarceration. We used an instrument (the discretionary portion of the drug arrest rate) that was analogous to the instrument we used to estimate the equations in table 6.4; this time, however, we used the discretionary portion of the levels of the drug arrest rates in 1987 and 1992 rather than the discretionary portion of the change in the drug arrest rates. We measured all of the variables in the models in natural logs, and the coefficients represent elasticities; thus we could compare the magnitudes of the effects more easily.

Table 6.5 shows two sets of results from these estimations of the impacts of prison admissions rates on crime rates. The results for the first model are based on nonzero values of variables. The results for the second model are based on adding 0.1 to all values before taking natural logs of the variables, thereby adding neighborhoods with zero values on variables. Each set of results shows again the importance of instrumenting the crime and incarceration relationship. For example, within each model, the set of results from the fixed-effects models without instruments yields a positive coefficient on the prison admissions rate; this would suggest that changes in prison admissions lead to increases in crime rates. However, as the instrumental variables results show (for both model 1 and model 2), after taking account of the simultaneity between crime and incarceration, we find that the effects of the prison admissions rate on the crime rate are negative and statistically significant. Between the two models, a 1 percent increase in the prison admissions rate resulted in a decrease in the crime rate of 0.13 to 0.29 percent.

Other variables exerting strong influences on the crime rate were the percentage of vacant housing units and the percentage of owner-occupied housing. The sign on the variable for vacant housing unit is positive, suggesting that increases in vacant housing lead to increases in crime. Conversely, the sign on the variable for owner-occupied housing is negative, indicating lower crime rates in neighborhoods with larger shares of owner-occupied housing.

These analyses of the impacts of prison admissions rates on crime lend support to the idea that incarceration at the neighborhood level is associated with reductions in crime in those areas. We must be somewhat cautious in asserting this claim, however, because of the impor-

Table 6.5   *Estimated Effects of Prison Admissions Rates on Crime Rates in Baltimore Neighborhoods, 1987 to 1992*

Variable[a]	Instrumental Variables Technique		Fixed-Effects Model (Without Instruments)	
	Estimate	Standard Error	Estimate	Standard Error
Model 1[b] (N = 53)				
Intercept	−1.5469	0.813	−0.8800	0.771
Prison admissions	−0.02885	0.148*	0.2514	0.087*
Vacant housing	0.42480	0.131**	0.1456	0.129
Owner-occupied housing	−0.39450	0.167*	−0.5072	0.153**
Percentage black	0.07400	0.042	0.0031	0.004
Model 2[c] (N = 60)				
Intercept	−1.2074	0.353	−0.9532	0.393*
Prison admissions	−0.1292	0.056*	0.0449	0.031
Vacant housing	0.2295	0.086**	0.1410	0.064*
Owner-occupied housing	−0.2151	0.073**	−0.2521	0.078**
Percentage black	0.0353	0.020	0.0177	0.023

Source: Authors' compilation.
Note: Dependent variable equals the natural log of the index crime rate.
[a]All variables in natural logs.
[b]Model 1 excludes observations with values of 0 before taking logs.
[c]Model 2 includes observations with values of 0 by adding 0.1 to each value before taking natural logs.
*p < .05 **p < .01

tance of instrumental variables in the correct specification of this relationship. Different instrumental variables can produce different results.[6] Nonetheless, it is better to use a number of instruments that may give somewhat different results than to ignore simultaneity bias in estimating the crime-incarceration relationship.

While these analyses suggest that incarceration may have a negative effect on crime at the neighborhood level, crime reduction does not seem to contribute to community organization or collective efficacy in the expected manner. Changes in the neighborhood crime rate are not significantly related to levels of membership in voluntary associations or, as noted earlier, to the exercise of informal social control; however, changes in crime rates are positively related to neighboring and community solidarity (table 6.4). The positive association between changes in crime rates and solidarity may occur because community residents mobilize rather than withdraw in the face of rising crime rates. This interpretation takes on added plausibility when we consider that the sample of thirty communities did not represent the extremes of social disorganization in Baltimore's 277 neighborhoods. Some of the worst areas with the highest levels of disorganization were omitted, leaving a larger proportion of neighborhoods with sufficient resources to mobilize in the face of crime.

The structural-equation models (in table 6.4) also indicate that increases in incarceration can have negative effects on aspects of community organization that, in turn, affect levels of informal social control. Specifically, increases in incarceration rates have a negative and significant effect on community solidarity, and solidarity has a strong positive effect on informal social control. The product of these two relationships is a negative effect of increases in incarceration on informal social control.

In sum, the structural-equation models that take account of simultaneity bias in the relationship between incarceration and crime find that

1. there is likely a negative effect of incarceration on crime at the neighborhood level;
2. reductions in crime at the neighborhood level do not enhance community organization and informal social control;
3. increases in incarceration are associated negatively with some of the community processes on which informal social control depends.

However, the results from the structural-equation models in table 6.4 do not take account of the nested nature of the data. When persons are nested within communities there is a lack of independence between observations that can lead to inefficient tests of significance and biased coefficients. In the following sections we employ hierarchical linear models to test the models from the previous section that include both individual- and neighborhood-level variables. The hierarchical linear model takes account of the fact that these data are nested.

TAKING ACCOUNT OF NESTED DATA

Using hierarchical linear models, we reestimated the models for voluntary associations, neighboring, community solidarity, and informal social control; these models used both neighborhood and individual level data. Table 6.6 shows the results from these efforts. Focusing on the effects of incarceration, we find that the changes in prison admissions rates are statistically significant and negatively associated with community solidarity; this is consistent with the results in table 6.4. We also find that

Table 6.6   *System of Simultaneous Equations for the Effects of Incarceration on Community Organization and Informal Social Control Using Hierarchical Linear Models: Standardized Coefficients*

	Dependent Variables			
Predictors	Voluntary Association	Neighboring	Community Solidarity	Informal Social Control
Area attribute				
Poverty[a]	.000970***	−.000899**	−.000104	.000347
Tenure	.006536**	.015925*	.004260*	.001143
Crime[a]	−.000384	.003710**	.009350***	.000423
Incarceration[a]	.015105	.007082	−.066940***	.040396**
Individual attribute				
Community solidarity	—	—	—	.079623**
Neighboring	—	—	.466860***	.145230***
Voluntary association	—	.228640**	.380020***	−.024585
Control				
Gender	.117647	−.022957	.277671	−.093963
Race	.096885	−.651000***	.642680**	−.078914
Education	.360006**	1.102330***	−.562260**	.274338**
Married	.189328**	.256211	−.339280**	.066102
Own	.316710***	.816560***	.356056*	−.005784
Children	.405410***	.327479*	−.178090	−.046876
Intercept	.557140**	4.01160***	9.24000***	1.61110***

Source: Authors' compilation.
[a]These three variables—crime, poverty scale, and incarceration—were measured by the change in rates. For incarceration and crime, the change was from 1987 to 1992; for poverty, the change was from 1980 to 1990.
*p < .05 **p < .01 ***p < .001

the direct effects of incarceration on informal social control that were insignificant in the structural-equation models are now significant and positive. As the incarceration rate in neighborhoods increases, the level of informal social control exercised by neighborhood residents also increases.

One interpretation of the positive effect of incarceration on informal social control is that increases in incarceration rates encourage informal social control through mechanisms such as fear reduction. We offer this explanation because our results do not support the contention that incarceration increases informal social control by promoting interaction among residents, such as involvement in voluntary associations or neighboring. Rather than working through these types of community-building processes, the positive effects of incarceration on informal social control may operate through individuals. Residents may see or know of persons being incarcerated for crime, and this may increase their confidence in engaging in informal social control. They may feel that the "bad guys" are gone and that the criminal justice system is working with them to increase safety. The importance for citizen reactions of fear of crime independent of actual levels of crime has been demonstrated in the community policing literature (Skogan 1990).

On the other hand, the finding that incarceration reduces community solidarity or feelings of attachment to communities can be explained as follows: To the extent that imprisonment "taints" a person such that neighborhood residents consider this person less desirable than before his or her incarceration, then increasing numbers of persons entering prison could reduce the perceived desirability of the area. When this occurs, feelings of solidarity within the community may diminish. One could envision, for example, a couple with a teenaged boy considering a neighborhood less desirable as an increasing number of their son's peers acquire prison records.

CONCLUSIONS AND IMPLICATIONS

In this chapter we have proposed and examined models of the effects of incarceration on community processes and ultimately informal social control in communities. We assessed some of the basic assumptions that the most punitive forms of crime control strategies can bolster community processes, thereby contributing to community building and ultimately to reductions in crime. Our answers are necessarily narrow and tentative, and more work with larger data sets must be done to replicate and elaborate the work done here.

We find empirical associations that suggest that incarceration had both a positive influence on informal social control in the neighborhoods studied and, at the same time, negative effects on the social processes on which informal social controls depend. Even in suburban communities, where informal social control is posited to occur without high levels of solidarity or neighboring, this occurs through participation in voluntary associations. Hence on the one hand, residents were more willing to engage in informal social control as incarceration increased, but on the other hand, they exhibited weaker feelings of attachment to their neighborhoods, and they were not influenced to change either their levels of involvement in voluntary associations or their neighboring activities. According to Rose and Clear's perspective, the negative association between incarceration and solidarity (attachments to the neighborhood) would decrease residents' willingness to participate in the setting and achieving of collective goals such as obtaining better schools or better service from the police. To the degree that this attachment is strongly associated with informal social control, the effect of incarceration could contribute to decreases in social control.

Our results do not support the common belief that incarceration promotes community organization through crime reduction. Although prison admissions rates are negatively correlated with crime rates, reductions in crime rates are not related to increased levels of interaction among community members and feelings of community solidarity or informal social control. Indeed, increasing crime seems to mobilize communities, resulting in high levels of interaction and high levels of attachment, both of which foster informal social control.

One plausible explanation for these effects stems from the following: During the period covered by our data (from 1987 to 1992), crime rates were generally increasing in the thirty neighborhoods in our sample. Thus the effects of crime on solidarity reflect the very real experience of crime rate changes. Alternatively, the negative effect of incarceration on crime may reflect the cross-sectional differences in crime rates associated with different levels of incarceration. The negative coefficient represents the counterfactual: What would crime rates have been were it not for incarceration rates? In reality, residents did not experience these reductions in crime; on the contrary, they observed their crime rates increase. Hence the mobilization that resulted from increases in crime reflected residents' actual experiences with crime; the negative effect of incarceration on crime reflected the counterfactual.

Finally, our results do not provide support for theories that incarceration negatively impacts communities by reducing the levels of interaction in them. We did not find incarceration rates to be negatively related to participation in voluntary associations or to neighboring. Hence removal through incarceration did not contribute to lessening the level of these community interactions.

These findings substantially complicate our view of how incarceration affects communities. They provide some support both for those who argue that high levels of incarceration undermine the ability of neighborhoods to perform their social control functions and for those who allege that incarceration is beneficial for communities. These results also raise some questions about the processes through which we have assumed that incarceration affects neighborhoods. Although increases in incarceration reduce crime, reductions in crime do not in themselves enhance community organization and promote informal social control. Similarly, increases in incarceration do not negatively affect the level of interactions in communities. Other processes by which incarceration can affect community organization must be identified, and these hypotheses must be tested.

It is important to verify that the results obtained here are reliable and can be generalized. The relationships among incarceration, community organization, and informal social control in this analysis are not particularly strong. More analyses of these data should be done to test the resilience of the findings. The findings might change with different measures of the concepts and different specifications of the models, especially with different instrumentation of the relationship between crime and incarceration. Given the importance of the use of coercion in the lives of citizens and communities, this kind of care seems warranted. Replicating this work in other neighborhoods would also increase our confidence in these results. This work was done in Baltimore, and it is important to know whether what is observed in Baltimore is applicable elsewhere. These replications should, if at all possible, provide for larger samples within the neighborhoods and a larger number of neighborhoods.[7]

Once we are confident in the results observed in this study, the processes by which coercion affects communities should be defined in greater detail. First of all, the definition of coercion should be refined. Admission and release from correctional institutions is one aspect of correctional policy that can influence communities, but probation and parole policies can affect the level of coercion in a community. A parole office who employs a stringent drug-testing and parole revocation policy may be more coercive than a court that simply incarcerates residents.

Second, more attention should be given to the issue of spatial autocorrelation in the relationship between incarceration and crime at the community level. Although we found a negative relationship between incarceration and crime rates at the neighborhood level, this relationship might be much stronger if we took account of free riding. Free riding can occur when incarcerations in community A reduce crimes in adjacent areas B and C; communities B and C then free ride on the incarceration policies of community A, thereby reducing the ability to observe the negative effect of incarceration on crime in these communities because both B and C will have reduced crime rates without increases in incarceration rates. We must explore this possibility before we can accurately gauge the effects of incarceration in a given community on crime in that community.

Third, the various models describing the link between coercion and community presented here should be modified in light of these findings. Specifically, if coercion does not seem to be related to beneficial outcomes for communities through crime reduction, then other processes must be identified that link coercion to these outcomes. The community policing literature suggests that coercion can encourage interaction within the community directly through reductions in fear or perceived reductions in risk rather than through actual reductions in crime. It is important that the theory behind various control programs and strategies be specified as clearly as possible so that these strategies can be assessed both logically and empirically.

Finally, more thought must be given to the desired outcome of applying coercion in communities so that these policy decisions can be seen in cost-benefit terms. In this analysis, we have emphasized community organization and informal social control as important community outcomes. These outcomes were chosen because they have been shown to affect the quality of life and the personal safety of community residents (Sampson, Raudenbush, and Earls 1997). Other neighborhood-level outcomes could have been chosen. For example, minimizing the negative and maximizing the positive social structural conditions of the neighborhood could be the desired outcome of coercion. Maintaining high property values in the area or minimizing the number of vacant houses, for example, could be considered more important than community organization or informal social control. The social organization of the community and the physical and social structural aspects of community are related but not perfectly. In a given time period, coercion policies may have very different effects on these two classes of outcomes. If we are to discuss in cost-benefit terms the use of aggressive arrest and incarceration to bolster communities, then we must be clearer about what the desired benefits are.

APPENDIX

Scale Construction and Factor Loadings

1. Informal social control (individual)   ($\alpha = .673$)

   Would neighbors try to stop a breaking and entering?
   Would neighbors get help to stop a breaking and entering?
   Would neighbors stop teenagers from shouting at night?
   Would neighbors get help to stop teenagers?

2. Community solidarity (individual)   ($\alpha = .754$)

   Do you feel part of the neighborhood?
   Do you feel a sense of the community?
   Do you feel an attachment to the block?
   Do you feel a sense of community on your block?

3. Neighboring (individual)   (α = .729)

   In the past year did you run an errand for a neighbor?
   In the past year did you visit a neighbor?
   In the past year did you borrow tools or household items?
   In the past year did you work together to improve your block?
   In the past year did you watch a neighbor's home?
   In the past year did you take in a neighbor's mail?
   In the past year did you give your keys to a neighbor?

4. Poverty scale   (α = .702)

   Percentage change from 1980 to 1990 in percentage under poverty line
   Percentage change from 1980 to 1990 in percentage of vacant homes

---

Partial support for this research was provided by Grant NIJ 98-CE-VX-0004 from the National Institute of Justice. We wish to thank David F. Weiman, Mary Pattillo, Bruce Western, and other anonymous reviewers for their helpful comments on previous versions of this chapter. We also wish to thank Ralph B. Taylor for his advice on using his data appropriately and on thinking about the role of community in social control. The views expressed in this paper are those of its authors and do not reflect those of the U.S. General Accounting Office.

NOTES

1. Stephen Gottfredson and Ralph Taylor (1988) include neighborhood-level incarceration rates in their study of recidivism outcomes. The rates are used to predict successful outcomes and not to assess the effects on neighborhood crime rates or the social organization of these areas.
2. Future research should investigate the degree to which residents in different communities systematically vary in their willingness to report crimes to the police, as systematic variations in this factor can introduce biases when using crime rates in these analyses of communities.
3. The endogeneity problem can also affect the relationship between coercion and informal social control. It is not immediately clear whether informal social control is affected by incarceration or incarceration is affected by informal social control. This problem is ameliorated somewhat in this model by the fact that informal social control is measured at the individual level and coercion is measured at the community level. It is less likely that collective and individual characteristics will derive from a common cause than it is that two phenomenon measured at the same level will.
4. We are grateful to David F. Weiman for this suggestion; personal email correspondence, July 31, 2003.
5. Here and throughout the discussion of results, we focus on the direction of

effects rather than the magnitudes of effects. We take this approach because our work in this chapter is primarily exploratory and, as becomes clear in the discussion of results, the case base of these findings is relatively small, despite the fact that Taylor's data are the best data available for examining these processes. Given the small samples of persons interviewed and the limited number of communities, discussion of magnitude of effects at this juncture seems premature.

6. In an earlier version of this chapter we used the ratio of drug arrests to total arrests in 1992 as an instrumental variable in our estimation of the relationship between incarceration and crime. The resulting coefficient for the effect of incarceration on crime was positive and significant. We deem the instrument used in the current analysis as superior because it has no relationship to crime, whereas the instrument used earlier had a significant but weak correlation with the change in crime rates ($r = .098$, $p < .05$).

7. Supplementing the data from the Chicago Neighborhoods Project in the way that we have supplemented Taylor's data would be an easy and inexpensive strategy for replicating this work. It would also provide for more communities and more cases within communities.

REFERENCES

Blumstein, Alfred. 1995. "Youth Violence, Guns, and Illicit Drug Industry." Working paper series. Pittsburgh, Penn.: H. John Heinz III School of Public Policy and Management, Carnegie Mellon University.

Blumstein, Alfred, and Allen J. Beck. 1999. "Factors Contributing to Growth in U.S. Prison Populations." In *Prisons*, edited by Michael Tonry and Joan Petersilia. Chicago: University of Chicago Press.

Bonczar, Thomas P. 2003. "Prevalence of Imprisonment in the U.S. Population, 1974–2001." *Bureau of Justice Statistics Special Report*. NCJ 197976. Washington: U.S. Department of Justice (August).

Bryk, Anthony, and Stephen Raudenbush. 1992. *Hierarchical Linear Models for Social and Behavioral Research: Applications and Data Analysis Methods*. Newbury Park, Calif.: Sage.

Bursik, Robert J. 1988. "Social Disorganization Theories of Crime and Delinquency: Problems and Prospects." *Criminology* 26(4): 519–52.

Bursik, Robert J., and Harold Grasmick. 1993. *Neighborhoods and Crime: The Dimensions of Effective Community Control*. New York: Lexington Books.

Caulkins, Jonathan P., C. Peter Rydell, William L. Schwabe, and James Chiesa. 1997. *Mandatory Minimum Drug Sentences: Throwing Away the Key or Throwing Away the Taxpayers' Money?* Santa Monica, Calif.: Rand.

Clear, Todd. 1996. "Backfire: When Incarceration Increases Crime." In *The Unintended Consequences of Incarceration*, edited by the Vera Institute. New York: Vera Institute of Justice.

Cohen, Jacqueline, and Jose A. Canela-Cacho. 1994. "Incarceration and Violent Crime: 1965–1988." In *Understanding and Preventing Violence*, vol. 4, *Consequences and Control*, edited by Albert J. Reiss and Jeffrey A. Roth. Washington, D.C.: National Academy Press.

Darity, William A., and Samuel L. Myers Jr. 1989. "The Effect of Homicides and

Imprisonment on Black Families." Paper presented at the Institute of Criminal Justice and Criminology. University of Maryland, College Park. (October 11).

————. 1994. *The Black Underclass: Critical Essays on Race and Unwantedness*. New York: Garland.

Gilliard, Darrell K., and Allen J. Beck. 1996. *Prison and Jail Inmates, 1995*. Washington: U.S. Department of Justice, Bureau of Justice Statistics.

Gottfredson, Stephen D., and Ralph B. Taylor. 1988. "Community Contexts and Criminal Offenders." In *Communities and Crime Reduction*, edited by Tim Hope and Michael Shaw. London: Her Majesty's Stationery Office.

Gowen, Rebecca. 2000. *Admissions from and Releases to Baltimore County from Maryland State Correctional Facilities*. Baltimore: Maryland Department of Public Safety and Correctional Services.

Grogger, Jeffrey. 1995. "The Effects of Arrests on the Employment and Earnings of Young Men." *Quarterly Journal of Economics* 110(1): 51–71.

Hackler, James, Kwai-yiu Ho, and Carol Urquhart-Ross. 1974. "The Willingness to Intervene: Differing Community Characteristics." *Social Problems* 21(3): 328–44.

Harrison, Paige M., and Allen J. Beck. 2003. "Prisoners in 2002." *Bureau of Justice Statistics Bulletin*. NCJ 200248. Washington: U.S. Department of Justice (July).

Kasarda, John D., and Morris Janowitz. 1974. "Community Attachment in Mass Society." *American Sociological Review* 39(3): 328–39.

Kling, Jeffrey R. 1999. "The Effect of Prison Sentence Length on the Subsequent Employment and Earnings of Criminal Defendants." Discussion Papers in Economics 208. Woodrow Wilson School of Economics, Princeton University (February).

Kuziemko, Ilyana, and Steven D. Levitt. 2001. "An Empirical Analysis of Imprisoning Drug Offenders." NBER Working Paper 8489. Cambridge, Mass.: National Bureau of Economic Research.

Levitt, Steven. 1996. "The Effect of Prison Population Size on Crime Rates: Evidence from Prison Overcrowding Litigation." *Quarterly Journal of Economics* 3(2, May): 319–52.

Lynch, James P., and William J. Sabol. 1992. "Macro-social Changes and Their Implications for Prison Reform: The Underclass and the Composition of U.S. Prison Populations." Paper presented at the American Society of Criminology annual meeting. New Orleans, La. (November 6).

————. 1997. *Did Getting Tough on Crime Pay?* Crime Policy Report 1. Washington, D.C.: Urban Institute.

————. 2000. "Prison Use and Social Control." In *Criminal Justice 2000*, vol. 3, edited by Julie Horney, Ruth Peterson, Doris MacKenzie, John Martin, and Dennis Rosenbaum. Washington, D.C.: National Institute of Justice.

Moore, Joan. 1996. "Bearing the Burden: How Incarceration Policies Weaken Inner-City Communities." In *The Unintended Consequences of Incarceration*, edited by the Vera Institute. New York: Vera Institute of Justice.

Myers, Samuel L., Jr. 2000. "Unintended Impacts of Sentencing Reforms." Paper presented at the annual meeting of the American Sociological Association. Washington, D.C. (August 13).

Nagin, Daniel. 1998. "Criminal Deterrence Research at the Outset of the Twenty-first Century." In *Crime and Justice: A Review of Research*, edited by Michael Tonry. Chicago: University of Chicago Press.

Nightingale, Demetra Smith, and Harold Watts. 1996. "Adding it Up: The Economic Impact of Incarceration on Individuals, Families, and Communities." In *The Unintended Consequences of Incarceration,* edited by the Vera Institute. New York: Vera Institute of Justice.

Putnam, Robert. 1993. "The Prosperous Community: Social Capital and Community Life." *American Prospect* 4(13, Spring): 35–42.

Rose, Dina, and Todd Clear. 1998a. "Incarceration, Social Capital, and Crime: Implications for Social Disorganization Theory." *Criminology* 36(3): 441–80.

———. 1998b. "Unintended Consequences of Incarceration: Exposure to Prison and Attitudes Toward Social Control." Paper presented to the Twentieth Annual Research Conference of the Association for Public Policy Analysis and Management. New York (October 30).

Rose, Dina, Todd Clear, and Elin Waring. 2003. "Coercive Mobility and Crime: A Preliminary Examination of Concentrated Incarceration and Social Disorganization." *Justice Quarterly* 20(1): 33–64.

Sabol, William J., and James P. Lynch. 2003. "Assessing the Longer-run Consequences of Incarceration: Effects on Families and Employment." In *Crime Control and Social Justice: The Delicate Balance,* edited by Darnell Hawkins, Samuel L. Myers Jr., and Randolph Stone. Westport, Conn.: Greenwood Press.

Sampson, Robert J. 1987. "Urban Black Violence: The Effects of Male Joblessness and Family Disruption." *American Journal of Sociology* 93(2): 348–82.

Sampson, Robert J., Jeffrey Morenhoff, and Felton Earls. 1999. "Beyond Social Capital: Spatial Dynamics of Collective Efficacy for Children." *American Sociological Review* 64(5): 633–60.

Sampson, Robert J., Stephen Raudenbush, and Felton Earls. 1997. "Neighborhoods and Violent Crime: A Multilevel Study of Collective Efficacy." *Science* 277(5328, August): 918–24.

Shaw, Clifford, and Henry McKay. 1942. *Juvenile Delinquency and Urban Areas.* Chicago: University of Chicago.

Skogan, Wesley. 1990. *Disorder and Decline: Crime and the Spiral of Decay in American Neighborhoods.* New York: Free Press.

Spelman, William. 2000. "What Recent Studies Do (and Don't) Tell Us about Imprisonment and Crime." In *Crime and Justice: A Review of Research,* edited by Michael Tonry. Chicago: University of Chicago.

Taylor, Ralph B. 1997. "Social Order and Disorder of Street Blocks and Neighborhoods: Ecology, Micro-ecology, and the Systemic Model of Social Disorganization." *Journal of Research on Crime and Delinquency* 34(1): 113–55.

———. 2001. *Breaking Away from Broken Windows.* Boulder, Colo.: Westview Press.

———. 2002. "Fear of Crime, Social Ties, and Collective Efficacy: Maybe Masquerading Measurement, Maybe Déjà vu All Over Again." *Justice Quarterly* 19(4): 773–92.

Western, Bruce. 2002. "The Impact of Incarceration on Wage Mobility and Inequality." *American Sociological Review* 67(4): 526–46.

Western, Bruce, Jeffrey R. Kling, and David F. Weiman. 2001. "The Labor Market Consequences of Incarceration." *Crime and Delinquency* 47(3): 410–27.

Wilson, William Julius. 1987. *The Truly Disadvantaged: The Inner City, the Underclass, and Public Policy.* Chicago: University of Chicago Press.

Christopher Uggen
Jeff Manza

Lost Voices: The Civic and Political Views of Disenfranchised Felons

7

Incarceration affects many aspects of community life, from demographic composition to public safety. In addition, it silences the political voices of millions of disenfranchised felons and dilutes the political strength of the groups to which they belong.

The criminal justice system in the United States is unique internationally not only for the relatively high rate at which it incarcerates citizens but also for the sharp restrictions it places on the political rights of offenders and former offenders. Nearly all states (forty-eight of the fifty) bar incarcerated felons from voting; most (thirty-three) bar either parolees or probationers, or both, from voting; and a minority (fourteen) ban some or all former felons from voting.[1] Based on a detailed, state-by-state canvass, we estimate that as a result of these various voting restrictions approximately 4.7 million felons and former felons were precluded from voting in the 2000 presidential election. This group represented approximately 2.3 percent of the 2000 voting-age population, more than tripling the 1976 disenfranchisement rate of .74 percent. The burden of disenfranchisement falls especially heavily on African American voters, both because of high conviction and incarceration rates and because they are disproportionately located in states with expansive disenfranchisement laws (Behrens, Uggen, and Manza 2003).[2]

When the United States is compared with other countries, the unique character of American felon disenfranchisement and the political consequences of the criminal justice regime are thrown into sharp relief (see Ewald 2003). In many countries (for example, Denmark, Iceland, Ireland, Finland, Greece, the Netherlands, Poland, Spain, Sweden, and Switzerland, as well as South Africa and Australia outside the European Union),

Figure 7.1   *Estimated Distribution of Legally Disenfranchised Felons in the United States, 2000*

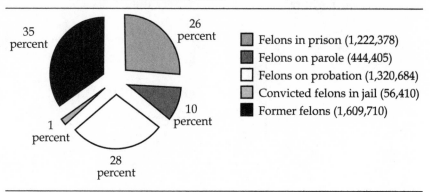

Source: Adapted from Uggen and Manza (2002).

even prison inmates are permitted to vote, while in a number of other nations only certain categories of prisoners are denied voting rights.[3] A handful of European countries—mostly from the former Soviet Union but the United Kingdom as well—restrict the voting rights of all prisoners. We are aware of no country (or region) in Europe that bans former offenders who have completed their sentences from access to the ballot.[4]

Figure 7.1 shows the distribution of U.S. disenfranchised felons at year-end 2000 across correctional supervision categories. We include a conservative estimate of the legally disenfranchised jail population, based on 10 percent of the inmate population at year-end 2000, though a much larger number of jail inmates are practically, if not legally, disenfranchised.[5] Although the precise distribution is shifting continuously as states alter their disenfranchisement laws, it remains the case that only a minority of disenfranchised felons are prison inmates. In 2000 almost three-fourths of those disenfranchised were either felons on probation or parole supervised in their communities or former felons who had completed their sentences. The rationale for disenfranchising current prison inmates would appear to be different from that for those who have completed their sentences (former felons) or those otherwise deemed fit to maintain community ties (probationers and parolees). Just as the loss of voting rights is a powerful symbol of a felon's "outsider" status, restoration of voting rights serves as a clear marker of reintegration and acceptance into a community of law-abiding citizens.

In discussions of the positive and negative community impacts of high criminal conviction and incarceration rates (including those explored in other chapters of this volume), one largely neglected question has been how these restrictions on the voting rights of felons impose costs on individual felons, on underrepresented groups, and on American democracy as a whole. The loss of the right to vote may be significant for individuals when it is experienced as a denial of a core right of citizenship (Shklar 1991) or on groups such as African Americans, who are disproportionately disenfranchised. For the polity as a whole, restrictions on the franchise matter if they influence election outcomes and change the balance of political power (Piven and Cloward 2000; Rueschemeyer, Stephens, and Stephens 1992; see also the historical examples in Keyssar 2000). If that is the case, rising incarceration rates may constitute a unique "democratic contraction," leading away from the universal trend toward franchise extension and the spread of democratic governance (Manza and Uggen forthcoming; Uggen and Manza 2002).

In previous work, we have considered the macro-level impact of felon disenfranchisement. We conducted a counterfactual analysis in which we asked what would have happened to election outcomes in the United States if felons had had the right to vote (Uggen and Manza 2002). Matching known demographic characteristics of the felon population to those of the electorate as a whole to estimate turnout and vote choice, and taking into account the size of the disenfranchised population in each state, we concluded that a number of Senate and gubernatorial elections won by Republican candidates in recent years would most likely have been reversed had felons been permitted to vote.[6]

In this chapter, we turn our attention to the political voices lost through disenfranchisement. Using data from an ongoing panel study of former students in St. Paul, Minnesota, and semistructured interviews with a group of convicted felons in Minnesota, we examine the substance of the political attitudes, preferences, engagements, and voting behavior of citizens convicted of crime and consider the extent to which franchise restrictions distance them from the political system. The information we present here provides a unique, if limited and primarily suggestive, portrait of the disenfranchised population.[7]

The chapter is organized as follows. The first section situates the study of political attitudes and behavior in a comparative frame of reference, noting that low levels of political knowledge and high levels of apathy can be found across the entire electorate. The second section reports our findings from the YDS (Youth Development Study) survey. In the third section, we allow felons to speak for themselves on politics, government, and public policy. A short conclusion summarizes our findings and suggests some policy implications.

A COMPARATIVE PERSPECTIVE ON
FELONS' POLITICAL ATTITUDES

An obvious starting assumption—based on widely held beliefs about criminal offenders—is that poor education and below-average citizenship norms make criminal offenders a low-information group with high levels of political apathy. On the basis of demographic information, we would further expect to find low levels of political participation among offenders who are eligible to vote (U.S. Department of Justice 1993, 2000).

Before jumping to such conclusions, however, it is important to keep in mind some well-documented aspects of the American electorate as a whole. First, consider political participation. In comparison with other postindustrial democratic countries, turnout rates in U.S. national elections are shockingly low. While 70 to 90 percent turnout rates are common in national legislative elections in Europe, only about half of the U.S. voting-age population has voted in recent presidential elections, and little more than one-third in midterm (nonpresidential) national elections.[8] Turnout rates are far lower in state and local elections without national contests and in primary elections in which major-party candidates are selected. Levels of political participation by criminal offenders (when they have been eligible) may be low, but so too is the electorate-wide average.

Next, consider political knowledge. Low levels of political information among the mass public have been widely documented since the pioneering work of the Michigan school in the early 1960s (most notably, Campbell et al. 1960; Converse 1964). Attempts to tie rising education levels and increasing availability of political information through the media to higher levels of political knowledge (Nie, Verba, and Petrocik 1979; Inglehart 1990) have generally not been supported (for example, Delli Carpini and Keeter 1996; Smith 1989). Indeed, as one recent textbook puts it, "many—often most—citizens are ignorant of rather basic facts. . . . The data suggest massive public ignorance" (Glynn et al. 1999, 251).

Finally, consider apathy and distrust of government. The production of nonpolitical orientations to the world around us, and the systematic avoidance of thorny political issues, are widely developed in American society and institutions (Eliasoph 1998). Distrust of politicians and the government are also common in American politics (Nye, Zelikow, and King 1997). Again, the existence of such beliefs among criminal offenders would be hardly unique.

In addition to properly situating the political consciousness of offenders alongside the limited competence and political apathy of the mass public, it is also worth noting that there may be ways in which—at least in some times and places for some inmates—incarceration actually stimulates political consciousness. In fact, the politicization of U.S. prisoners attracted some degree of scholarly attention in the 1960s and 1970s (Brody 1974; Burdman 1974; Fairchild 1977; Wright 1973). Although both the prisoners' rights movement (Smith 1993) and rehabilitation programs have eroded significantly over the past three decades (Lin 2000), inmates often acquire more education or have time to reflect about the outside world in ways that they did not while on the street. In chapter 3 of this volume, Kathryn Edin, Timothy Nelson, and Rechelle Paranal report on the transformative impact of incarceration for some men who, with time and distance, were able to recognize the ties they had destroyed by their behavior and make plans to restore those relationships (also see Maruna 2001, 97).

In unusual cases, prisoners have used their time for intensive study and activism. As Malcolm X (1965, 180) put it, "Where else but in a prison could I have attacked my ignorance by being able to study intensely sometimes as much as fifteen hours a day?" The Norfolk Prison Colony afforded Malcolm X other opportunities for political action, including a forum for educating or radicalizing other inmates and a weekly debating program that provided a "baptism into public speaking" (Malcolm X 1965, 182). Upon entering San Quentin a generation later, Sanyika Shakur was told, "You'll feel the comrade strong here. Bro, you'll read books here, see things that are gonna change the way you walk, talk, and think. This is the best place for an aspiring young revolutionary. This is repression at its best" (Shakur 1994, 341). Progressive or radical politics are embedded in several first-person accounts of prison life, both because such messages echo the experiences of "caged-up" men (Malcolm X 1965, 182) and because the radical press is viewed as more trustworthy in describing prison conditions and events (Abbott 1981). Various forms of collective action among prisoners, including, in extreme cases, riots (Goldstone and Useem 1999; Pallas and Barber 1973; Useem and Kimball 1991), provide an opportunity for political involvement and may also stimulate a broader sense of political efficacy. More typically, perhaps, many inmates simply develop greater interest in politics and its implications for community life as they begin to cultivate a prosocial identity for themselves upon release (Maruna 2001; Uggen, Manza, and Behrens 2004).

In view of all of these considerations, then, it is important not to exaggerate the degree of political apathy, disinterestedness, or low levels of political participation on the part of criminal offenders but rather to treat it as a question to be interrogated. Both our survey questions and in-depth interviews are designed to explore the extent and depth of political consciousness among convicted felons in the United States.

SURVEY RESULTS: THE 2000 YOUTH DEVELOPMENT STUDY

We begin our analysis by drawing upon some unique survey data to compare the political preferences and involvement of offenders and non-offenders. This portion of our investigation is based on the Youth Development Study (YDS), a survey of a thousand persons who began the study in 1988 as ninth-graders in St. Paul, Minnesota, public schools. Self-reported crime and arrest data were collected from 1988 to 1998. Political participation questions are taken from the twelfth survey wave in 2000, when a total of 757 respondents, then aged twenty-six to twenty-seven years, remained in the sample.[9] To our knowledge, the YDS is the only representative survey containing information about the political preferences and behaviors of both offenders and nonoffenders.

In table 7.1, we contrast four groups: YDS respondents who had never been arrested; YDS respondents who had been arrested but not incarcerated; YDS respondents who had been incarcerated in jail or prison; and, to place these Minnesota data in a national context, twenty-four- and twenty-five-year-old prison inmates surveyed as part of the 1997 National Survey of Inmates in State and Federal Correctional Facilities (U.S. Department of Justice 2000). As the table shows, by 1998 approximately three-fourths of YDS respondents had never been arrested, one-fourth had been arrested or incarcerated, and 10 percent had been incarcerated. About 36 percent of the YDS nonarrestees were male, 83 percent were white, and 29 percent were married. Arrestees and inmates in the YDS sample were much more likely than nonarrestees to be male, nonwhite, and unmarried, though to a lesser extent than state prisoners. Similarly, YDS arrestees and inmates reported lower levels of education than other YDS respondents but much higher levels of education than those of comparable age in the national survey of prisoners. When offenses are ranked by severity (with violence ranked as most severe, followed by property, drug, and other offenses), the most serious offense among YDS arrestees was a violent crime in 19 percent of cases, a property crime for 39 percent, a drug crime for 24 percent, and some other offense (such as a weapons or public order violation) for 17 percent, with a similar distribution observed among those who had been incarcerated. Overall, table 7.1 suggests that YDS respondents who had experienced criminal sanctions were generally less advantaged than the Minnesota cohort from which they were drawn but more advantaged than the typical U.S. inmate serving time in a state penitentiary. Respondents in the YDS sample who had been arrested or incarcerated also reported far fewer arrests for violent crimes relative to the national sample of prison inmates.

Political Orientation, Attitudes, and Engagement

The 2000 YDS contains a number of items that tap aspects of respondents' political attitudes, political efficacy, and political engagement. Table 7.2 presents a summary of the main results, again contrasting nonarrestees, those who had been arrested but not incarcerated, and those who had been incarcerated. Many of the questions we used are identical to long-standing items on the biennial National Election Study (National Election Studies 1995–2000), thereby incorporating tested items and enabling comparison to national election survey results.[10]

The results shown in table 7.2 underscore the extent to which the political beliefs of respondents who have been arrested or incarcerated conform to our starting assumptions but also reveal that not all of the differences with nonarrestees are statistically or (perhaps) substantively significant. Arrestees and inmates are significantly more likely to claim independent partisan identification than the rest of the sample, though this result must be interpreted cautiously in view of the strong attraction of Jesse Ventura's successful 1998 independent gubernatorial campaign to Minnesota offenders (discussed later in this chapter). Fully 54 percent of the incarcerated or formerly incarcerated respondents say they "do not lean toward either the Republican or Democratic Party." Lack of partisan identification among the remaining YDS sample is also high by comparison with the national mean.

Ideological self-identification and identification with the Christian right are not markedly different across groups, though incarcerated respondents reported somewhat greater conservatism than the remainder of the sample. The latter may be somewhat surprising at first glance but is less so in view of the interview results reported later in this chapter.

Attitudes toward government reflect some of the most striking and consistent differences between inmates, arrestees, and the remainder of the sample. One of the most widely discussed trends in U.S. public opinion over the past decade has been declining levels of public confidence in the government (for example, Brooks and Cheng 2001; Hetherington 1998; Nye, Zelikow, and King 1997). Several questions were asked of YDS respondents about their trust in politicians and in their government. On all of these questions, arrestees and inmates exhibited significantly less trust than those who had not been arrested or incarcerated. They were also much more likely to express no confidence in the criminal justice system, a hardly surprising result but one that may have been produced by conflicting responses, as our interview data reported later in this chapter suggest.

We also probed respondents about their beliefs in the efficacy of

Table 7.1   Comparison of Youth Development Study Arrestees and Inmates with 1997 National Survey of State Prison Inmates

Characteristic	Youth Development Study			National Inmate Survey: State and Federal Prisoners Aged Twenty-four to Twenty-five (N = 85,661)
	Never Arrested (N = 568) 74.3 percent	Arrested but Not Incarcerated (N = 118) 15.4 percent	Incarcerated (N = 78) 10.2 percent	
Percentage male*	35.6	67.6	70.5	95.3
Race				
Percentage white*	82.5	73.0	68.8	25.1
Percentage black*	5.2	9.6	16.9	51.5
Percentage Hispanic	4.3	4.3	3.9	18.6
Percentage other[a]	7.9	13.0	10.4	4.7
Family				
Percentage currently married	29.0	20.0	22.0	11.4
Number of children*	0.5	0.8	1.0	1.1
	(0.9)	(1.2)	(1.2)	(1.2)
Age	24.4	24.5	24.5	24.5
	(0.6)	(0.6)	(0.6)	(0.5)

Mean years of education*	14.2	13.4	13.0	10.5
	(1.7)	(1.8)	(1.7)	(2.0)
Employment				
Percentage employed full-time	58.3	58.1	58.5	45.4
Annual income	$19,150	$19,110	$18,490	$18,269
	($10,788)	($10,656)	($12,403)	($22,789)
Most serious offense				
Percentage violent	0	19.1	14.8	59.9
Percentage property	0	39.1	40.7	11.6
Percentage drug	0	24.4	22.2	23.8
Percentage other	0	17.4	22.2	4.7

Source: Data from U.S. Department of Justice (2000).

[a]"Other" category includes those reporting "mixed" race in Youth Development Study data (Mortimer 2003).

*The significance of the differences across the nonarrest, arrest, and incarceration groups was tested by analysis of variance (ANOVA). To obtain direct comparisons (arrested versus nonarrested and incarcerated versus nonincarcerated), we also conducted a supplementary set of t tests (tables available from authors). An asterisk indicates that the F test is statistically significant at $p < .05$ and that we can reject the null hypothesis that the three groups are equivalent on the characteristic. Standard deviations for continuous variables are in parentheses.

Table 7.2   *Relationship Between Criminal Sanctions and Political Attitudes and Experiences (YDS)*

Characteristic	Never Arrested	Arrested but Not Incarcerated	Incarcerated
Party identification			
Percentage Republican	15.4	14.3	7.9
Percentage Democrat	48.3	37.8	38.2
Percentage neither party*	36.3	48.0	54.0
Ideological self-identification[a]			
Liberal or conservative	2.75	2.86	2.96
Percentage Christian right	13.20	12.80	14.10
Trust in government[b]			
Government cannot be trusted*	2.53	2.79	2.82
People running government are crooked*	2.78	2.94	3.08
No confidence in criminal justice system*	2.75	3.07	3.09
Political efficacy[b]			
People like me have no say*	2.31	2.49	2.70
Get nowhere talking to public officials*	2.29	2.44	2.69
Political engagement			
Percentage talk with spouse or partner, 2000*	49.2	29.9	35.9
Percentage talk with friends, 2000	40.0	40.2	28.2
Percentage talk with relatives, 2000*	44.3	33.0	30.8

Source: Authors' compilation.

[a]On a scale of 1 to 5: 1 is extremely liberal, 5 is extremely conservative.

[b]On a scale of 1 to 4: 1 strongly disagrees, 4 strongly agrees.

*The significance of the differences across the nonarrest, arrest, and incarceration groups was tested by analysis of variance (ANOVA). To obtain direct comparisons (arrested versus nonarrested and incarcerated versus nonincarcerated), we also conducted a supplementary set of t tests (tables available from authors). An asterisk indicates that the F test is statistically significant at $p < .05$ and that we can reject the null hypothesis that the three groups are equivalent on the characteristic.

political action. A sense that political activity can be meaningful has long been identified as an important factor stimulating participation in civic life (Almond and Verba 1963; Verba, Scholzman, and Brady 1997). Arrestees and inmates are significantly less likely to think that they can influence public officials or even have some say in politics. The differences between those who have been incarcerated and those who have never been arrested (more than one-third of one point on a four-point scale) are statistically and, we suspect, substantively significant.

Conversations with friends, co-workers, and family members represent an important source of political information and a stimulus for interest in politics (Lipset 1981). Although inmates may discuss political issues with staff or among themselves, their access to friends, relatives, and co-workers is likely to be restricted during periods of incarceration. We find that when it comes to discussing politics, those who have experienced criminal justice sanctions are indeed somewhat less likely than nonarrestees to engage in such conversations with their spouses or relatives.

Political Behavior

Voting is the most fundamental form of political expression in democratic polities. Table 7.3 shows YDS turnout rates in the 1996 and 1998 elections and plans for participating in the 2000 elections. We find large and statistically significant differences between the groups, the greatest differences being between those who had been incarcerated and those who had never been arrested. Individual self-reports of voting always produce inflated estimates, however, so it is the gap, rather than the percentages reporting having voted, that is of greatest interest. In the 1996 election, arrestees were 18 percent less likely to vote than nonarrestees, and inmates were 27 percent less likely to have voted than nonarrestees. The turnout gap between arrestees and nonarrestees is smaller for the 1998 midterm elections, when participation is much lower overall, and for respondents' intentions (in May 2000) to vote in the 2000 election. The gap between those who had been incarcerated and those who had never been arrested remains consistently high across the different electoral contexts.

Because better-educated and more affluent citizens are more likely to report having voted (Bernstein, Chadha, and Montjoy 2001) and criminal offenders have mean levels of income and education significantly below those of nonoffenders (U.S. Department of Justice 1993), some of the observed turnout gap reflects sociodemographic differences. In other analyses, we have shown that a large portion of the differences in political participation and vote choice between offenders and nonoffenders in the

Table 7.3   *The Relationship Between Criminal Sanctions and Voter Turnout and Vote Choice (YDS)*

Variable	Never Arrested	Arrested but Not Incarcerated[a]	Incarcerated[b]	Turnout Gap[c]
Turnout				
Percentage voted in 1996*	70.5	52.7	43.6	26.9
Percentage voted in 1998*	54.5	46.9	28.6	25.9
Percentage planned to vote in 2000*	82.3	69.1	59.7	22.6
Vote choice				
1996				
Percentage Clinton (Dem.)	72.9	71.9	81.3	8.4
Percentage Perot (Ind.)	13.7	19.3	12.5	1.2
Percentage Dole (Rep.)	9.5	5.3	6.3	3.2
Percentage other	3.9	3.5	0.0	3.9
1998				
Percentage Ventura (Ind.)	56.3	74.4	69.6	13.3
Percentage Humphrey (Dem.)	22.0	11.6	13.0	9.0
Percentage Coleman (Rep.)	19.8	11.6	17.4	2.4

Source: Authors' compilation.

[a]For the 1996 election, arrest refers to an arrest before 1997. For the 1998 and 2000 elections, arrest refers to an arrest before 1999.

[b]For the 1996 election, incarceration refers to incarceration before 1996. For the 1998 and 2000 elections, incarceration refers to incarceration before 1999.

[c]Turnout among those never arrested minus turnout of those who have been incarcerated.

*The significance of the differences across the nonarrest, arrest, and incarceration groups was tested by analysis of variance (ANOVA). To obtain direct comparisons (arrested versus nonarrested and incarcerated versus nonincarcerated), we also conducted a supplementary set of t tests (tables available from authors). An asterisk indicates that the F test is statistically significant at $p < .05$ and that we can reject the null hypothesis that the three groups are equivalent on the characteristic.

YDS is attributable to sociodemographic differences between the two groups (see Uggen and Manza 2002). Once factors such as education level, marital status, employment history, race, and gender are taken into account, the turnout gap and differences in voting behavior diminish dramatically.[11] In other words, we should be cautious in attributing too much weight solely to the experience of having been incarcerated or having received a felony conviction.

In presidential politics, the former public school students in urban Minnesota exhibited strong support for the Democratic incumbent Bill Clinton in the 1996 election, so much so that there were only small differences between arrestees, inmates, and the remainder of the YDS sample. The most startling differences, however, register in the highly unusual 1998 Minnesota gubernatorial race, in which those who had been arrested exhibited significantly greater support for former professional wrestler Jesse Ventura. Among those who reported having voted, fully 74 percent of arrestees and 70 percent of inmates supported Ventura. Ventura, like Clinton, drew strong support among the entire sample of young Minnesota adults, but his appeal was even higher among those who had been arrested or incarcerated. Further analyses (not shown here) suggest that those who had been arrested for drug- and alcohol-related offenses were particularly likely to favor both Bill Clinton in 1996 and Jesse Ventura in 1998 (Uggen and Manza 2002).

THE POLITICAL VIEWS OF CRIMINAL OFFENDERS: EVIDENCE FROM IN-DEPTH INTERVIEWS

The new survey results discussed in the previous section provide some baseline information about the political orientations of respondents who have had contact with the criminal justice system, relative to a comparison group of nonoffenders. In this section, we go beyond those survey results to detail the underlying attitudes and dispositions of convicted offenders, based on a series of intensive, semistructured interviews with thirty-three Minnesota prisoners, probationers, and parolees, undertaken in the spring and summer of 2001.[12] The questions we posed addressed political participation, partisanship, trust in government, and attitudes about other civil disabilities. The interviews were designed to elicit in more detail the political attitudes of offenders and the deeper significance of the loss of voting rights posed by felon disenfranchisement.[13] We asked our respondents questions such as the following: What kinds of political experiences have you had? Do you expect to participate in the future, and why or why not? Are any political issues especially salient to you? How does losing the right to vote affect your ideas about being a part of a community and about your government? Do politics and voting affect your ability to stay away from crime on the outside?

We carried out these interviews at two state correctional facilities and one county community corrections office. Although the interviews were conducted within these facilities, we arranged for a private room with a closed door so that correctional and administrative staff would not overhear the interview questions or responses. The interviews generally ran from forty-five minutes to more than an hour and (with the permission of the interviewees) were recorded and later transcribed. To protect the participants' confidentiality, we identify neither their race nor their real names when quoting from the transcripts. All major offense categories were represented among the interviewees, and almost all respondents had been convicted of serious or index crimes.

Table 7.4 provides some descriptive information about the interviewees. Respondents varied in race and gender and ranged from twenty to fifty-four years of age; we interviewed people in prison, on parole, and on probation. Relative to national prison populations, women are significantly overrepresented among our interviewees. In view of the broader questions about citizenship and political rights we are posing in this chapter, however, we do not necessarily anticipate large gender differences in respondent preferences on most topics.[14] Reflecting in part the unusual demographic profile of the felon population in Minnesota, white respondents constituted a majority (67 percent) of the interviewees, and Native Americans comprised an additional 15 percent. Our sample is probably somewhat more conservative politically than the population of U.S. felons and former felons (Manza and Uggen forthcoming; Uggen and Manza 2002): 24 percent expressed a preference for George W. Bush in the 2000 presidential election.

We began each interview by confirming that the respondent had been convicted of a felony and asking whether he or she had ever voted. When we asked about voting rights, we discovered that few respondents were aware exactly how long they would be disenfranchised, though all knew that they were not permitted to vote for some period. Some respondents had learned about disenfranchisement from probation and parole officers, Department of Corrections officials, or other convicted felons, though a few "just knew" beforehand that a criminal conviction would deprive them of the right to vote.[15] We then asked a series of open-ended questions concerning political involvement, attitudes, and awareness; partisanship, efficacy, and trust; and community involvement and reintegration. Finally, we asked whether respondents wanted to add anything that had yet to be discussed and whether they had any questions for us. Voting was a salient issue to most respondents, and they readily shared their political views.

Table 7.4   *Characteristics of Felon Interviewees*

Characteristic	Frequency	Percentage
Race		
White	22	67
Black	6	18
Native American	5	15
Sex		
Male	23	70
Female	10	30
Age		
Twenty to twenty-nine	15	45
Thirty to thirty-nine	11	33
Forty and over	7	21
Party		
Democrat	18	55
Republican	9	27
Independent	2	6
"Don't know" or unknown	4	12
Political label		
Conservative	9	27
Liberal	7	21
Moderate	2	6
Conservative or moderate liberal	3	9
"Independent"	1	3
"Everything"	1	3
"Don't know" or unknown	10	30
Correctional status		
Prison	23	70
Probation	7	21
Parole	3	9
Ever voted?		
Yes	22	67
No	11	33
Plan to vote in future?		
Yes	24	73
No	1	3
Unknown	8	24
2000 presidential choice		
Gore	16	48
Bush	8	24
Nader	3	9
No preference or unknown	6	18

Source: Authors' compilation.
Note: n = 33.

Political Participation

We found great variation in respondents' self-reported political participation before their most recent felony conviction. Of the thirty-three interviewees, twenty-two reported having voted at least once in the past,
and a few were active and enthusiastic voters before their convictions.
For example, Lynn, a thirty-eight-year-old prisoner, tried to impress the
importance of voting upon her disinterested son:

> I take [voting] very seriously.... This was the first year my son was
> able to vote, and he wasn't going to, and I literally put him in the car
> and took him to vote. I mean it was [a] "You're living in my house,
> you're going to vote" kind of thing because I can't.... I've voted every
> time I can since I've been eighteen, and I think this is the worst, one of
> the worst things about being a felon, having a felony, is not being able
> to vote.

To be sure, to admit that one has not voted is awkward; failure to
vote is perceived as a dereliction of basic citizenship duty that is reflected, for example, in the overreporting of turnout by all survey respondents (including those in the YDS). Of those who had been old
enough to vote in a previous election but volunteered that they had not,
justifications for the failure to participate were similar to those often expressed by other Americans. Henry, a twenty-five-year-old parolee who
had never been eligible to vote, felt that his one vote was unlikely to
have much impact:

> I feel that I'm not too involved. The reason I say that is 'cause I feel one
> person doesn't have enough power. It takes a group. A majority, you
> know? And I've kind of lowered my standards on how much to give
> off. I figure if I don't count for much, why get involved, you know? But
> they say one can make [a] difference sometimes. So ... you can look at
> it either way, but I look at it as I wouldn't make a difference politically.

Ironically, however, Henry also told us that when he did attempt to vote
in the 2000 presidential elections, he was denied the right to participate
because of his current parole status. Some respondents suggested that
though felon disenfranchisement was a barrier, they might not have
voted anyway. Michael, a twenty-three-year-old probationer who had
been old enough to vote since the 1996 presidential election, explained,
"I never voted. Never.... I couldn't 'cause I just caught that felony [in
1996]," before adding, "I really don't think I'd vote anyway."
Our interviews also suggested an interaction between the right to

vote and the willingness to invest in political knowledge, awareness, or interest, which might stimulate participation in the first place. A thirty-one-year-old prisoner named Susan told us that her disenfranchisement was a source of frustration that discouraged her from thinking about politics:

> I was thinking about getting involved with politics when I get out, and how I'd love to, and then I'm like, "Well, I can't vote," so it's so discouraging. I'm not gonna read this article on this candidate's views or, you know, I'm not going to research on it. But then the only thing that motivates me is that the people around me don't know I'm an ex-con and can't vote, and so I don't want them to think I'm just lame and ignorant because I can't participate in their political conversations. So that's like my only motivation, and that's not a lot of motivation because, I mean, being able to vote, my vote making a difference, would be more motivation than the rare political conversation.

Susan's position—echoed in different ways in other interviews—is a rational response to disenfranchisement. If one is categorically prevented from participating, there is little incentive to maintain an interest in an activity. Viewed in this way, it is probably surprising that our interviewees have as much political interest and engagement as they do.

In addition to the disincentives prison or a felony conviction creates for political participation, a number of incarcerated or formerly incarcerated felons also noted substantial barriers to acquiring information about the outside world while in prison. These barriers include limited contact with family and friends (and the reduced likelihood that precious time for interaction would be used to discuss political matters—as reflected in our survey evidence); restricted access to television in a communal setting where the daily news may already be a low priority for many inmates; and, of course, the inability to access political life outside prison walls. Lynn, the politically enthusiastic mother quoted earlier, described some of these problems:

> I [used to] go to city council meetings. I want to know what's going on. That's the one thing I hate about being in here. Nobody wants to watch the news. And so I . . . broke down and spent the $250 and got a TV. . . . I like to know what's going on. I'm part of this world, whether I'm in here or not. I'm not going to be here that long, I'm still going to be out in the real world. I want to know what's going on, and I want to know what's changed since I've been in here. You try to watch news in here, oh no. . . . And that really irritates me.

Despite these barriers, prison cannot be viewed simply as a roadblock to political interest and consciousness. We were struck in our conversations, paralleling the findings of Edin, Nelson, and Paranal in chapter 3 in this volume, about the degree to which time in prison encourages reflection on civic duties and responsibilities (see also Uggen, Manza, and Behrens 2004). Many of the inmates we spoke with told us that their time in prison made them more interested in political issues. Dylan, a twenty-nine-year-old who had been incarcerated continuously since the age of sixteen for a serious violent offense, described how he gradually developed an interest in politics:

> [E]arly on, when I was a teenager and I was first incarcerated, obviously, if [politics] ever came to mind, it was, "I don't care." You know? Or "It doesn't affect me," and the whole attitude of that, I suppose. But as I've matured over the years in prison, and started looking forward to all the trappings of society and what it's going to mean to be free again, . . . that was one of the considerations. . . . I start[ed] forming actual political opinions. . . . You watch these politicians on TV and say, "This guy's a scumbag. I wouldn't vote for him," or whatever. Or you see someone that actually has a good agenda. . . . I've gotten more and more interested in it over the years in talking to other guys, my age or older, that have more of a political opinion, that have been following politics longer than I have. Just get pulled into discussions there.

Several other respondents echoed Dylan's burgeoning interest in political life. Asked whether he had ever voted, Louis replied, "No, . . . but after being incarcerated and having that time to reflect on all the issues, I see how important it really can be." A thirty-eight-year-old prisoner named Alan described the change in his television viewing habits, and increased attention to political news, while in prison:

> [I]t's weird because before my crime . . . I really didn't follow the elections or anything that close. And since I've been in prison, I've been watching the way the Senate works on . . . channel 17. . . . I've been watching the political process a lot since I've been in here. . . . I'd say 200 percent more at least. You know? 'Cause before I didn't even turn on the TV. . . . I rarely watched the news or anything like that. Now I watch the city council meetings sometimes if they have them.

Like most Americans, many of our interviewees reported closely following the 2000 presidential election and its aftermath, although here it is hard to separate the entertainment value of that unique event from its substantive political meaning. We were, however, also surprised to learn from Alan that inmates in several housing units or "cottages" had organized their own mock election:

> Yeah, they were [talking about the 2000 election in here]. There was a lot of going back and forth on it [between wanting Bush or Gore to

win]. . . . [P]eople were going around doing kind of a silent mock election just to see how people would vote even in our cottage. And, you know, the winner . . . was Bush. But not by very much. It was, you know, out of seventy-four people in our cottage, I think it was pretty split down the middle. . . . I know that was happening in other cottages, but I didn't really pay attention.

Such a striking example of protodemocratic action—even when the votes do not "count" in any meaningful sense—is hard to square with models of complete disinterest and lack of concern about politics among inmates.

Views About the Right to Vote

With a few exceptions, our respondents were well aware of the restrictions on their right to vote, and they offered a variety of articulate responses to questions about the implications of this loss. Particularly striking were the connections between the right to vote and the process of reintegration back into their communities. Pamela, a forty-nine-year-old prisoner, described the loss of her right to vote as rubbing "salt in her wounds":

I think that just getting back in the community and being a contributing member is difficult enough. . . . And saying, "Yeah, we don't value your vote either because you're a convicted felon from how many years back." . . . But I, hopefully, have learned, have paid for that and would like to someday feel like a, quote, "normal citizen," a contributing member of society, and you know that's hard when every election you're constantly being reminded, "Oh yeah, that's right, I'm ashamed." . . . It's just like a little salt in the wound. You've already got that wound and it's trying to heal . . . and you're trying to be a good taxpayer and be a homeowner. . . . Just one little vote, right? But that means a lot to me. . . . [I]t's just loss after loss after loss. And this is just another one. Another to add to the pile. . . . Me being able to vote isn't going to just whip up and heal that wound. . . . I am looking forward to and trying to prepare to be that productive member of society that I've always wanted to be. . . . I have this wound and it's healing. . . . But it's like it's still open enough so that you telling me that I'm still really bad because I can't [vote] is like making it sting again. . . . It's like haven't I paid enough yet?

For others, the restoration of voting rights serves as a powerful symbol signifying the recovery of manifold privileges of citizenship. In the words of Karen, a thirty-nine-year-old prisoner,

I voted every single solitary year from the day I was granted voting privileges when I was eighteen until I was convicted. . . . For me it's important because I like to know that when I leave here, I will start—I will continue my life because I won't start it over—although there's a whole new part of me coming out of here—I will continue my life, and I would like to have that position back. To be able to vote.

Finally, a number of respondents noted that losing the right to vote marks them as noncitizens, as people without voices. This noncitizenship status has definite local community repercussions, as highlighted in the following comment. Voting does not simply decide national leaders; through referendums and other ballot measures, voting can impact local schools, property tax proposals, resource allocation, and the like. Consistent with our survey results showing diminished political efficacy among arrestees and inmates, Paul, a thirty-seven-year-old prisoner, commented,

I have no right to vote on the school referendums that will affect my children. I have no right to vote on how my taxes is going to be spent or used, which I have to pay whether I'm a felon or not, you know? So basically I've lost all voice or control over my government. . . . [I]n this system, once you're a felon you're punished for life. And you don't have a voice. . . . People don't want to recognize that we can still be citizens and still be patriotic, even though we made a mistake. And that's a hard pill to swallow. . . . I can't say anything because I don't have a voice. Or 'cause I can't vote about it. . . . I'm not saying give back gun rights or anything like that to people that definitely don't deserve them. But giving back voting rights is another way to make a person feel part of that community. How can you feel that you're giving back to a community that you're a part of when you're exiled from it by not being able to vote and have a voice in it?

One thing that was particularly startling to us—and is reflected in Paul's comments—was that many of our respondents assumed that they were disenfranchised for ten years or more (with several assuming they had lost the right to vote for life). In fact, Minnesota law permits all former felons to vote once they are "off paper," having completed incarceration and any probation or parole supervision. Although we lack systematic data on this question, it is entirely possible that such misperceptions about voting rights, combined with hesitancy to inquire about eligibility for fear of being denied, may extend the impact of voting restrictions far beyond a formal period of legal disenfranchisement.

Views about Government and Public Policy

Our survey findings that arrestees and inmates—in comparison with nonoffenders—lack confidence in government and believe the political system is corrupt were reflected in many of our conversations. As we probed deeper into these sentiments, however, we also heard some more nuanced explanations of these views. We asked our respondents to define in their own words what "politics" means to them, and we were told many times that "politics" is about politicians who are corrupt or greedy. For example, Thomas, a twenty-three-year-old parolee, told us that for him, politics is

> [c]rap. Or, as in my man, he says, "Who wants to be a millionaire?" 'Cause in politics everyone wants the prize.... I know a lot of things cost money.... Just to make that next dollar. So I'm going to politics, Congress, it's money, yeah. Nobody goes to Congress, or into politics just to go "Okay, I'm gonna make a lot of laws." No, it's too much money. It's too much money.

Such blanket dismissals leave little room for a positive appreciation of government as a potentially valuable social institution. But other interviewees, while endorsing a similar view of corruption, articulated substantive reasons why the political system falls short of an ideal democracy. Consider the views of a twenty-eight-year-old prisoner named Nathan:

> To me a politician's nothing but a crook.... They're making laws, but I never thought it would never affect me.... "Go make your laws." Because I believe the government's all wrong. We've gotten so much with politicians and with the governor, but yet they don't hear what the people have to say. I mean I thought we were based on the Constitution and "we the people" have the say over what the government has to say. I thought ... they're the ones who are supposed to look up to us and say, "What do you want us to do? We're working for you. What do you want us to do?" ... It's like, "well, if they're working for us, why aren't they in my community asking what we want?"

Nathan's broad characterization of politicians as "crooks" is combined in this context with a real and substantive conception of what a noncorrupt democratic politician would do: go to the community and "ask what we want," and then act as an honest delegate. Such a vision of democracy, in which politicians act as brokers of majoritarian opinion, is a view embraced by some sophisticated models of democratic representation.[16]

For those whose primary contact with the state occurs through the criminal justice system, levels of trust and confidence in the government are undoubtedly shaped by that engagement. Scott, a twenty-six-year-old probationer, described how his experiences with the police had eroded his overall level of trust in government:

Well, who can you trust anyway? . . . I think a lot of it's superficial. . . .
I grew up where the police, you know, the police beat up people. And
that didn't happen in every instance, you know, but you learn to not
have trust. . . . I don't think I have a say about what the government
does. They look good for awhile, then they get elected and you hear all
kind of junk. [The police,] that's the immediate government right there.

Mary, a forty-year-old prisoner who believes she was wrongly convicted, detailed how her views of government had changed as a result
of her experience with the criminal justice system:

Five years ago I was sitting on the streets, . . . doing my own thing and
. . . [being] a law-abiding citizen, and I didn't have these problems, I
didn't have these concerns, I didn't even think about things like that,
. . . you know? I thought, . . . "Geez, believe in the judicial system. Believe in the politics of the system because they're what's going to support you." That's a mistake.

Disgust with politics was sometimes accompanied by a preference
for local government over the state or federal governments. Consider the
views of two respondents. The first is that of Karen, a thirty-nine-year-
old inmate:

[S]ince . . . I've been incarcerated, . . . not as strongly would I focus on
national politics, as I have always been far more concerned about the
politics right here and now. You know, more grassroots. How it affects—I don't want to say small-town community, because I think that
small-town communities, farming communities, all those types of
things . . . have a lot of power, but I think more things like the sheriff
being elected, appellate court judges, supreme court judges, legislators,
you know. . . . [M]aybe because it was just closer to home for me. . . .
[I'm] closer to [being a] Democrat, and I think, a good chunk of that is
the born-and-raised, Iron Range union person inside of me.[17]

Andrew, a twenty-nine-year-old probationer, expressed a similar preference: "I think it's easier to trust the local government, which is why my
beliefs are as they are. National government, I just think there's so much
money involved that corruption might be a little more likely. Not saying
that it's, you know, ruined society. I'm not that big of a naysayer, but I
just think accountability is a little easier locally. I think we can trust our
local governments more."

Preferences for local government—and for the possibility of greater
citizen control—are quite common in American society. In the comments
of Karen and Andrew, we see two distinct and serious theories of why
localism might be preferred. For Karen, a more viable democracy with

higher levels of citizen activism is more likely at the local level. For Andrew, local governments are more trustworthy and accountable.

In explaining their political views, most interviewees stressed specific policy concerns rather than making generalizations about politics, parties, candidates, or voting. For example, Sally commented,

> Here amongst us, we don't do a lot of talking about like politics type stuff. We just . . . don't really do it that often. We talk more about specific issues that have to do with politics, but we don't sit and talk about "Are you a Republican, are you a Democrat, who would you vote for?" We talk about specific issues, you know? . . . We talk about same-sex marriages or raising children. You know, like . . . the rights of same-sex couples, stuff like that. Well, I've mentioned the welfare stuff. Sex offenders. You know, the laws with the sex offenders. . . . Those are mainly the three issues that we talk about that have a lot to do with the government, the political stuff.

Specific policy areas of concern came up frequently in our interviews. Among the most common concerns were new time limits on receipt of public assistance (especially salient among female inmates), education, health care, and more generally, inequality in American society.

Not surprisingly, given their direct connection to the criminal justice system, numerous interviewees expressed strong and articulate views about criminal justice, although many of these views did not tend toward leniency for their fellow inmates. Peter, a young probationer, explained his opposition to George W. Bush as follows: "I heard he's supposed to hire more police officers and all that, and I think Bush would have been looking out more for the rich and less for the poor." Others discussed specific laws. Minnesota applies restrictive civil commitment laws to certain sex offenders, under which "sexually dangerous persons" may face an indefinite and involuntary period of confinement beyond any court-imposed criminal sentence (Minn. §253B.02 Subd. 18b–c). The anomalies of these laws occasioned comment from several of our interviewees who were serving time as sex offenders. Alan, for example, noted, "When I get committed [as a sexually dangerous person under the civil commitment law], one of my projects is to try and overturn the Sexually Dangerous Predator law because right now it's so broad. The legislature has worded it so broad that you could have five parking tickets and be committed."

Alan also made clear, however, that he supported laws against child pornography and had begun active lobbying: "One of things I'm doing is calling . . . [a state legislator who is] . . . trying to get a child pornography law through. . . . I've been calling there a couple times a week, going, 'Yeah, I still support it. Keep pushing.'" Others drew similar distinctions, critiquing the apparent irrationality of particular laws and policies (including disenfranchisement) and advocating their replacement with more reasoned—though not necessarily more lenient—approaches.

Political and Partisan Preferences

Some of our interviewees expressed clear political and partisan identities. We asked each about the hotly contested 2000 presidential election and, of those who indicated a preferred candidate, why they supported that candidate. Among Al Gore supporters, a number of respondents invoked class- or race-based themes similar to those Gore emphasized during the campaign. For example, Sally, a thirty-year-old prisoner, told us that in her opinion, George W. Bush "just doesn't care about lower-class people. . . . [He seems to be] more about people who have money. I just don't see that—I see that there's more middle- and lower-class people than there is, you know, upper class. . . . [Gore] seems like a . . . more caring person. Like he cares about the people."

For Sally, as for many of our interviewees, Bush's upper-class origins contrasted sharply with a view of Gore as "for the average person." Steven, a fifty-two-year-old probationer, invoked similar themes in describing his support for Gore: "Gore's more for the people and the average person, and Bush, he's more for the rich. And I have nothing against rich people if they make it fair and square, but there's a lot of things that are going on that ain't right. But I got nothing against rich people otherwise, but you gotta, you know, you gotta care about people . . . even if they're not rich." Similarly, Marvin, a twenty-four-year-old prisoner, noted that he supported Gore "because Gore seems like a person that's there for the people."

We also found a healthy sampling of support for George W. Bush. As with Gore, the themes endorsed by Bush supporters often paralleled those invoked by Bush on the campaign trail. James, a twenty-four-year-old prisoner, said, "Since this incarceration I'm kind of anticriminal. And he did some good stuff in Texas." Daniel, a thirty-one-year-old prisoner, endorsed Bush's positions on gun control and education: "Well, I liked a lot of what Gore had to say, but his politics on guns kind of turned me off that. So I was more [for] Bush . . . if he does anything about what he said. Education, . . . 'cause some areas do get more money allocated to them than poor areas. I kind of like his voucher system."

In talking about politics and elections, we also heard many references to what is sometimes called "candidate-centered politics," which some believe has become increasingly common in contemporary American political life (Wattenberg 1991). For example, Pamela, a forty-nine-year-old prisoner, told us that "character" was important in shaping her views of Bush as a candidate. Asked whether she would have voted in the last presidential election, had she had the legal right to do so, Pamela replied that yes, she would have voted for Bush.

> Mainly because . . . [of] his opinion on abortion. I found him much more real as a person. It's a character thing. I just felt like he had so much more character, and he was much more consistent. He wasn't like a chameleon like changing. . . . I just felt that Bush was more honest, and . . . I liked his wife. . . . I think he has an honor for our original amendments and everything, you know, that I haven't seen in anyone for a while. I didn't see it in Clinton. Just that . . . kind of a reverence. Or an honor looking at how our forefathers really set up the country, 'cause it was all about God. It was all about God. And it just got neutralized, neutralized, neutralized as the time went on.

When it comes to ideological labels, however, most of our respondents were less engaged, and it is important to try to understand why such labels appear less salient to them. Only about half of our respondents identified themselves as either liberal or conservative, and in many cases these broad labels were given meaning in personal rather than political terms. For example, for many respondents the term "conservative" connoted maturity, sophistication, or an aversion to risk rather than the economic and social approaches of the Republican Party or the preservation of existing political institutions. Thomas, a twenty-three-year-old parolee, thinks of himself as "[c]onservative, definitely. . . . Because I look at myself as a more mannerable and very conscious man. I wouldn't become more disrespectful, I would just become more persistent. I wouldn't become mad. . . . Can't nobody make me mad but myself. I become angry of mistakes I've made and try again to be a more conservative-type person." Dennis, a thirty-seven-year-old prisoner, said, "I'd probably put myself as a conservative 'cause I'm a very casual, respectable-type person. When I'm out there in the real world, and freedom, I—Suits—[I] gotta look good. Very respectable looking. You know, very respectful towards other people and carrying myself very proper. It's a little different in here. . . . But otherwise, I'm a very casual, respectable kind of person."

Steven, a fifty-two-year-old probationer, had been

> a liberal Democrat most of my life, but due to my problems I have to be conservative 'cause I can't cope with my problems and be liberal. I'll admit, like when I got drunk and became . . . sexually prone, you know? It was like the alcohol and the sex were one and the same. . . . Yeah, I grew up in a liberal environment. . . . And I grew up, you know, I grew up in the sixties when a lot of changes in this country happened. . . . And that, now, that actually hurt me because even though alcohol af-

fected me so severely, I was liberal, you know, and I didn't, I wasn't proud of not drinking. I was, "If I want to go out and get drunk with the guys, well, so what? I'm gonna go out and get drunk with the guys." But . . . now I . . . have to be conservative 'cause . . . [w]ith my medications and stuff, and my mental problems, . . . without being conservative, I'll be in trouble.

By contrast, party labels held greater meaning for most respondents, as a negative heuristic if nothing else. Eighteen of the thirty-three interviewees identified with the Democratic Party, most doing so in class or race terms. The following comments from two respondents about the reasons for identifying with the Democrats present typical class-based perceptions about the parties. Peter, a twenty-four-year-old probationer, expressed a preference for the Democrats "because I feel they look out more for the poor. And Republicans, you know, they gonna look out more for the rich, and less for the poor really. That's how I see it." Mary, a forty-year-old prisoner, said, "I feel that the little people is what needs the help. Not the big businesses and the big people, you know? And that's what the Republicans represent, you know, I feel essentially. You know the rich get richer and the poor get poorer, and there's really no in between."

Race emerged as a clear factor in Democratic Party identity for a number of African American respondents, with some suggesting that disenfranchisement laws are intended to dilute the voting strength of racial minorities. Michael, a twenty-three-year-old African American probationer, characterized the different social bases of the two parties (and his reasons for supporting the Democrats) in the following terms:

It seems like the Republicans don't really be for the minorities, they're like for the majority. And the Democrats seem like they . . . [are] more minority based, trying to help . . . better the community, our community. . . . I think the Republicans [are] more based in the middle-class area. . . . They try to do for them. But the Democrats, you know, try to help out with child care. . . . They really don't want people on welfare, you know, they try to help you get off welfare and get a stable job. Whereas, the Republicans, they just, they just want you to be based how you already is, you know. . . . That's . . . my view, that's my opinion, I really don't know too much about politics, but from what I be seeing . . . Democrats can more help, you know, my people out more."

Other respondents cited a family history of support for one of the major parties as helping to crystallize their own partisanship. Lynn, a thirty-eight-year-old prisoner, told us,

I vote Democratic. I'm not ashamed to say it. I'm a Democrat. . . . The thing is, from what I've gathered through the years and what I guess I grew up with—my parents were, are, both Democratic— . . . it always seems that the Democrats fight a little harder for the middle class, the underdogs. . . . The education issue. . . . Welfare . . . I've used the system, but only when I've needed to, so I think the five years and off is great, and it's not just a kick-you-off program. They go out of their way to try and help you get jobs, to make you self-sufficient. . . . Basically, any issue that is on the Democratic side, I'm pretty much, pretty much with.

A perception that the Republicans are less receptive to the needs and interests of low-income urban communities provided some interviewees with another basis for identification with the Democratic Party. A twenty-three-year-old former gang member named Thomas, recently out on parole, described his experiences with big-city party politics:

I look at myself more as a Democrat. . . . Where I come from, Chicago, we did a lot of talking. We did a lot of, you know, men organizations, that I was in organizations, you know what I'm saying? A lot of people would say gang, but I call it organization. We did a lot of . . . community work. . . . In Chicago, they came, and you know, there's a lot of Democrats. . . . Democrats gonna speak out more. The Republicans gonna, in my eyes, . . . be like a snake, a serpent. You know, reach out for the weak. And they're gonna use you, twist you, spit you out, whatever. They don't need them, throw them away. That's why so many people are in prison now, you know? Anything to send a person to prison. . . . There was one guy . . . he was a part of the organization once before, and he . . . kind of turned his life around. . . . [H]e came and talked to us . . . and we wasn't feelin' it at first. . . . But he said, "Well, listen to me. They're having an election downstairs." . . . They said, "You have a chance to . . . do some type [of] justice because you're probably gonna get this chance again. You know, "Just do the time, just do . . . the time with Million Man March" . . . and things like that. And they were grassroots. And the Republicans, they was like, you know, "Why are they marching?"

Those who identified with the Republicans (a quarter of the respondents) frequently linked a preference for limited government to Republican partisanship. In the words of Larry, a thirty-year-old prisoner,

I like the idea that Republicans are more in favor of the smaller government, and they're not so interested in the push towards socialism that our country seems to be heading for right now. You know, like socialized medicine and . . . trying to take control of everything. . . . [Money is] one thing that would make me lean toward the Republican viewpoint. . . . [T]hey think that, you know, the government shouldn't have so much money and, you know, shouldn't be as big as it is and have so much power and authority, which all really comes from money, I guess. But they think it should be more of the people.

We also spoke with a number of respondents who characterized themselves as political "independents." Many of these people expressed a basic distrust of both major parties or disaffection from political life more generally. Their views were often accompanied by a pragmatic nonpartisan approach to politics, although in practice these two meanings of political independence overlapped.[18] Roger, a fifty-four-year-old probationer, characterized his political independence in candidate-centered terms:

> I consider myself to be an independent voter. . . . I let the man dictate how I vote and not the party. I would have voted for Jesse Ventura had I been able to vote. 'Cause he made the most sense. . . . [In the past] . . . I supported Jimmy Carter. I supported Ronald Reagan. Especially John Kennedy. Because he was a mover and a shaker. And I tend to probably vote more so that way. Towards the movers and the shakers. Because it just makes a lot more sense. Yeah, [I put Ventura in that camp]. I don't care for some of his antics. But I do care for the way he carries on the office as governor. And I guess if you have to put up with one thing, you know, the antics I'll put up with because you see him doing some stuff that is, so to speak, against the political machinery. . . . [M]yself, I'm middle income, and I would say that . . . basically, we've been the class of people that have been where everything falls onto. And because of that, you know, that's where I would see the need for change. You've got the Democrats, of course, for the working person, you've got the Republicans, so to speak, for the upper class, and, you know, in the midst of that, the middle class gets trampled.

By contrast, Craig, a twenty-two-year-old prisoner, said he supported independents because in their nonpartisanship they cut "against the grain" of conventional politics: "I do like some of . . . the independents and . . . the alternatives just because it's just that. It's not so polarized. So I do tend to side when it will come to voting with Independent or somebody that at least sounded like they were against the grain and not just the same old talk. Somebody that sounded genuine and didn't sound like maybe a career politician." For both Roger and Craig, political independence allows them to choose, rather than be forced out of habit or convention, whether to support major-party candidates (Rose and McAllister 1986).

Learning from the Interviews

In contrast to images of offenders as an ill-informed, apathetic group with low citizenship norms, sophisticated underlying political views and concerns emerged in our in-depth interviews, only a sample of which we have reported here. As Louis, a thirty-seven-year-old prisoner, argued,

For me not to participate in all the inevitable rights that are given unto me is to just give 'em away. You know, that's foolish. . . . These things that are given to me make me a part of society. And if I continue to run from them, I'm just furthering myself away from society. So by participating in those little things that we don't think about—Because maybe one day they may just say, "If you . . . ain't had a perfect life and your income is such here you can't vote." . . . I don't know where that's gonna go, but before I allow all that to get out of hand, I need to let my voice be heard. Whether it be publicly or on paper as a vote.

As Edin, Nelson, and Paranal point out (chapter 3 in this volume), qualitative data both address some of the limitations of survey research and raise important new themes that had not previously been apparent to researchers. Our interviews sensitized us to a number of issues that we had not considered in planning and executing our survey and macro-level analysis of voting behavior (Uggen and Manza 2002; Manza and Uggen forthcoming). Most important, we have gained a sense of the sa-lience of disenfranchisement to felons who may have more pressing se-curity and survival needs. The denial of voting rights is perceived as "another loss to add to the pile" of things, such as their decreased em-ployability (documented by Harry Holzer, Steven Raphael, and Michael Stoll in chapter 8 in this volume) and the damaged ties with parental partners and children (as illustrated in part I of this volume)—all of which are piled atop confinement itself. Within this array of punish-ments, disenfranchisement carries a powerful sting for those citizens convicted of crimes.

In addition, we learned that convicted felons do not speak with one voice. We were struck by the diversity of political views and concerns expressed by offenders, even within a single institution. Although disen-franchisement laws generally treat "felons" as a homogeneous mass, those affected by such laws make important distinctions by offense type and other status markers. This led some respondents to advocate for more narrowly tailored restrictions on their political behavior, asking what their particular crime had to do with voting and why disenfranchisement was imposed as a collateral consequence of their sentence.

Our interviews suggest that, in crafting subsequent surveys on the basis of these results, researchers should devote greater attention to the broader political impacts of felony convictions. One respondent noted, for example, that although he would like to participate in "peaceful dem-onstrations" upon release from prison, he was reluctant to do so because an arrest at such an event could result in his return to the penitentiary. Several interviewees also commented on the influence of their felon sta-tus on political conversations with nonfelons and their level of attentive-ness to political and civic affairs. We also learned that the connotations of labels such as "liberal" and "conservative" among convicted felons are far different from those among the general population. In a correctional setting, it is vitally important to present oneself as "conservative" in manner and dress, regardless of one's political beliefs.

Finally, the interviews also illustrate that social divisions along race, class, and gender lines remain important for understanding the political attitudes and behaviors of convicted felons. In particular, our African American interviewees generally expressed much greater distrust of the criminal justice system and of government more generally; several argued that disenfranchisement laws intentionally curb African American political power (see also Behrens, Uggen, and Manza 2003). Although few of our respondents would be considered middle class by conventional criteria, our discussions showed substantial variation in the sort of class-based themes invoked in expressing preferences for particular political parties and candidates. Although we are reluctant to generalize from the small number of female inmates we interviewed, these women expressed much greater concern for issues such as welfare reform, education, and health care than did the male interviewees. Despite important differences in the orientations and social positions of our interviewees, however, it is important to reiterate that a disproportionate number of the lost political voices in the United States are those of young men of color. Criminal punishment and disenfranchisement directly dilute the political power of African Americans, males, and poor and working-class U.S. citizens and, by extension, the communities to which they return.

CONCLUSION

Although some measure of criminal punishment surely benefits families and communities by increasing safety and stability, it is clear that felon disenfranchisement has become a growing impediment to the political participation of an expanding group of U.S. citizens. With more than 2 percent of the electorate now disenfranchised owing to past or current felony convictions (approximately three-fourths of whom are living in the community, and some 35 percent of whom have completed their sentence entirely), there are good reasons to be concerned that rising rates of criminal punishment affect communities by influencing political outcomes in a highly competitive, two-party system.

Several points from the results of our investigation are especially striking. First, to a certain extent, felons are distinct from the rest of the population in their political tastes, preferences, and dispositions. They have below-average levels of political interest and political participation. They are significantly more Democratic and more likely than the rest of the electorate to express independent political partisanship. Not surprisingly, the YDS results suggest that offenders are also far less trusting of government and the criminal justice system than are nonoffenders.

Second, we think these results confirm that offenders, though they may be more alienated from mainstream politics than the rest of the population, have valuable political views and interests to contribute. Something is lost, as a consequence, when they are written out of the political system by criminal punishment and disenfranchisement. Of course, low rates of political participation are endemic in the United States as a whole, and indeed a majority of felons (like a majority of Americans in general), given the opportunity to vote, would not do so in most elections. The difference between convicted felons and other citizens who do not vote, however, is profound: felons have no choice in the matter. Although many Americans do not exercise their right to vote, the right itself is fundamental to citizenship, and few nonvoters would willingly opt for an authoritarian system of government.

While the reduction of these voices at the margins may appear politically insignificant, we think that is not likely to be the case. Our macro-level investigations suggest that several Senate races since 1978, and two presidential elections in the past forty years, have been influenced by felon disenfranchisement (Uggen and Manza 2002). It is likely that election outcomes beneath the state level are also influenced by felon disenfranchisement, although we currently lack the fine-grained data needed for such investigations.

Finally, there is also some evidence that felon disenfranchisement has an impact at the legislative-district level that may magnify these effects (albeit in ways that are hard to measure). Felons are drawn disproportionately from low-income urban areas (see, for example, Rose and Clear 1998); removing them from the electorate reduces the weight of the votes from those areas, quelling not only felon voices but also those of other poor people. Moreover, because the U.S. Census counts prisoners as living wherever their prison is located, the placement of prisons in more conservative rural areas further diminishes urban representation (Beale 1996; Peter T. Kilborn, "Rural Towns Turn to Prisons to Reignite Their Economies," *New York Times*, August 1, 2001, p. A1).

POSTSCRIPT

When we began work on this project a few years ago, there was virtually no public discussion of the issue of felon disenfranchisement and the implications for the reintegration of felons back into society. Much has changed since that time. Disenfranchisement of former felons in states that impose lifetime bans has been the subject of considerable discussion and policy activity. Democrats in the House of Representatives have

Table 7.5   *Changes in State Disenfranchisement Laws Since 1980*

Year	State	Expanded Voting Rights	Restricted Voting Rights
1981	South Carolina	Automatic restoration upon completion of sentence	
1983	Georgia	Automatic restoration upon completion of sentence	Disenfranchised felons convicted in any state
	Texas	Automatic restoration two years after completion of sentence	
1993	Colorado		Disenfranchised parolees
	Nebraska		Disenfranchised for non-pardoned out-of-state convictions
1995	Pennsylvania		Five-year post-prison voting ban
1997	Colorado		Disenfranchised felons convicted in federal court
	Texas	Automatic restoration upon completion of sentence	
1998	New Hampshire	Inmates received voting rights through court decision	
	Utah		Disenfranchised inmates
1999	Oregon		Disenfranchised federal inmates
2000	Delaware	Voting rights restored five years after completion of sentence	
	Massachusetts	Disenfranchised inmates	
	New Hampshire		Court redisenfranchised prison inmates
	Pennsylvania	Five-year post-prison waiting period eliminated	

Table 7.5   *Continued*

Year	State	Expanded Voting Rights	Restricted Voting Rights
2001	New Mexico	Automatic restoration upon completion of sentence	
2002	Connecticut	Expanded franchise to probationers	
	Kansas		Disenfranchised probationers
2003	Maryland	Automatic restoration three years after completion of sentence (recidivists only)	
	New Mexico	Automatic restoration for first-time, non-violent offenders upon completion of sentence	

Source: Authors' compilation.

sponsored legislation that would prevent the states from maintaining voting bans on former felons; on February 14, 2002, the Senate defeated an amendment to electoral reform legislation sponsored by Harry Reid (D-Nev.), on a 63–31 vote. The bill gained the striking support of at least one Republican, former prosecutor Arlen Spector of Pennsylvania, who commented that "this provision would aid ex-convicts in being reintegrated into society and would be a fair provision on the basic proposition that these people have fully paid their debt to society" (U.S. Congress 2002, S804).

In addition to federal action, efforts have been mounted in many states to eliminate voting restrictions on former felons, parolees, probationers, and even incarcerated felons. In the past few years New Mexico eliminated its former-felon ban, Texas eliminated its two-year waiting period for former felons, Maryland narrowed its ban to include only violent recidivists, and Connecticut restored the voting rights of felony probationers. On the other hand, we should note that there is not a one-sided movement toward liberalization; states such as Massachusetts and Utah have added new restrictions on felon voting rights (see table 7.5). Over the past two decades, an approximately equal number of states have liberalized and restricted their disenfranchisement provisions (see

Behrens, Uggen, and Manza 2003; Manza and Uggen forthcoming). The debate over these questions is likely to intensify in the near future, as this and other collateral consequences of large-scale incarceration are subjected to greater scrutiny.

Earlier versions of this paper were presented at the 2001 annual meetings of the American Sociological Association in Washington, D.C., and at the University of Wisconsin, the University of Washington, and the Institute for Policy Research at Northwestern University. Our research was supported by grants from the National Science Foundation (grant 9819015) and the Individual Project Fellowship Program of the Open Society Institute. We thank the editors of this volume as well as Clem Brooks, John Hagan, Marc Mauer, Jeylan Mortimer, Katherine Pettus, and Sara Wakefield for helpful suggestions or materials and Melissa Thompson, Angie Behrens, and Kendra Schiffman for research assistance.

NOTES

1. The only states that allow currently incarcerated felons to vote are Vermont and Maine, although even in these states those convicted of treason, bribery, or election offenses may be permanently disenfranchised (Olivares, Burton, and Cullen 1997; U.S. Department of Justice 1996). As of May 2002, ten states (Alabama, Florida, Iowa, Kentucky, Mississippi, Nevada, Tennessee [for those convicted before 1986], Virginia, Washington [for those convicted before 1984], and Wyoming) permanently deny convicted felons the right to vote (unless reinstated by a pardon or executive clemency procedure). Additionally, Arizona and Maryland permanently disenfranchise recidivists (those with two or more felony convictions), and Delaware requires a five-year waiting period (effective June 2000). As of January 2003, Maryland restored voting rights to recidivists upon completion of sentence, unless convicted of more than one violent offense.
2. According to our estimates, 1.8 million of the 4.7 million disenfranchised felons and former felons are African American; in a number of states, the disenfranchisement rate of black men exceeds 30 percent (see Uggen and Manza 2002; Uggen, Manza, and Thompson 2000).
3. Among the countries restricting the voting rights of some categories of prisoners are Austria, Belgium, France, Germany, Italy, and Norway. In Austria and Belgium, length of sentence is the determining factor in the loss of voting rights (more than one year in Austria, more than four months in Belgium). In France and Germany, judges can restrict voting rights as an additional sanction (for the details of the German case, see Demleitner 2000). In Italy and Norway, some specific offenses trigger the loss of voting rights. Only eight European countries, most of them in the former Soviet bloc, impose complete bans on all incarcerated offenders (the only non–

Eastern European case is the United Kingdom). Some countries make direct provisions to enable incarcerated individuals to vote. For example, Australia provides a mobile polling staff to visit prisons to facilitate inmate voting (Australian Electoral Commission 2001). We thank Joe Levinson, at the Prison Reform Trust, and Femke van der Meulen, at the International Centre for Prison Studies, both in London, for making the results of their international survey of felon voting rights in Europe available to us. See also Allard and Mauer (1999); Fellner and Mauer (1998); and Ewald (2003).

4. The sole exception is France, where the loss of civil rights (including the right to vote) can be applied to noninmates (who are, however, still serving at least part of their sentence) as long as the civil penalty remains in force. Outside the Organization for Economic Cooperation and Development countries, Alec Ewald (2003) finds that at least one country (Mali) denies voting rights to some former offenders after completion of the sentence.

5. For details, see Uggen and Manza (2002). At year-end 2000, we estimate that there were 57,708 legally disenfranchised jail inmates, but more than 600,000 were "practically" disenfranchised (lacking access to a polling place) on election day (U.S. Department of Justice 2001).

6. If not for disenfranchisement, control of the U.S. Senate may have shifted from Republican to Democratic control during the Clinton presidency in the 1990s. Perhaps not surprisingly, we also found that the 2000 presidential election would have been reversed, if former felons in a single state (Florida) had had the right to vote. Our analysis focused only on the most significant state-level elections; it is quite likely that the effects of these lost votes would have been decisive in lower-level elections as well, but in the absence of sufficiently disaggregated data it is difficult to make those calculations.

7. There are a number of appropriate cautions about the results presented in this chapter. First, our survey and interview data are drawn entirely from the state of Minnesota. This state is unique in having one of the lowest incarceration rates in the United States (U.S. Department of Justice 2001). It has a relatively low proportion of African Americans both in the state and in the criminal justice system (although, as in other states, African Americans are significantly overrepresented). Minnesota also had an unusual political context at the time these data were collected, as the state's governor was political Independent Jesse Ventura, who changed the tenor of political discussion through his upstart 1998 gubernatorial campaign and resulting term as governor (and, indeed, he proved popular among offenders). It is conceivable that Ventura both reinforced antigovernment sentiment and heightened general awareness of conventional political institutions among offenders.

8. For comparative evidence on cross-national voting trends, see Norris (2002, chapter 3). In recent presidential elections, turnout rates of the entire voting-age population have been around 50 percent (50.1 percent in 1988, 49.8 percent in 1996, 51.1 percent in 2000), with the 55 percent turnout in 1992 (the year of the first H. Ross Perot campaign) as an outlier. Turnout rates in nonpresidential midterm elections, analogous to parliamentary elections in European countries without a presidential system, have been in the mid–30 percent range.

9. As in other longitudinal surveys, race and family income are associated

with sample attrition in the YDS. In supplementary analysis, however, we found no evidence that estimates reported here are biased by sample selectivity or attrition. More complete information about the YDS can be found in Mortimer (2003) and Uggen and Janikula (1999).

10. Lack of space precludes a detailed discussion of that comparison here. See Manza and Uggen (forthcoming, chapter 4) for more information.

11. We found that when the independent variables in our multivariate models were set to their mean values, the predicted probability of having voted in 1996 was about .63 for arrestees and .69 for nonarrestees. It is likely that at least part of the remaining turnout gap is a function of the legal disenfranchisement of arrestees still under correctional supervision. In Minnesota, those convicted of felonies may not vote until they are "off paper," having completed probation or parole supervision in addition to any prison sentence. Unfortunately, we cannot determine from these data whether individual arrestees were legally eligible to vote at the time of the election.

12. Prison respondents were recruited by including an invitation to participate in "a study about voting and politics" in the daily announcements at each facility. Prisoners then sent a response to a staff contact person to schedule interviews. Probation and parole participants were recruited by office staff who mentioned the study at the conclusion of their daily interviews and through an invitation (again inviting participation in "a study about voting and politics") posted outside the door to the interview room. Probationers and parolees were paid $10 upon completion of the interview. Unfortunately, prisoners could not be similarly compensated; staff suggested that such payments were likely to create a surplus of respondents that would introduce potential inequities among volunteers not selected to participate. Moreover, we also encountered logistical difficulties in setting up a payment transfer system to credit inmates' institutional accounts. For these reasons, we suspect that the inmate volunteers were likely to have a higher degree of political interest and experience than nonvolunteers but that the probation and parole volunteers were perhaps more representative of the daily clientele visiting the large, urban, community corrections office.

13. Use of in-depth interviews to explore political attitudes in ways not well captured in conventional survey research has a long history; see especially the classical work of Robert Lane (1962) and, more recently, the work of William Gamson (1992). For a historically informed critique of survey research as a measure of public opinion, see Herbst (1993) and Lee (2002, chapter 3).

14. To be sure, clear evidence of a growing political gender gap in the United States (Manza and Brooks 1999, chapter 5) means that there are some important policy and partisan differences between men and women.

15. Participants were also asked about other rights they may have lost, prompting most to discuss the right to "bear arms" or own a gun. While this was inconsequential to many of the felons we interviewed, others were passionate about gun rights.

16. Another inmate, Diana, complained in a similar manner about the lack of openness in the political system as undermining her trust in government: "I think the government should open up and feel what the people need.

Some countries don't have any say in the matter at all. But United States, we're supposed to be more open and [have] more freedom, and [be] more proud, we should be able to open up more, and expand more. You know there's a lot out there that the government's not taking care of, and people aren't able to voice their opinion."

17. The Iron Range is a Minnesota mining region with a reputation for prolabor politics.

18. In response to specific questions about party affiliations, those who classified themselves as "independents" often mentioned independent political parties, whereas those who were unfamiliar with political parties responded with "I don't know." Many respondents referred to themselves as independent thinkers but still indicated a preference for either the Republican or (more typically) the Democratic Party.

REFERENCES

Abbott, Jack Henry. 1981. *In the Belly of the Beast: Letters from Prison.* New York: Vintage.

Allard, Patricia, and Marc Mauer. 1999. *Regaining the Vote: An Assessment of Activity Relating to Felon Disenfranchisement Laws.* Washington, D.C.: The Sentencing Project.

Almond, Gabriel, and Sidney Verba. 1963. *The Civic Culture.* Boston: Little, Brown.

Australian Electoral Commission. 2001. *Frequently Asked Questions: Voting.* Canberra: Commonwealth of Australia.

Beale, Calvin L. 1996. "Rural Prisons: An Update." *Rural Development Perspectives* 11(2, February): 25–27.

Behrens, Angela, Christopher Uggen, and Jeff Manza. 2003. "Ballot Manipulation and the 'Menace of Negro Domination': Racial Threat and Felon Disenfranchisement in the United States, 1850–2002." *American Journal of Sociology* 109(3, November): 559–605.

Bernstein, Robert, Anita Chadha, and Robert Montjoy. 2001. "Overreporting Voting: Why It Happens and Why It Matters." *Public Opinion Quarterly* 65(1, Spring): 22–44.

Brody, Stuart A. 1974. "The Political Prisoner Syndrome: Latest Problem of the American Penal System." *Crime and Delinquency* 20(2, April): 97–106.

Brooks, Clem, and Simon Cheng. 2001. "Declining Government Confidence and Policy Preferences in the U.S.: Devolution, Regime Effects, or Symbolic Change?" *Social Forces* 79(4, June): 1343–75.

Burdman, Milton. 1974. "Ethnic Self-Help Groups in Prison and on Parole." *Crime and Delinquency* 20(2, April): 107–18.

Campbell, Angus, Philip E. Converse, Warren E. Miller, and Donald E. Stokes. 1960. *The American Voter.* New York: John Wiley.

Converse, Philip E. 1964. "The Nature of Belief Systems in Mass Publics." In *Ideology and Discontent,* edited by David Apter. New York: Free Press.

Delli Carpini, Michael X., and Scott Keeter. 1996. *What Americans Know About Politics and Why It Matters.* New Haven, Conn.: Yale University Press.

Demleitner, Nora V. 2000. "Continuing Payment on One's Debt to Society: The German Model of Felon Disenfranchisement as an Alternative." *Minnesota Law Review* 84(4, April): 753–804.

Eliasoph, Nina. 1998. *Avoiding Politics: How Americans Produce Apathy in Everyday Life.* New York: Cambridge University Press.

Ewald, Alec C. 2003. "Of Constitutions, Politics, and Punishment: Criminal Disenfranchisement Law in Comparative Context." Unpublished paper. Department of Political Science, University of Massachusetts, Amherst.

Fairchild, Erika S. 1977. "Politicization of the Criminal Offender: Prisoner Perceptions on Crime and Politics." *Criminology* 15(3, November): 287–318.

Fellner, Jamie, and Marc Mauer. 1998. *Losing the Vote: The Impact of Felony Disenfranchisement Laws in the United States.* Washington, D.C.: Human Rights Watch and The Sentencing Project.

Gamson, William. 1992. *Talking Politics.* New York: Cambridge University Press.

Glynn, Carroll, Susan Herbst, Garrett O'Keefe, and Robert Shapiro. 1999. *Public Opinion.* Boulder, Colo.: Westview Press.

Goldstone, Jack, and Bert Useem. 1999. "Prison Riots as Microrevolutions: An Extension of State-Centered Theories of Revolution." *American Journal of Sociology* 104(4, January): 985–1029.

Herbst, Susan. 1993. *Numbered Voices: How Opinion Polling Has Shaped American Politics.* Chicago: University of Chicago Press.

Hetherington, Marc J. 1998. "The Political Relevance of Political Trust." *American Political Science Review* 92(4, December): 791–808.

Inglehart, Ronald. 1990. *Culture Shift in Advanced Industrial Society.* Princeton, N.J.: Princeton University Press.

Keyssar, Alexander. 2000. *The Right to Vote: The Contested History of Democracy in the United States.* New York: Basic Books.

Lane, Robert. 1962. *Political Ideology.* New York: Free Press.

Lee, Taeku. 2002. *Mobilizing Public Opinion: Black Insurgency and Racial Attitudes in the Civil Rights Era.* Chicago: University of Chicago Press.

Lin, Ann Chih. 2000. *Reform in the Making: The Implementation of Social Policy in Prisons.* Princeton, N.J.: Princeton University Press.

Lipset, Seymour Martin. 1981. *Political Man.* Baltimore, Md.: Johns Hopkins University Press.

Malcolm X. 1965. *The Autobiography of Malcolm X,* assisted by Alex Haley. New York: Grove Press.

Manza, Jeff, and Clem Brooks. 1999. *Social Cleavages and Political Change: Voter Alignments and U.S. Party Coalitions.* New York: Oxford University Press.

Manza, Jeff, and Christopher Uggen. Forthcoming. *Locked Out: Felon Disenfranchisement and American Democracy.* New York: Oxford University Press.

Maruna, Shadd. 2001. *Making Good: How Ex-Convicts Reform and Rebuild Their Lives.* Washington, D.C.: American Psychological Association.

Mortimer, Jeylan T. 2003. *Working and Growing Up in America.* Cambridge, Mass.: Harvard University Press.

National Election Studies. 1995–2000. *The NES Guide to Public Opinion and Electoral Behavior.* Ann Arbor, Mich.: University of Michigan, Center for Political Studies.

Nie, Norman H., Sidney Verba, and John R. Petrocik. 1979. *The Changing American Voter.* 2d ed. Cambridge, Mass.: Harvard University Press.

Norris, Pippa. 2002. *Democratic Phoenix: Political Activism Worldwide*. New York: Cambridge University Press.

Nye, Joseph S., Philip D. Zelikow, and David C. King, eds. 1997. *Why People Don't Trust Government*. Cambridge, Mass.: Harvard University Press.

Olivares, Kathleen M., Velmer S. Burton, and Francis T. Cullen. 1997. "The Collateral Consequences of a Felony Conviction: A National Study of State Legal Codes 10 Years Later." *Federal Probation* 60(3, September): 10–17.

Pallas, John, and Robert Barber. 1973. "From Riot to Revolution." In *The Politics of Punishment: A Critical Analysis of Prisons in America*, edited by Erik O. Wright. New York: Harper Torchbooks.

Piven, Frances Fox, and Richard A. Cloward. 2000. *Why Americans Don't Vote*. New York: Free Press.

Rose, Dina R., and Todd R. Clear. 1998. "Incarceration, Social Capital, and Crime: Implications for Social Disorganization Theory." *Criminology* 36(3, August): 441–79.

Rose, Richard, and Ian McAllister. 1986. *Voters Begin to Choose*. Newbury Park, Calif.: Sage Publications.

Rueschemeyer, Dietrich, Evelyne Huber Stephens, and John D. Stephens. 1992. *Capitalist Development and Democracy*. Chicago: University of Chicago Press.

Shakur, Sanyika. 1994. *Monster: The Autobiography of an L.A. Gang Member*. New York: Viking Penguin.

Shklar, Judith N. 1991. *American Citizenship: The Quest for Inclusion*. Cambridge, Mass.: Harvard University Press.

Smith, Christopher E. 1993. "Black Muslims and the Development of Prisoners' Rights." *Journal of Black Studies* 24(2, December): 131–46.

Smith, Eric R. A. N. 1989. *The Unchanging American Voter*. Berkeley: University of California Press.

Uggen, Christopher, and Jennifer Janikula. 1999. "Volunteerism and Arrest in the Transition to Adulthood." *Social Forces* 78(1, September): 331–62.

Uggen, Christopher, and Jeff Manza. 2002. "Democratic Contraction? The Political Consequences of Felon Disenfranchisement in the United States." *American Sociological Review* 67(6, December): 777–803.

Uggen, Christopher, Jeff Manza, and Angela Behrens. 2004. "Stigma, Role Transition, and the Civic Reintegration of Convicted Felons." In *After Crime and Punishment: Ex-Offender Reintegration and Desistance from Crime*, edited by Shadd Maruna and Russ Immarigeon. Devon, U.K.: Willan Publishing.

Uggen, Christopher, Jeff Manza, and Melissa Thompson. 2000. "Crime, Class, and Reintegration: The Socioeconomic, Familial, and Civic Lives of Criminal Offenders." Paper presented at the annual meeting of the American Society of Criminology. San Francisco (November 18).

U.S. Congress. 2002. *Congressional Record*. 107th Congress, 2nd session S565.

U.S. Department of Justice, Bureau of Justice Statistics. 1993. *Survey of State Prison Inmates, 1991*. NCJ-136949. Washington: U.S. Government Printing Office.

———, Office of the Pardon Attorney. 1996. *Civil Disabilities of Convicted Felons: A State-by-State Survey*. Washington: U.S. Government Printing Office.

———. 2000. *Survey of Inmates in State and Federal Correctional Facilities, 1997*. Computer file compiled by the U.S. Department of Commerce, Bureau of the Census. Ann Arbor, Mich.: Inter-university Consortium for Political and Social Research.

———. 2001. *Prisoners in 2000.* Washington: U.S. Government Printing Office.

Useem, Bert, and Peter Kimball. 1991. *States of Siege: U.S. Prison Riots, 1971–86.* New York: Oxford University Press.

Verba, Sidney, Kay L. Scholzman, and Henry E. Brady. 1997. *Equality and Voice.* Cambridge, Mass.: Harvard University Press.

Wattenberg, Martin. 1991. *The Rise of Candidate-Centered Politics.* Cambridge, Mass.: Harvard University Press.

Wright, Erik O. 1973. *The Politics of Punishment: A Critical Analysis of Prisons in America.* New York: Harper Torchbooks.

Harry J. Holzer
Steven Raphael
Michael A. Stoll

8 | Will Employers Hire Former Offenders?: Employer Preferences, Background Checks, and Their Determinants

The U.S. Bureau of Justice Statistics (BJS) estimates that, at current incarceration rates, approximately 9 percent of all men residing in the United States will serve some time in state or federal prisons. For certain subgroups of the population, the proportion likely to serve time is quite large. For example, according to these estimates, nearly 30 percent of African American men and 16 percent of Hispanic men will serve prison sentences at some point in their lives (U.S. Department of Justice 1997). The BJS also estimates that the median time served for prisoners released during the late 1990s was less than two years. In consort, these two pieces of information (high incarceration rates and a relatively low median sentence) suggest that a large minority of noninstitutionalized men have served time in state or federal prisons.

Although the state and federal prison populations appear to be leveling off, the rapid increase in incarceration rates over the past two decades indicates that the number of former offenders among the noninstitutionalized population is likely to be large into the foreseeable future.[1] The successful reintegration of this growing population into their families and communities depends in part on the employment potential of former offenders. In addition to the low education, poor cognitive skills, and other personal factors that would restrict employment opportunities for offenders even without their having been incarcerated, there are several reasons to suspect that serving time may further reduce their future earnings and employment prospects. The incarcerated do not accumulate work experience and may experience an erosion of skills while serving time. Furthermore, any ties to legitimate employers are likely to be severed by an initial arrest and by a prison spell. From the viewpoint of employers, a criminal record may signal an untrustworthy or otherwise problematic employee. Employers may avoid such workers based on a perceived increased propensity to break rules, steal, or harm customers.

Several studies have analyzed the labor market consequences of involvement in the criminal justice system by testing for direct effects on future employment and earnings of having been arrested (Grogger 1995) or of having served time (Kling 2000). An alternative approach that we use is to analyze employer self-reported preferences with respect to applicants with criminal histories. In this chapter we seek answers to the following questions: To what extent are employers willing to hire workers with criminal backgrounds? Does this willingness to hire vary with different job and firm characteristics and over time with the tightness of the labor market? To what extent do employers act on these preferences by investigating the criminal history of applicants? Does the propensity to check backgrounds also vary with specific job and firm characteristics? Finally, how do these measures of employer demand for former offenders compare with their potential supply to the labor market, and what do these comparisons imply about employment prospects for former offenders in the current environment and in the near future?

EMPLOYERS' WILLINGNESS TO HIRE FORMER OFFENDERS AND THEIR USE OF CRIMINAL HISTORY RECORDS

On average, former offenders tend to be mostly younger (that is, under the age of thirty-five) minority men from poor urban or rural areas. Large percentages of them are high school dropouts or functionally illiterate (or both); many suffer from substance abuse and other health problems (Travis, Solomon, and Waul 2001). Employers might reasonably be reluctant to hire many of them based on these personal characteristics alone, even had they not been incarcerated. As other authors in this volume have recognized (see especially chapters 2, 6, and 7), these disadvantageous characteristics similarly negatively affect their marriageability, their impact on the communities to which they return, and their political participation, again regardless of incarceration status. In the labor market, for example, "hard" and "soft" skill requirements by employers, transit and locational factors, slack urban labor markets, employer discrimination, and weak social networks are all likely to adversely affect the employment and earnings of low-skilled workers in general and the former-offender population in particular (Freeman and Rodgers 2000; Stoll, Holzer, and Ihlanfeldt 2000; Moss and Tilly 2000; Holzer 1996). Nonetheless, former-offender status may create additional barriers to employment (as well as to marriage and voting) above and beyond those experienced by other low-skilled workers.

Employers may be unwilling to hire workers with criminal backgrounds (all else held equal) owing to several considerations. Like political participation, certain occupations are legally closed to individuals with felony convictions under state and, in some cases, federal law (Hahn 1991; chapter 7 in this volume). Examples include jobs requiring contact with children, certain health services occupations, and employment with firms providing security services. In addition, employers may place a premium on the trustworthiness of employees, especially when the ability to monitor employee performance is imperfect. Jobs that require significant customer contact or the handling of cash or expensive merchandise require dependable, honest employees. To the extent that past criminal activity signals something less, employers may take such information into account when making hiring decisions.

Furthermore, in many states employers can be held liable for the criminal actions of their employees under the theory of negligent hiring. Legally, negligence is premised on the idea that employers have a duty of care to others in their organization and to the public and are legally liable for any damages that result from breach of that duty (Glynn 1988); thus employers may be held liable for the risk created by exposing the public and other employees to potentially dangerous individuals. As articulated by Shawn Bushway (1996, 4), "Employers who know, or should have known, that an employee has had a history of criminal behavior may be liable for the employee's criminal or tortuous acts." Thus employers may be exposed to punitive damages as well as liability for loss, pain, and suffering as a result of negligent hiring.[2] Employers have lost 72 percent of negligent hiring cases, with an average settlement of more than $1.6 million (Connerley, Arvey, and Bernardy 2001).[3] The high probability of losing such a suit coupled with the magnitude of settlement awards suggest that fear of litigation may substantially deter employers from hiring applicants with criminal history records.

The ability of employers to act effectively on an aversion to hiring former offenders, and the nature of the action in terms of hiring and screening behavior, will depend on the accessibility of criminal history record information to non-criminal-justice entities. Information on arrest, conviction, and time served for nonfederal offenses is compiled by the state in which the offense occurred. All states and the District of Columbia maintain a central repository where this information is housed and from which criminal history information is disseminated. All law enforcement agencies within a state are required to report arrest and disposition information for all serious offenses to the central repository (U.S. Department of Justice 1999). The information in the repository is used to generate rap sheets for law enforcement officials and is the source for criminal history records for non-criminal-justice purposes.

In its most recent review of state privacy and security legislation, the U.S. Department of Justice concludes that information from criminal history records is increasingly becoming more available to non-criminal-justice users, although the degree of openness varies from state to state (U.S. Department of Justice 1999). Nearly all states make a distinction between arrest records and conviction records. In general, states are less likely to freely disseminate information on arrest records, especially arrests for cases that are still open or have occurred within the previous year. States tend to place fewer restrictions on non-criminal-justice access to conviction records. Currently, twenty-three states have some form of public access or freedom-of-information statutes that pertain to some aspect of information from criminal history records.[4]

Given the availability of criminal history records to non-criminal-justice users, employers are likely to check the criminal backgrounds of potential employees. Certainly, the extent to which they do so is likely to be in part a function of their aversion to hiring former offenders, for all the reasons discussed earlier. In addition, the propensity to check an applicant's background is likely to be related to the size of the local population of former offenders as a proportion of the local labor force. This proportion varies from state to state owing to interstate differences in sentencing and other criminal justice policies.

To be sure, employers can act on an aversion to hiring former offenders in the absence of information on applicants' criminal history records by screening job applicants on the basis of characteristics that are predictive (either in actuality or in perception) of previous criminal activity. For example, employers who believe that African Americans, welfare recipients, or workers with unaccounted-for breaks in their employment histories are more likely to have past criminal convictions may statistically discriminate against such individuals. Although imperfect information will clearly lead to instances of "false-positive" and "false-negative" assessments of previous criminality, basing employment decisions on such discriminatory rules of thumb may minimize the likelihood of hiring former offenders.

DESCRIPTION OF THE DATA

To examine employers' willingness to hire former offenders and their use of criminal background checks, we use an establishment survey collected through the Multi-City Study of Urban Inequality. The survey, which covers slightly more than three thousand establishments, was conducted between June 1992 and May 1994 in the Atlanta, Boston, Detroit, and Los Angeles metropolitan areas. The sample of firms is drawn from two sources: employers of the respondents to a household survey conducted in conjunction with the Multi-City Study, which provided approximately 30 percent of the observations, and a sample of establishments generated by Survey Sampling Incorporated. The latter is a random-stratified sample in which the initial lists are stratified by establishment size and firms are sampled according to the proportion of metropolitan-area employment accounted for by their respective size categories. Hence the sample is representative of the set of establishments faced by a job seeker in any of the four metropolitan areas. We use sample weights in all calculations to account for the nonrepresentative portion of the sample from the household survey.

Establishments were screened according to whether during the previous year they had hired an employee into a position that did not require a college degree. The response rate for firms that passed the initial screen was 67 percent. This compares favorably with other establishment surveys (Kling 1995).[5]

Telephone surveys were conducted with individuals in charge of hiring at each firm. The survey asked two questions vital to the current analysis: a question on employer preferences with respect to workers with criminal histories and a question on whether employers use criminal background checks. The exact wording of the questions, including the possible responses, is as follows: The question on employer preferences, referring to the most recently filled position, reads, "Would you accept for this position an applicant who had a criminal record? Definitely will, probably will, probably not, absolutely not?" For criminal background checks, the question reads, "For the last position hired into, how often do you check the applicant's criminal record? Always, sometimes, or never?"

CHARACTERIZING THE DEMAND FOR FORMER OFFENDERS

Figure 8.1 presents the distribution of employer responses to the question about the likelihood that the employer would be willing to accept an applicant with a criminal record. More than 60 percent of employers indicated that they would "probably not" or "definitely not" be willing to hire an applicant with a criminal record, "probably not" being the modal response.[6] Only 38 percent of employers indicate that they would definitely or probably consider an applicant with a criminal history, 12.5 percent indicating that they definitely would consider hiring a former offender. Hence the simple distribution of the responses to this question reveals a relatively widespread aversion to applicants with criminal histories.

To put these employer responses into perspective, figure 8.2 presents the distributions of employer responses to similarly worded questions

Figure 8.1 *Distribution of Employer Responses to the Question Concerning the Likelihood That the Employer Would Accept an Applicant with a Criminal Record*

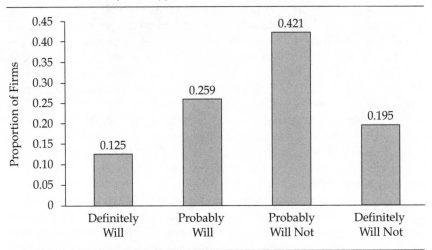

Source: Data from Multi-City Employer Survey.

concerning the likelihood that employers would accept applicants from other groups of low-skilled and possibly stigmatized workers. The figure illustrates employer preferences with respect to the acceptability of welfare recipients, applicants with a certificate of general educational development (GED) but no high school diploma, applicants with spotty work histories, and applicants who have been unemployed for a year or more. Approximately 92 percent of employers indicated that they would definitely or probably hire former or current welfare recipients, 96 percent indicated that they would probably or definitely hire workers with a GED in lieu of a high school diploma, 59 percent indicated that they would hire workers with a spotty employment history, and 83 percent indicated that they would probably or definitely consider an application from an individual who has been unemployed for a year or more. In contrast, only 38 percent of employers said that they definitely or probably would accept an application from an former offender (figure 8.1). Hence employers' aversion to hiring applicants with criminal histories is not only widespread, it is also considerably stronger than their aversion to hiring applicants from other commonly stigmatized groups of workers.

Do employer attitudes concerning the employability of former offenders differ across the metropolitan areas represented in our sample? Figure 8.3 presents results comparable to those in figure 8.1 for each of

Figure 8.2   Distribution of Employer Responses to the Questions
Concerning the Likelihood That the Employer Would
Accept an Application from Various Disadvantaged
(Low-Skilled) Groups

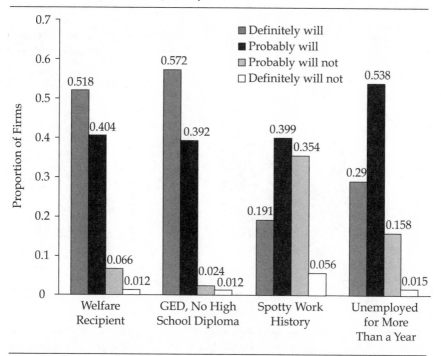

Source: See figure 8.1.

the four metropolitan areas (Atlanta, Boston, Detroit, and Los Angeles).
Employer responses are comparable across areas. In all metropolitan areas, approximately 60 percent of employers indicated that they would
probably not or definitely not consider applicants with criminal histories.
This uniformity is particularly striking considering interarea differences
in size, demographic composition, and economic conditions (see Holzer
1996 for a discussion of the exact differences in these metropolitan areas).
Given that the data pertain to employers who have recently hired low-
skilled workers (employers who are perhaps the most likely to employ
former offenders), the simple distributions in figures 8.1 and 8.3 imply
that a substantial majority of employers are unwilling to hire former
offenders and that this unwillingness appears uniform across cities.

An alternative indirect manner of gauging employer aversion to hiring applicants with criminal histories would be to assess whether em-

Figure 8.3   *Distribution of Employer Responses to the Question Concerning the Likelihood That the Employer Would Accept an Applicant with a Criminal Record, by Metropolitan Area*

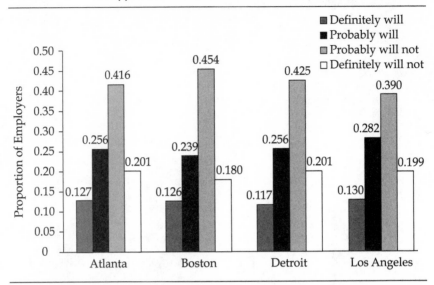

Source: See figure 8.1.

ployers investigate the criminal backgrounds of their potential employees. Figure 8.4 presents the distribution of employer responses to the question concerning the frequency with which employers check the criminal backgrounds of job applicants. Approximately 32 percent of employers in our sample said that they always check, 17 percent indicated that they sometimes do so, and 51 percent responded that they never check criminal backgrounds. Although the time period covered in our sample probably precedes the emergence of Internet services providing low-cost criminal background checks, the use of such checks by a sizable minority of employers is evident in the data.

To the extent that the question concerning employer willingness to hire former offenders and the question concerning the use of background checks both measure employer aversion to hiring applicants with criminal histories, the responses to the two questions should be systematically related. Figure 8.5 explores this possibility. The figure presents the distribution of responses to the question about criminal background checks by the responses to the question concerning the likelihood that the employer would consider hiring an former offender. There is a clear associ-

Figure 8.4   *Employer Responses to the Question Concerning the Frequency with Which the Employer Checks the Criminal Backgrounds of Job Applicants*

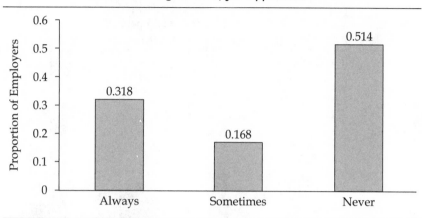

Source: See figure 8.1.

ation between the responses to these two questions. While only 19 percent of employers who say they definitely will consider hiring an former offender always check criminal backgrounds, 56 percent of employers who say that they would definitely not hire an applicant with a criminal history always do so. Conversely, while 32 percent of those least willing to hire former offenders never check criminal backgrounds, the comparable figure for those employers who are most willing to hire former offenders is 61 percent. Hence employer responses to the two questions are largely consistent with one another and suggest considerable employer reluctance to hire former offenders.

In contrast to the uniformity in the responses to the willingness to hire question displayed in figure 8.3, there are significant differences in the propensity to check criminal backgrounds across metropolitan areas. Figure 8.6 presents this comparison for the four metropolitan areas in our sample. As the figure shows, the propensity to check criminal backgrounds among firms in Atlanta, Detroit, and Los Angeles is generally comparable, but employers in Boston were much less likely to use criminal background checks as a screening device. Potential explanations for this difference may lie in interarea differences in the size of the population of former offenders or in differences in the ease with which employers can access criminal justice information for non-criminal-justice purposes.

Figure 8.5   *Frequency of Criminal History Record Checks by Employer Willingness to Hire Applicants with Criminal Records*

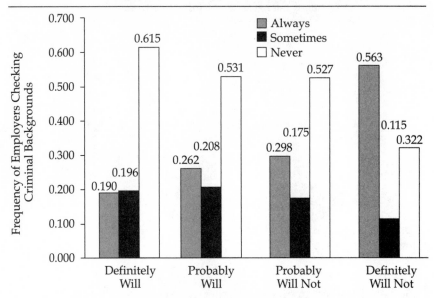

Likelihood That the Employer Would Accept an
Applicant with a Criminal Record

Source: See figure 8.1.

To investigate the first possible explanation, table 8.1 presents estimates of the incarcerated and former-offender populations for the four states in which the metropolitan areas are located during the time period covered by our sample (metropolitan-level estimates are not available). As can be seen, the incarceration and probation rates, as well as the proportion of the population that are recently released offenders (all expressed per 100,000 state residents) are considerably lower in Massachusetts than in the other three states. Hence the lower propensity of Boston firms to investigate the criminal background of employees may derive in part from the relatively small former-offender population of the host state.

Concerning differences in the stringency of state laws governing non-criminal-justice uses of criminal history records, an examination of the most recent *Compendium of State Privacy and Security Legislation: 1999 Overview* (U.S. Department of Justice 1999) does not reveal glaring interstate differences in who can legally access criminal history records. How-

Figure 8.6   *Employer Responses to the Question Concerning the Frequency with Which Employer Checks the Criminal Backgrounds of Applicants, by Metropolitan Area*

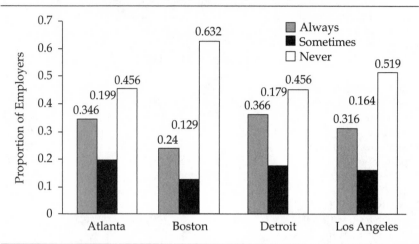

Source: See figure 8.1.

ever, in a review of earlier issues of the compendium, Bushway (1996) concludes that around the beginning of the 1990s criminal history records were considerably less available in Massachusetts to non-criminal-justice entities than they were in the other three states in our sample.

Figures 8.1 through 8.6 and table 8.1 indicate clear patterns. Through their stated hiring preferences and as revealed by their actions (running background checks), employers reveal considerable reluctance to hire workers with criminal histories. This aversion appears to be stronger than the aversion to hiring workers from other commonly stigmatized groups. Moreover, the correlation between the stated preferences and checking behavior are consistent with one another. How do these measures correlate with employer demand for former offenders?

Which Employers Are Most Likely to Avoid Applicants with Criminal History Records and Which Employers Check Criminal Backgrounds?

To be sure, employer attitudes toward applicants with criminal histories are likely to depend on the nature of the employer's business and on the nature of the position that is being filled. One would expect that employers who cannot perfectly monitor their employees or those who hire

Table 8.1   *Offender and Recent Former-Offender Populations for Selected States, 1992 to 1994 Average*

	Georgia	Massachusetts	Michigan	California
Population	6,759,474	5,993,474	9,528,015	31,113,435
Incarcerated population (state and federal)	28,832	10,525	39,687	118,513
Released prisoners annually (state and federal)	12,554	4,698	11,564	89,693
On probation	146,359	47,379	139,135	293,645
On parole	20,438	4,590	13,432	84,550
Recent former-offender population[a]	179,351	56,667	164,071	467,888
Incarceration rate per 100,000	427	176	417	381
Recently released prisoners per 100,000	186	78	121	288
Recent former offenders per 100,000	2,653	945	1,722	1,504

Source: Data from U.S. Department of Commerce (1993, 1994, 1995); U.S. Department of Justice (1993, 1994, 1995).
Note: All figures presented here are based on averages using 1992 to 1994 data.
[a]The recent former-offender population is the total of the annual released prisoner, probation, and parole populations.

workers into positions that deal frequently with the public would be more averse to hiring former offenders. One might also suspect that employers filling jobs that require the handling of expensive merchandise, large amounts of cash, or costly equipment may be differentially averse to applicants with a criminal past.

To explore these possible differences, table 8.2 presents averages of establishment characteristics, recruiting and screening methods, required job tasks and qualifications, and desired employee characteristics for the sample of employers stratified by the four possible responses to the question concerning willingness to consider former offenders. Establishment characteristics include the number of employees at the establishment, industry sector, the percentage of workers represented by a union, dummy variables indicating that the hiring agent is black and that the firm is located in the central city, a variable measuring the average distance to blacks in the metropolitan area, and a variable measuring the average distance to whites in the metropolitan area.[7] Our measures of recruiting and screening methods used are a set of dummy variables

Table 8.2   *Establishment Characteristics by Employer Self-Reported Likelihood of Hiring Applicants with Criminal Backgrounds*

Characteristic	Definitely Will	Probably Will	Probably Will Not	Definitely Will Not
Size				
Fewer than twenty employees	0.26	0.31	0.37	0.36
Twenty to ninety-nine employees	0.29	0.33	0.32	0.33
One hundred to four hundred ninety-nine employees	0.31	0.27	0.23	0.20
Five hundred to nine hundred ninety-nine employees	0.06	0.04	0.04	0.03
One thousand or more employees	0.08	0.05	0.04	0.07
Industry				
Mining	0.00	0.00	0.00	0.00
Construction	0.02	0.03	0.03	0.01
Manufacturing	0.32	0.29	0.18	0.12
Transportation, communications, and utilities	0.05	0.05	0.06	0.06
Wholesale trade	0.05	0.10	0.09	0.04
Retail trade	0.20	0.15	0.19	0.17
Finance, insurance, and real estate	0.02	0.05	0.11	0.16
Services	0.30	0.31	0.32	0.36
Percentage union	15.94	13.17	12.48	17.67
Central city	0.33	0.27	0.27	0.28
Black hiring agent	0.05	0.07	0.06	0.06
Distance black	17.35	17.97	17.80	17.19
Distance white	22.57	22.63	22.58	22.26
Recruitment methods				
Help Wanted signs	0.31	0.28	0.24	0.27
Newspaper ads	0.45	0.46	0.48	0.50
Walk-ins	0.78	0.74	0.67	0.66
Referrals from				
Current employees	0.84	0.84	0.83	0.81
State agency	0.46	0.40	0.31	0.30
Private agency	0.23	0.21	0.21	0.17
Community agency	0.33	0.26	0.24	0.25
School	0.40	0.34	0.34	0.38
Union	0.08	0.06	0.06	0.06
Affirmative action	0.61	0.55	0.50	0.56

(*Table continues on p. 218.*)

Table 8.2   *Continued*

Characteristic	Definitely Will	Probably Will	Probably Will Not	Definitely Will Not
Screening methods				
Drug test or physical exam	0.20	0.15	0.15	0.19
Aptitude test	0.09	0.09	0.14	0.14
Knowledge test	0.16	0.17	0.16	0.15
Personality test	0.03	0.05	0.07	0.09
Background check				
Criminal background	0.39	0.45	0.47	0.67
Education	0.66	0.69	0.68	0.70
References	0.92	0.95	0.96	0.97
Daily job tasks				
Customer contact	0.52	0.49	0.60	0.71
Phone conversations	0.48	0.49	0.55	0.55
Reading	0.53	0.56	0.52	0.58
Writing	0.28	0.29	0.30	0.34
Math and computations	0.63	0.66	0.67	0.64
Computer work	0.48	0.47	0.54	0.51
Job qualifications				
High school diploma	0.57	0.68	0.74	0.79
Recent work experience	0.63	0.68	0.70	0.69
Specific experience	0.55	0.60	0.60	0.62
References	0.69	0.67	0.74	0.78
Vocational education	0.34	0.40	0.38	0.39
Desired characteristics of new employees				
Physical attractiveness	0.09	0.10	0.11	0.17
Physical neatness	0.44	0.45	0.56	0.62
Politeness	0.71	0.70	0.80	0.83
Verbal skills	0.54	0.54	0.64	0.72
Motivation	0.71	0.70	0.76	0.76
Speaks English	0.44	0.47	0.59	0.65
Type of applicant who would probably not be hired				
On welfare	0.01	0.04	0.10	0.18
With only GED	0.01	0.02	0.03	0.11
Spotty work history	0.21	0.36	0.51	0.46
Unemployed for a year	0.06	0.13	0.21	0.26

Source: Authors' compilation.
Note: All figures use the sample weights.

equal to one if the employer regularly uses the described methods. Similarly, the daily job tasks are the means of dummy variables describing daily tasks performed on the job, such as interacting with customers, reading, writing, or using a computer. Job qualifications refer to applicant qualifications that the employer expressed are either absolutely necessary or strongly preferred, while desired employee characteristics are employee traits that employers deem important and types of applicants that employers would not consider hiring.

There are several clear patterns in table 8.2. First, the establishment size distribution among the least willing employers is skewed toward smaller firms, while large firms are disproportionately represented among employers most willing to hire workers with criminal histories. Among employers willing to hire former offenders, manufacturing firms are disproportionately represented, while establishments in the finance, insurance, and real estate sector and the service sector are underrepresented. The opposite pattern holds among employers who are the least willing. There is little relationship between the remainder of the establishment characteristics and employer aversion to hiring former offenders, although employers located in the central city are slightly more likely to be among the firms willing to hire applicants with criminal records.

Concerning recruiting and screening methods, employers who are averse to hiring former offenders are less likely to consider applications from walk-ins or to post Help Wanted signs, less likely to consider referrals from state and community agencies, and less likely to use affirmative action in recruiting for the position. There are also positive relationships between employer aversion and several of the screening methods, including the use of aptitude and personality tests, checking criminal backgrounds, and the verification of educational attainment and references.

One of the strongest associations evident in table 8.2 is the positive relationship between employer unwillingness to hire former offenders and whether the recently filled job involves frequent customer contact. Among employers most willing to hire former offenders, 52 percent of the positions required customer contact. Among employers least willing to hire former offenders, 71 percent of the positions required customer contact. There also are weaker positive correlations between unwillingness to hire and several of the other job tasks, including phone conversations, reading, and writing. Employers who are the least willing to hire former offenders are more likely to require high school degrees, recent and specific work experience, references, and some vocational education. Such employers are also more likely to indicate that physical attractiveness, neatness, politeness, motivation, verbal skills, and the ability to speak English well are important employee characteristics.

Table 8.2 indicates that employers in smaller, nonmanufacturing firms whose employees interact with customers are the most averse to hiring former offenders. The patterns also indicate that averse employers are less likely to use informal recruiting techniques (walk-ins, for example). Regression analysis (not shown here) confirms these basics patterns. These patterns are sensible and support our earlier discussion of the possible reasons employers may be reluctant to hire former offenders.

Table 8.3 presents average characteristics for the sample of establishments stratified by the response to the question concerning employer use of criminal background checks. The variables presented are exactly the same as those presented in table 8.2. There are notable differences in the size and industrial distributions between employers who check and those who do not. Despite their greater reluctance to consider applicants with criminal histories, employers in small firms are most represented among establishments that never use criminal background checks. Nearly 40 percent of employers who never check have fewer than twenty employees, compared with 24 percent of employers who always check. Concerning industry, manufacturing firms are the least likely to use criminal background checks, while establishments in finance, insurance, real estate, and services are the most likely. There is a negative relationship between a firm's spatial proximity to black neighborhoods and use of criminal background checks. In addition, establishments with a greater union presence screen criminal history records more often than less unionized establishments.

In comparing the use of various recruitment methods, several interesting patterns emerge. Employers who check criminal backgrounds are more likely to use informal recruiting methods (accepting walk-ins and posting Help Wanted signs), more likely to accept referrals from state and community agencies, and more likely to use affirmative action in recruiting. Firms unwilling to hire workers with criminal histories are less likely to use these tools, as shown in table 8.2. The combination of these two findings suggests that in the absence of explicit inquiries into an applicant's criminal history, employers use these alternative recruiting and screening methods to avoid taking applications from former offenders. Concerning screening methods, the use of background checks is strongly associated with the use of various forms of tests (such as drug and aptitude tests) and with the likelihood that the employer will attempt to verify the stated educational attainment of the applicant and the applicant's references.

Employers who are filling positions that require customer contact are more likely to check criminal backgrounds, a pattern consistent with the patterns displayed in table 8.2. In addition, employers who check are more likely to require high school diplomas, though the association is

Table 8.3   *Establishment Characteristics by the Frequency with Which Employers Check the Criminal Backgrounds of Applicants*

Characteristic	Always	Sometimes	Never
Size			
Fewer than twenty employees	0.24	0.28	0.38
Twenty to ninety-nine employees	0.31	0.31	0.32
One hundred to four hundred ninety-nine employees	0.28	0.27	0.24
Five hundred to nine hundred ninety-nine employees	0.08	0.06	0.03
One thousand or more employees	0.10	0.09	0.04
Industry			
Mining	0.00	0.00	0.00
Construction	0.02	0.03	0.02
Manufacturing	0.10	0.20	0.27
Transporation, communications, and utilities	0.08	0.04	0.05
Wholesale trade	0.04	0.10	0.09
Retail trade	0.15	0.19	0.17
Finance, insurance, and real estate	0.14	0.08	0.06
Services	0.40	0.34	0.33
Percentage union	23.65	13.23	11.23
Central city	0.28	0.31	0.26
Black hiring agent	0.09	0.07	0.04
Distance black	17.36	17.59	17.78
Distance white	22.42	22.55	22.42
Recruitment methods			
Help Wanted signs	0.29	0.30	0.23
Newspaper ads	0.51	0.50	0.46
Walk-ins	0.72	0.73	0.66
Referrals from			
Current employees	0.85	0.85	0.80
State agency	0.40	0.40	0.29
Private agency	0.22	0.23	0.20
Community agency	0.32	0.30	0.22
School	0.47	0.35	0.32
Union	0.10	0.08	0.04
Affirmative action	0.69	0.57	0.48

(*Table continues on p. 222.*)

Table 8.3   *Continued*

Characteristic	Always	Sometimes	Never
Screening methods			
Drug test or physical exam	0.24	0.18	0.11
Aptitude test	0.15	0.13	0.10
Knowledge test	0.18	0.18	0.15
Personality test	0.09	0.05	0.06
Background checks			
Criminal background	1.00	1.00	0.00
Education	0.83	0.83	0.58
References	0.98	0.98	0.93
Daily job tasks			
Customer contact	0.69	0.62	0.52
Phone conversations	0.55	0.54	0.54
Reading	0.62	0.56	0.54
Writing	0.38	0.29	0.34
Math and computations	0.65	0.62	0.68
Computer work	0.54	0.52	0.54
Job qualifications			
High school diploma	0.76	0.74	0.68
Recent work experience	0.70	0.72	0.69
Specific experience	0.63	0.60	0.63
References	0.80	0.75	0.69
Vocational education	0.40	0.42	0.39
Desired characteristics of new employees			
Physical attractiveness	0.14	0.10	0.10
Physical neatness	0.55	0.54	0.52
Politeness	0.81	0.74	0.77
Verbal skills	0.70	0.56	0.63
Motivation	0.76	0.73	0.76
Speaks English	0.60	0.53	0.56
Type of applicant who would probably not be hired			
On welfare	0.09	0.07	0.09
With only GED	0.04	0.02	0.04
Spotty work history	0.40	0.41	0.43
Unemployed for a year	0.15	0.16	0.20

Source: Authors' compilation.
Note: All figures use the sample weights.

considerably weaker than that with the variable measuring employer unwillingness to hire former offenders.

The positive association with firm size, unionization rates, and the use of other screening tests suggests that employers with more-formal human resources systems are more likely to run background checks. The positive association between checking and positions with customer contact indicates that employer aversion, and possibly state law, are also important determinants of whether an employer checks an applicant's criminal background. However, there are several patterns in table 8.3 in which the differences in the averages between employers who run background checks and those who do not are the reverse of what one might predict from the patterns in table 8.2.[8] Hence a further dissection of the data may better illuminate the relationship between employer aversion, the use of criminal background checks, and recruiting and screening.[9]

Table 8.4 provides this more detailed cross-tabulation of the data. We first define all employers who indicated that they would "definitely" or "probably" hire applicants with criminal records as willing to hire former offenders and employers who responded that they would "definitely" or "probably" not do so as being unwilling. Next, we dichotomize the criminal background checks variable by defining employers who said they sometimes or always check backgrounds as checking and those who said they never check backgrounds as not checking. Table 8.4 presents means for the variables in tables 8.2 and 8.3 for the four categories defined by these two dichotomized variables. The first two columns in the table present means for firms that are willing to hire former offenders, while the third and fourth columns present means for employers who are unwilling to do so.

Stratifying the sample in this manner reveals several patterns that are masked in tables 8.2 and 8.3. First, the firm-size distributions indicate that small firms constitute a large portion of firms that are unwilling to hire former offenders and do not check criminal backgrounds. Fully 45 percent of establishments in this category have fewer than twenty employees.

Concerning the distributions by industry, manufacturing establishments are quite likely to be among firms that are willing to hire former offenders and never review criminal history records, while establishments in the finance, insurance, real estate, and service sectors are most likely to be unwilling to hire and most likely to check backgrounds. Retail and wholesale trade establishments are disproportionately represented among firms who will not hire former offenders and never check backgrounds (a pattern consistent with the size distributions). Skipping ahead to daily job tasks, customer contact is positively associated with

Table 8.4   *Establishment Characteristics by Employer Self-Reported Likelihood of Hiring Applicants with Criminal Backgrounds Crossed with Whether the Employer Checks the Criminal Backgrounds of Job Applicants*

Characteristic	Willing to Hire, Does Not Check	Willing to Hire, Checks	Not Willing to Hire, Does Not Check	Not Willing to Hire, Checks
Size				
Fewer than twenty employees	0.33	0.24	0.45	0.29
Twenty to ninety-nine employees	0.33	0.31	0.33	0.32
One hundred to four hundred ninety-nine employees	0.29	0.27	0.18	0.27
Five hundred to nine hundred ninety-nine employees	0.03	0.07	0.02	0.06
One thousand or more employees	0.03	0.11	0.02	0.07
Industry				
Mining	0.00	0.00	0.00	0.00
Construction	0.03	0.03	0.02	0.02
Manufacturing	0.38	0.19	0.22	0.11
Transporation, communications, and utilities	0.04	0.07	0.05	0.07
Wholesale trade	0.08	0.08	0.10	0.05
Retail trade	0.16	0.18	0.20	0.17
Finance, insurance, and real estate	0.04	0.04	0.09	0.16
Services	0.26	0.36	0.30	0.36
Percentage union	11.99	17.28	8.22	19.59
Central city	0.26	0.32	0.28	0.27
Black hiring agent	0.05	0.08	0.03	0.07
Distance black	18.21	17.22	17.82	17.45
Distance white	22.89	22.26	22.35	22.60
Recruitment methods				
Help Wanted signs	0.24	0.34	0.21	0.28
Newspaper ads	0.43	0.50	0.45	0.53
Walk-ins	0.72	0.80	0.64	0.70

Table 8.4   *Continued*

Characteristics	Willing to Hire, Does Not Check	Willing to Hire, Checks	Not Willing to Hire, Does Not Check	Not Willing to Hire, Checks
Referrals from Current				
employees	0.82	0.86	0.80	0.85
State agency	0.36	0.50	0.24	0.36
Private agency	0.20	0.25	0.19	0.20
Community				
agency	0.23	0.35	0.20	0.28
School	0.31	0.42	0.29	0.41
Union	0.05	0.10	0.03	0.09
Affirmative action	0.52	0.64	0.43	0.60
Screening methods				
Drug test or				
physical exam	0.11	0.24	0.11	0.21
Aptitude test	0.07	0.13	0.13	0.15
Knowledge test	0.15	0.20	0.15	0.17
Personality test	0.04	0.06	0.07	0.08
Background Checks				
Criminal				
background	0.00	1.00	0.00	1.00
Education	0.57	0.82	0.55	0.81
References	0.91	0.98	0.94	0.98
Daily job tasks				
Customer contact	0.43	0.59	0.57	0.70
Phone conversations	0.47	0.50	0.58	0.53
Reading	0.55	0.55	0.50	0.58
Writing	0.28	0.28	0.31	0.31
Math and				
computations	0.65	0.64	0.69	0.63
Computer work	0.46	0.48	0.55	0.51
Job qualifications				
High school				
diploma	0.60	0.69	0.73	0.77
Recent work				
experience	0.67	0.66	0.68	0.71
Specific experience	0.60	0.58	0.61	0.61
References	0.62	0.75	0.71	0.78
Vocational				
education	0.39	0.39	0.38	0.39

(*Table continues on p. 226.*)

Table 8.4   *Continued*

Characteristics	Willing to Hire, Does Not Check	Willing to Hire, Checks	Not Willing to Hire, Does Not Check	Not Willing to Hire, Checks
Desired characteristics of new employees				
Physical				
attractiveness	0.08	0.12	0.12	0.14
Physical neatness	0.42	0.49	0.59	0.56
Politeness	0.70	0.72	0.82	0.81
Verbal skills	0.53	0.55	0.65	0.66
Motivation	0.59	0.73	0.78	0.74
Speaks English	0.46	0.47	0.62	0.60
Type of applicant who would probably not be hired				
On welfare	0.03	0.04	0.15	0.11
With only GED	0.01	0.02	0.07	0.04
Spotty work history	0.30	0.32	0.54	0.45
Unemployed for a				
year	0.12	0.10	0.26	0.19

Source: Authors' compilation.

Note: All figures use the sample weights. Employers who answer that they "definitely will" or "probably will" hire applicants with criminal histories are coded as willing. Employers who check criminal background "always" or "sometimes" are coded as checking.

checking among both firms that are willing and those that are unwilling to hire former offenders. In addition, employers who check criminal backgrounds are more likely to demand certain job qualifications of applicants, relative to employers who do not check.

Perhaps the most interesting patterns in table 8.4 are found in the differences in the means of the dummy variables indicating types of applicants that the employer avoids. Among firms that are willing to hire former offenders, background checking is basically unrelated to these variables. Among firms that are unwilling to hire former offenders, firms that check are less averse to hiring these types of workers than firms that do not check. For both firms that check and firms that do not, unwillingness to hire former offenders is associated with a greater unwillingness to hire the types of applicants described by the dummy variables. However, this differential aversion is greatest among employers who do not run criminal background checks. Specifically, among employers who do not check criminal history records, the difference between those who are unwilling to hire former offenders and those who are willing to do so is 12 percentage points for the dummy variable indicating unwillingness to welfare recipients, 6 percentage points for the dummy indicating unwillingness to hire workers with a GED, 24 percentage points for the spotty-work-history dummy, and 14 percentage points for the dummy indicating an applicant who has been unemployed for more than a year. The comparable differences among firms who do check are 7, 2, 13, and 9 percentage points, respectively. These differences among employers who check criminal backgrounds are uniformly lower (and by considerable magnitudes) than those for employers who do not.

These patterns indicate that employers who do not review criminal history records and are unwilling to hire former offenders are more likely to exclude from consideration applicants with characteristics that may be indicative of a criminal history.[10] The results in table 8.4 indicate that educational attainment, prior participation in public assistance program, and gaps in one's employment history are perceived by employers to signal such information. An alternative signal that may be taken into account by employers is race. Specifically, African Americans are considerably more likely to have past criminal convictions than are members of other racial and ethnic groups. Moreover, employers may overestimate the average incidence of prior conviction among blacks, owing to prejudice or a general lack of experience with black employees.

To explore this possibility, table 8.5 presents average values of a dummy variable indicating that the last worker hired into a position that does not require a college education is black. We present averages for the whole sample, the sample stratified by whether the firm checks criminal backgrounds, the sample stratified by whether the employer is willing to hire former offenders, and the four categories defined by the cross of these two variables. The final column of the table presents the differences in means between firms that are unwilling to hire former offenders and firms that are willing to do so, while the final row presents differences in means between establishments that check criminal backgrounds and establishments that do not.

For the sample overall, there is no discernable overall difference in the likelihood of hiring a black worker between firms that are willing to hire former offenders and firms that are unwilling to do so. There is a large significant difference, however, between firms that check criminal backgrounds and firms that do not. Relative to firms that do not check, firms that check criminal backgrounds are 8.4 percentage points more likely to have hired an African American applicant into the most recently filled position. This difference is statistically significant at the 1 percent

Table 8.5   *Averages of the Dummy Variable Indicating That the Last Worker Hired Is Black by Whether the Firm Checks the Criminal Background of Applicants and by the Willingness of the Employer to Hire Applicants with Criminal Backgrounds*

	All Firms	Firms Willing to Hire	Firms Not Willing to Hire	Difference[a]
All firms	0.199 (0.008)	0.193 (0.013)	0.203 (0.010)	0.010 (0.017)
Checks	0.244 (0.012)	0.223 (0.021)	0.254 (0.015)	0.031 (0.026)
Does not check	0.159 (0.010)	0.175 (0.016)	0.148 (0.013)	−0.027 (0.021)
Difference[b]	0.084 (0.016)***	0.048 (0.026)*	0.107 (0.021)***	0.058 (0.033)*

Source: Authors' compilation.
Note: Standard errors are in parentheses. Firms that always check or sometimes check criminal backgrounds are coded as checking. Firms that state that they "definitely will" or "probably will" hire a worker with a criminal background are coded as willing to hire, while firms stating "probably not" or "absolutely not" are coded as unwilling to hire.
[a]Firms not willing to hire minus firms willing to hire.
[b]Firms that check backgrounds minus firms that do not.
*p < .10 **p < .05 ***p < .01

level of confidence. Among firms willing to hire former offenders, this difference is 4.8 percentage points and is marginally significant. Among employers who are unwilling to hire former offenders, this difference is 10.7 percentage points and is highly significant. Moreover, the difference between these two differences (shown in the last row of the last column) is statistically significant at the 8 percent level. This latter finding indicates that the relatively larger positive effect of background checks for firms that are unwilling to hire former offenders is larger than and statistically distinguishable from the effect for firms that are willing to do so. Hence the patterns observed for the groups of stigmatized workers in table 8.4 are reproduced for the hiring outcomes of African Americans in table 8.5.

The statistical discrimination implied by the results in tables 8.4 and 8.5 raises interesting policy questions with respect to state laws governing non-criminal-justice access to criminal history records. To the extent that employers substitute such screening for actual information on criminal histories, some workers will be unfairly discriminated against. In addition, workers from groups with high rates of previous criminal activity (for example, young men, African Americans, and workers with gaps in their employment histories) are likely to be considerably impacted by such discrimination. Hence while more-liberal access policies may adversely impact the employment prospects of applicants with criminal histories, the information infusion may positively impact the employment prospects of workers from groups with high incarceration rates. This is a provocative trade-off that needs to be explored in further detail.

Does Employer Demand for Former Offenders Vary over Time or with the Business Cycle?

Regardless of whether employers check backgrounds, the data presented here indicate relatively limited demand by employers for former offenders. However, given that these data are based on surveys administered during a period of relatively slack labor markets earlier in the decade (from 1992 to 1994), the figures may substantially understate this component of labor demand. It is widely known that tight labor markets tend to disproportionately increase demand for less-skilled and disadvantaged workers (Hoynes 2000) and that African Americans benefited particularly from the recent boom (Freeman and Rodgers 2000). It is also quite possible that any improvements in demand that initially result from cyclical factors could generate secular changes in employer behavior. For example, employer attitudes and hiring behavior may adjust with experience in a manner that reduces the stigma attached to a prior conviction.[11]

Thus the timing of the survey used to generate the results presented here begs the question of whether such demand has improved over time, particularly given the dramatic tightening of U.S. labor markets that occurred over the remainder of the 1990s.[12] To shed some light on this question, we turn to an additional source of data: a more recent set of surveys that were administered to roughly three thousand employers by phone in several metropolitan areas during the period 1998 to 1999. The metro areas in which the latter surveys were administered are Chicago, Cleveland, Los Angeles, and Milwaukee.[13]

A certain amount of overlap exists in the questions asked on the two surveys. Hence we can make some limited inferences about changes over time in employer demand for former offenders and the responsiveness of such demand to business cycle conditions. Specifically, the latter survey asks the same questions as the early survey concerning willingness to hire former offenders and other stigmatized workers into the last noncollege job that was filled.[14] This more recent survey also includes some additional questions on current willingness to hire former offenders.

Table 8.6   *Measures of Employer Demand for Former Offenders over Time, by Industry and Metropolitan Area*

	Employers' Willingness to Hire Former Offenders into Most Recently Filled Job		Employers' Current Willingness to Hire Former Offenders (1998 to 1999)	
Employer Category	1992 to 1994	1998 to 1999	Employers	Jobs
All employers	0.38	0.41	0.19	0.014
Metropolitcan area				
Milwaukee	—	0.49	0.24	0.015
Other	0.38	0.38	0.17	0.014
Major industry				
Manufacturing	0.54	0.56	0.22	0.008
Retail trade	0.38	0.45	0.25	0.021
Services	0.36	0.33	0.16	0.015

Source: Data from Holzer and Stoll (2001); Multi-City Study of Urban Inequality.

Specifically, employers were asked whether they would be willing to hire any former offenders at the current time and, if so, how many they would hire.

Tabulations using these data are presented in table 8.6. The first column of the table presents the percentages of employers in both surveys who answered that they would "definitely" or "probably" have hired persons with criminal backgrounds into their last-filled noncollege job. The data are presented for the overall sample of establishments and also for subsamples by metropolitan area (Milwaukee and other) and by selected industries. The second column then presents data from the more recent survey only on current willingness to hire former offenders: the percentage of employers who indicated they would currently hire former offenders and the percentage of all jobs in the sample establishments that could potentially be filled with former offenders. Tabulations are presented for the total sample of establishments and the same subsamples that are used in the first column of the table.

The comparison of results from the two surveys indicates a small increase between the two periods (from 1992 to 1994 and from 1998 to 1999) in the proportion of all employers willing to hire former offenders, from 38 to 41 percent. However, all of the increase is accounted for by the relatively greater willingness of employers in Milwaukee to hire former offenders (49 percent). This result contrasts somewhat with the experience of other potentially stigmatized groups over this same period. Our data (not shown here) indicate that employer willingness to hire welfare recipients and those with spotty employment histories over this boom period increased by 5 and 12 percentage points, respectively, and that these results are not accounted for by the Milwaukee phenomenon.

By industry, we find some substantial increases in the willingness of retail trade establishments to hire former offenders and much smaller changes within the manufacturing and service sectors, though the relative rankings of industries in terms of willingness to hire former offenders does not change. Still, this increase in demand is not as striking as that for other stigmatized groups. For example, our data (not shown here) indicate that employer willingness to hire those with spotty employment histories increased by 4, 15, and 8 percentage points in manufacturing, retail trade, and service establishments, respectively. Employer willingness to hire welfare recipients also increased across these industries over this period, though at somewhat smaller rates than for those with spotty employment histories (between 4 to 6 percentage points from the first period [1992 to 1994] to the second [1998 to 1999]).

How should we interpret these numbers? The relatively greater willingness of employers in Milwaukee to hire former offenders no doubt at least partly reflects the tight labor market conditions in Wisconsin in the late 1990s, though other factors might also be at play here.[15] The tightening of labor markets in other areas should have led to at least some improvements in the demand for former offenders as well. However, the characteristics of firms and jobs in our samples of employers changed across the two surveys in a manner that is likely to partially offset any increases in demand for former offenders caused by the business cycle.[16] Moreover, since labor markets nationwide continued to be very tight at least through the end of the year 2000, it is also possible that our data (which reflect the period only through early 1999) do not fully capture the extent of rising demand for former offenders during this time period.[17] Still, in comparison with other stigmatized groups, it appears that demand for former offenders is not as sensitive to business cycle fluctuations, though more research is needed on this question.

Some additional light is shed on this issue by the data on current willingness to hire former offenders from the later survey. Overall, just under 20 percent of surveyed employers expressed a current willingness to hire former offenders, to whom 1.4 percent of all jobs in their establishments would be available. Once again, those in Milwaukee are more willing to hire former offenders than those elsewhere, though the distinction is much clearer among proportions of employers than among proportions of all jobs open to former offenders. By industry, however, we now find a relatively greater current availability of jobs to former offenders in retail trade than in manufacturing or the services. This pattern is consistent with the much higher rates of gross hiring and job vacancies in the retail sector.[18]

Indeed, the data on the current willingness of employers to hire former offenders suggests a somewhat greater sensitivity to demand conditions than was seen in the earlier measure of employer demand based on the last-filled job. This seems largely to reflect differences in the sampling used to generate each. Since each establishment in the sample reports on one recently filled noncollege job, that measure is based on a sample of employers weighted only by their number of employees.[19] In contrast, current job availability measures differences across these establishments in hiring and job vacancy rates as well. The latter measure may thus be better suited than the former for evaluating the effects of demand conditions on employer hiring of former offenders and other groups. The latter measure also more accurately captures the shift in hiring toward retail trade and services that may impede the demand for former offenders (and other less-skilled workers) over time.

Taken together, the data available do suggest that employer willingness to hire former offenders is at least partly responsive to business cycle conditions and did increase somewhat over the course of the 1990s. However, the magnitudes of these increases were modest, at best, especially in comparison with other potentially stigmatized groups such as welfare recipients and those with spotty employment histories. Moreover, employer demand for former offenders remained quite limited even in the boom conditions that existed at the end of the decade.

Prisoners, Former Offenders, and Potential Supply to the Labor Market

This final section is most germane to the focus of this volume, as former incarcerees disproportionately return to low-income, minority communities; thus their prospects for employment have special spatial repercussions. The relatively limited employer demand for former offenders that exists even in very tight labor markets raises an important set of questions. Is such demand sufficient, at least in the short run, to absorb the numbers of offenders who are being released from prison? Moreover, who among the population of individuals who are either currently or previously incarcerated might contribute (at least potentially) to the supply of former offenders seeking legitimate employment in the labor market?

Some data on the numbers of currently incarcerated prisoners, former prisoners, and former felons are presented in table 8.7. The data are for the year 1999, to facilitate comparisons with the demand-side data for the period from 1998 to 1999 in table 8.6. The current inmate popula-

Table 8.7   *Potential Supply of Prisoners and Former Offenders to the Labor Market, 1999*

Category	Numbers (Thousands)	Percentage of Civilian Labor Force
Civilian labor force	139,368	100.00
Current prisoners		
Federal and state prison	1,299	0.93
Local jail	606	0.43
Felons in local jail	61	0.04
Total prisoners	1,905	1.36
Total felons incarcerated	1,360	0.97
Current status		
On parole	696	0.50
On felony probation	1,966	1.41
Total	2,662	1.91
Former offenders		
Total former prisoners	2,932	2.10
Total former felons	8,961	6.43
Annual releases	561	0.40

Source: U.S. Department of Labor (2000); U.S. Department of Justice (1999); Uggen and Manza (2001).
Note: All figures are for 1999.

tions of federal and state prisons, as well as the jail population, are presented here. For the latter, the table presents figures for both the total jail-inmate population and the subset of jail inmates who have been convicted of felonies.[20] The numbers of prisoners currently on parole and the number of convicted felons on probation are also presented, as well as the flow of prisoners released during 1999 and estimates of the total current stock of former prisoners and former convicted felons.[21]

In addition to the raw numbers in each category, we also present percentages of the civilian labor force in 1999 that each category would constitute. These can then be compared with the percentages of all jobs available to former offenders on the demand side of the labor market as presented in the table 8.6.

The data in table 8.7 indicate that there are currently close to 2 million individuals incarcerated in prisons and jails in the United States, of whom about 1.4 million are convicted felons. Including those on parole and felony probation would add roughly 2.7 million to those counts. The total stock of former prisoners and former felons is estimated to be close to 3 million and 9 million, respectively. If the numbers of current parolees and felons on probation are added to the latter figures, the result would be nearly 6 million former prisoners and nearly 12 million former felons at least potentially available in the labor market.[22] In addition, the data indicate an annual flow of roughly six hundred thousand from prison each year. Combining annual flows of new parolees and those on felony probation with those of released prisoners generates as many as 2 million individuals added to the potential labor force each year.[23]

As percentages of the civilian labor force, these numbers are quite striking. For instance, those currently incarcerated represent 1 percent or more of the labor force. The totals currently on parole or felony probation together constitute nearly 2 percent of the labor force, while the total stock of former prisoners and former felons represents more than 2 percent and 6 percent, respectively. When those on parole or felony probation are combined with the overall stock of former prisoners and former felons, the totals constitute about 4 and 8 percent of the civilian labor force, respectively. Considering annual flows out of prison rather than stocks, we find that the flow of new prisoners constitutes just 0.4 percent of the labor force each year; but when combined with the flow of new parolees and felons on probation, they generate estimates of well over 1 percent of the labor force being released each year.

How can we compare these estimates with those of jobs that employers would fill with former offenders? Combining former prisoners or former felons with those currently on parole or probation, and remembering that many former prisoners and former felons are already likely to be working, we estimate that the total stock of unemployed former felons at any point in time might be 4 million to 6 million, or 3 to 4 percent of the labor force; while that of former prisoners might be 2 million to 3 million, or 1.5 to 2 percent of the labor force.[24] At least the latter figures (those for former prisoners) do not suggest a huge imbalance between the potential labor supply from former offenders and the aggregate job availability they might face (at 1.4 percent of all jobs), though the former figures (those for former felons) are somewhat less reassuring.

Alternative approaches might consider annual labor market flows on the two sides of the market. A net flow of new former prisoners to the labor market of more than 1 percent per year for each of the next several years almost certainly exceeds the average net flow of new jobs available to them, which by our estimates would be about 0.6 percent per year.[25] On the other hand, relative to the gross flow of new hiring (which reflects hiring generated by turnover as well as net new job growth), a great deal more employment might be potentially available—

along with a good deal more competition from other low-skilled workers in the workforce.

Of course, any such exercise in which quantities on the supply and demand sides of the labor market are compared is suggestive at best and based on many strong assumptions.[26] Even in the short run, the magnitudes of any potential "mismatches" in the labor market will be sensitive to factors such as the numbers of former felons or former prisoners who would actually be seeking work, the extent to which employer aversion to hiring them varies with whether they were incarcerated, the number and nature of their offenses, their experiences since conviction or incarceration, and so forth. Furthermore, new supplies of workers over time will help generate new jobs as wage rates adjust in response to the growing supplies of workers. Indeed, estimates of the ability of labor markets to absorb an additional 3 million welfare recipients before the fact of their entry frequently proved to be too pessimistic (Burtless 2000) and to have ignored the dynamic nature of that market (as well as the extraordinary labor market tightness that existed during that time).

On the other hand, the data in our surveys indicate a much greater reluctance of employers to hire former offenders than to hire welfare recipients (as noted earlier in this chapter). Furthermore, it seems as though the labor market that former offenders will enter during the next few years will be much less tight than it was during most of the previous decade, while the flow of new former offenders will remain quite large. Moreover, that flow is highly concentrated in poor minority neighborhoods and among minority (especially African American) men, so that even an aggregate balance of potential supply and demand in the short run may overstate the true availability of jobs facing these former offenders. That is, a disproportionate share of former offenders is likely to live in, come from, or return from prison to poor neighborhoods that are racially segregated (Travis, Solomon, and Waul 2001). These neighborhoods, however, are relatively jobs-poor, especially for low-skill jobs (Stoll, Holzer, and Ihlanfeldt 2000). Thus a resulting spatial mismatch between former offenders and jobs is likely to further overstate the employment demand facing these workers. In addition, of course, the very limited skills and work readiness of this population means that even jobs that are potentially available may be out of reach for a large part of this population (Travis, Solomon, and Waul 2001; chapter 9 in this volume).

In sum, there may or may not be an aggregate imbalance between the number of former offenders returning to neighborhoods and the number of jobs potentially available to them. Given their personal characteristics and their concentration in poor neighborhoods and minority groups, however, it is likely that job availability facing this group will be quite limited.

CONCLUSION

Our data indicate a number of important findings. Employer willingness to hire former offenders is limited, even relative to other groups of disadvantaged workers (such as welfare recipients). Employer willingness to hire is highly correlated with establishment and job characteristics and is much lower in financial or service jobs and in those involving a variety of tasks, particularly direct customer contact, than elsewhere. Employer tendencies to check criminal backgrounds also vary greatly with characteristics of the establishment such as its size, which presumably reflects both the resources and expertise available for human resource functions.

The fact that many smaller firms refuse to hire former offenders but also do not check criminal backgrounds suggests that they may engage in statistical discrimination against a broader range of applicants, such as less-educated young black men. Paradoxically, efforts to make background checks easier for employers to perform and less costly might therefore improve job prospects for these latter groups, even while they weaken them for those who actually have criminal backgrounds.

Our comparisons of employer data at different points in the 1990s suggest some sensitivity to demand conditions and some modest improvements in demand for former offenders over the decade, though these were to some extent offset by a continuing shift in employment away from manufacturing toward the retail trade and service sectors and toward jobs with direct customer contact. Comparisons between our estimated quantities of labor demand for and supply of former offenders also suggest that there may be some imbalance between the two, particularly as large numbers of offenders continue to be released over the coming decade and are heavily concentrated in poor minority communities.

Overall, then, it seems that the employment prospects for former offenders are quite restricted. The low rates of employment that they suffer not only will mean lower incomes and higher rates of recidivism for them but will also adversely affect their families and communities. For instance, the families of former offenders will have lower incomes and higher poverty rates than they otherwise would; and there may be intergenerational effects, in which their sons also become more likely to avoid the labor market or to engage in crime.[27] Poor employment prospects for former offenders will also weaken informal job networks in these neighborhoods and may lead to higher crime rates there than would occur if their employment prospects were better.

These results suggest that policies should attempt to reduce the barriers faced by former offenders in the labor market. Some possible approaches might include revisiting the legal barriers to employment that many states have implemented; providing special training, job placement services, or transitional employment to offenders upon release; and exploring the extent to which employer reluctance to hire former offenders might be reduced by making tax credits or bonding more readily available.[28] Our results do not suggest that we should restrict employer access to background information, as the provision of such information might reduce employer discrimination against young black men in general. But it is important that the information available be accurate—in other words, that it not contain arrest records as opposed to records on convictions and that it not mistakenly identify individuals as offenders.

A good deal more research is also needed to understand more about employer demand for former offenders. To what extent do employers distinguish between those convicted and those incarcerated? How important are the nature and quantities of the offenses, as well as when they occurred and offender records since the time of the offense? Are employers engaging in more criminal background checks over time? If so, how does this affect demand for offenders as well as other disadvantaged groups more broadly? In the meantime, we can say with some certainty that employer demand limits the job prospects facing former offenders in the labor market, in addition to the many other disadvantages and difficulties they face.

We thank the Russell Sage Foundation for their generous support of this project.

NOTES

1. As of December 31, 2000, there were 1,381,392 inmates in state and federal prisons. This is an increase of 1.3 percent over the previous year, far lower than the average annual growth rate of 6 percent since year-end 1990.
2. Scott Craig (1987) cites several examples of employers who were held responsible for the criminal acts of their employees under the theory of negligent hiring, including judgments against the owner of a taxi company and the owner of a security services firm for sexual assaults committed by employees. In one cited instance involving a sexual assault committed by an apartment manager, the owner of an apartment complex was found negligent for not taking into account gaps in the manager's work history in the hiring decision. More recent examples are found in Connerley, Arvey, and Bernardy (2001). In one instance, a home health hiring agency was found negligent for not conducting a criminal background check before hiring an aide who subsequently murdered a quadriplegic in his care and the patient's mother. The aide had in fact six larceny-related convictions.

3. Although as of this writing we have found no data on the number of negligent hiring suits, anecdotal evidence suggests that the number of such suits is increasing. Furthermore, it is argued that the possible increase in such suits is attributable to several factors, including the potential liability of employers, under negligent hiring theory, for actions taken by employees who are off the job; the possibility that the amount of compensation awarded in negligent hiring cases may be higher than in other cases; the statue of limitations for negligent hiring claims being longer than for other claims; and the possibility that evidence of prior acts of the employee's negligence may be introduced in negligent hiring cases (Extejt and Bockanic 1991).

4. In addition to the greater openness of state repositories, several services have emerged that perform nationwide reviews of criminal history records for small fees. An Internet search of the term "criminal history record" turns up several companies who will perform nationwide criminal background checks (allegedly accounting for offenses in all fifty states) for as little as $15. In addition, well-known security services firms such as Pinkerton offer basic and extensive background checks for employers as well as other non-criminal-justice clients.

   All of this suggests that criminal history records are potentially available to non-criminal-justice users, but whether the employer can legally access and consider such information in making hiring decisions is another matter. A 1976 Supreme Court decision ruled that arrest and prior conviction records are public, given that the initial source of information was from public records (Bushway 1996). Hence it is not a violation of the right to privacy for non-criminal-justice employers to access criminal history records. Moreover, as noted earlier, who can access records and the extent of information available (for example, arrests and prior convictions versus prior conviction only) are determined by individual states (U.S. Department of Justice 1999). For most jobs, the Equal Employment Opportunities Commission guidelines prohibit "blanket exclusions" of applicants with criminal records. However, employers can consider criminal histories as long as the severity of the offense is related to the applicant's ability to effectively perform the job and as long as the employer considers the time lapsed since the offense in coming to a decision (Bushway 1996).

5. Harry Holzer (1996) provides detailed comparisons of response rates by industry, location, and establishment size and finds no substantial differences in response rates. He also provides evidence that the distribution of firms in the Multi-City Study of Urban Equality sample within areas by industry and firm size is comparable to those found in the *County Business Patterns*.

6. Evidence presented by Walter Jensen and William Giegold (1976) suggests that employers are not unwilling to hire former offenders and are in fact engaged in activities to absorb the flow of partially rehabilitated former offenders. However, this study used data that is now more than twenty-five years old and was therefore conducted in a very different time and under very different circumstances.

7. The average distances are calculated using linear distances (in miles) be-

tween the centroid of the employer's census tract and the centroids of all other census tracts in the area. The variable for each employer is the weighted average of distance to all other census tracts, where the weights are the number of persons of a particular race residing in the destination tract. Hence the variable "distance black" measures the firm's distance to the average black person in the metropolitan area. See Holzer and Ihlanfeldt (1996) and Raphael, Stoll, and Holzer (2000) for a more detailed discussion of these indexes.

8.   Since background checking and employer aversion to hiring former offenders are positively correlated, one might predict that variables that are positively correlated with employer aversion should be positively correlated with the likelihood that firms check backgrounds and the opposite for variables that are negatively correlated with firm aversion. The patterns in table 8.3 contrast these predictions for firm size, several of the recruiting methods variables, and the means for the variables indicating the types of applicants that the employer would avoid hiring.

9.   We also used regression analysis to examine these basic patterns and found that the most statistically significant predictors of criminal background checks at firms (that is, always or sometimes checked) included smaller establishments, jobs with customer contact, and firms that used testing, net of all other factors included in table 8.3. On the other hand, the strongest predictor of establishments that did not check was industry, especially manufacturing and wholesale trade. These results are consistent with the basic patterns shown here.

10.   Regression analysis of firms that are willing to hire former offenders and do not check criminal backgrounds as a function of all other variables listed in table 8.4 confirms these same patterns. The most statistically significant predictors of being willing to hire and not checking are whether the firm would hire those with spotty work histories or those on welfare. Other significant predictors include whether the job required a high school diploma or customer contact, whether the firm used tests during screening, and whether the firm was a manufacturing, wholesale trade, retail trade, or service establishment.

11.   For instance, the labor market gains experienced by blacks during World War II and the late 1960s did not dissipate with the passing of those boom periods, and their entry into new sectors of the economy and the labor force was not reversed after those periods.

12.   Unemployment rates nationally averaged about 7 percent during the period in which the survey was administered, and even a bit higher in the four metropolitan areas considered here. In contrast, by the last few years of the decade unemployment rates averaged about 4 percent.

13.   For more information about this survey see Holzer and Stoll (2001). The focus of the survey was employer demand for welfare recipients. However, a shortened section of the survey focused on the last worker hired in the firm into a job that did not require a college education, posing questions comparable to those asked in the Multi-City Study between June 1992 and May 1994.

14.   Unfortunately, the questions on whether or not employers are checking

criminal backgrounds were not included for most recently filled jobs on the later survey.

15. Unemployment rates in Wisconsin averaged just about 3 percent over much of the decade, reflecting one of the tightest state labor markets of that period. But the greater willingness to hire former offenders in Milwaukee could also reflect other factors, such as a more tolerant political climate or greater efforts by state agencies to place disadvantaged workers into the labor market.

16. For instance, the proportions of employers in manufacturing and retail trade were roughly 0.22 and 0.17 in the earlier (1992 to 1994) survey but 0.18 and 0.22 in later (1998 to 1999) one. Proportions of jobs requiring direct customer contact rose as well. Some of this may reflect changes in the metropolitan areas sampled between our two surveys as well as secular changes over time in firm and job composition.

17. If former offenders are the last group employers are willing to hire, the demand for them might well reflect not only the level of labor market tightness but also the period of time during which such tightness was experienced. Indeed, it appeared as though various employer organizations and those that work with them, such as the Welfare to Work Partnership, began to focus their efforts on the placement of former offenders only toward the end of this period.

18. For instance, the mean job vacancy rates in manufacturing, retail trade, and services in the later survey (1998 to 1999) data are 0.029, 0.056, and 0.065, respectively.

19. The stratification of the sample by establishment size and the oversampling of larger firms (in proportion with the percentage of employment at such firms) implicitly weights the sample by establishment size.

20. Owing to overcrowding in state prisons, felons with sentences of a year or longer sometimes serve part or all of their sentences in county jails.

21. The total numbers of former prisoners and former felons are drawn from Uggen and Manza (2001). Their measure of prisoners includes those who have been in prison or on parole, while their measure of felons includes prisoners plus those on felony probation and those convicted of felonies in jail. However, the measures of former prisoners and former felons do not include those currently on parole or felony probation. Uggen and Manza estimate these numbers based on annual flows of prisoners released from jail over time, along with assumptions of recidivism and mortality rates by race among those released. Their estimates are for the years 1998 and 2000, so we interpolate their numbers to obtain estimates for 1999.

22. It is not completely clear whether employers are as averse to hiring convicted felons who have not been incarcerated as they are to hiring those that have been incarcerated. For some evidence on this matter see Freeman (1992).

23. This last estimate is based on the assumption that at least half of all individuals on parole or probation represent new flows within any year. We thank Chris Uggen for providing us with some estimates to this effect.

24. These estimates assume employment rates for former offenders of 0.50 to 0.66. Estimated employment rates based on the National Longitudinal Survey of Youth from the 1980s (see Freeman 1992) are closer to the higher end

of this range, while employment rates of male high school dropouts currently are closer to the lower end. Estimates of preincarceration employment rates for inmates of federal prisons presented in Kling (2000) are at the low end of this range.

25. Roughly, the Bureau of Labor Statistics projects 1.4 percent annual growth in employment for the next decade, and our estimates suggest that employers would fill about 40 percent of these jobs with former offenders.

26. For another such exercise in which the hypothetical quantities of less-skilled labor demanded and supplied are matched to each other, see Holzer and Danziger (2000).

27. Even if the father is a noncustodial parent, the employment barriers he faces will reduce his family's income by limiting his ability to pay child support. The poor employment prospects of fathers may limit those of their children either through role-model effects or by limiting their labor market information and contacts.

28. The Work Opportunity Tax Credit is now available to employers who hire former offenders and other disadvantaged groups, though employer take-up of the credit is quite low. A federal program also now provides low-cost bonds to employers that insure them for up to $5,000 in damages or liabilities that might be incurred if they hire former offenders.

REFERENCES

Burtless, Gary. 2000. "Can the Labor Market Absorb Three Million Welfare Recipients?" In *The Low-Wage Labor Market: Challenges and Opportunities for Economic Self-Sufficiency*, edited by Kelleen Kaye and Demetra Smith Nightingale. Washington, D.C.: Urban Institute Press.

Bushway, Shawn D. 1996. "Labor Market Effects of Permitting Employer Access to Criminal History Records." Working paper. University of Maryland.

Connerley, Mary L., Richard D. Arvey, and Charles J. Bernardy. 2001. "Criminal Background Checks for Prospective and Current Employees: Current Practices Among Municipal Agencies." *Public Personnel Management* 30(2, Summer): 173–83.

Craig, Scott R. 1987. "Negligent Hiring: Guilt by Association." *Personnel Administrator* (October): 32–34.

Extejt, M. M., and W. N. Bockanic. 1991. "Issues Surrounding the Theories of Negligent Hiring and Failure to Fire." *Business and Professional Ethics Journal* 8(4): 21–33.

Freeman, Richard. 1992. "Crime and the Employment of Disadvantaged Youth." In *Urban Labor Markets and Job Opportunity*, edited by George Peterson and Wayne Vroman. Washington, D.C.: Urban Institute Press.

Freeman, Richard, and William M. Rodgers III. 2000. "Area Economic Conditions and the Labor Market Outcomes of Young Men in the 1990's Expansion." In *Prosperity for All? The Economic Boom and African Americans*, edited by Robert Cherry and William M. Rodgers III. New York: Russell Sage Foundation.

Glynn, T. P. 1988. "The Limited Viability of Negligent Supervision, Retention, Hiring, and Infliction of Emotional Distress Claims in Employment Discrimination Cases in Minnesota." *William Mitchell Law Review* 24: 581.

Grogger, Jeffrey. 1995. "The Effects of Arrest on the Employment and Earnings of Young Men." *Quarterly Journal of Economics* 110(1): 51–71.

Hahn, J. M. 1991. "Pre-Employment Information Services: Employers Beware." *Employee Relations Law Journal* 17(1): 45–69.

Holzer, Harry J. 1996. *What Employers Want: Job Prospects for Less Educated Workers.* New York: Russell Sage Foundation.

Holzer, Harry J., and Sheldon Danziger. 2000. "Are Jobs Available for Disadvantaged Workers in Urban Areas?" In *Urban Inequality,* edited by Alice O'Connor, Lawrence Bobo and Chris Tilly. New York: Russell Sage Foundation.

Holzer, Harry J., and Keith R. Ihlanfeldt. 1996. "Spatial Factors and the Employment of Blacks at the Firm Level." *New England Economic Review: Federal Reserve Bank of Boston* (May–June): 65–68.

Holzer, Harry J., and Michael A. Stoll. 2001. *Employers and Welfare Recipients: The Effects of Welfare Reform in the Workplace.* San Francisco: Public Policy Institute of California.

Hoynes, Hilary. 2000. "The Employment, Earnings and Income of Less-Skilled Workers Over the Business Cycle." In *Finding Jobs: Work and Welfare Reform,* edited by David Card and Rebecca Blank. New York: Russell Sage Foundation.

Jensen, Walter, Jr., and William C. Giegold. 1976. "Finding Jobs for Ex-Offenders: A Study of Employers' Attitudes." *American Business Law Journal* 14(2): 195–225.

Kling, Jeffrey. 1995. "High Performance Workplaces." *Monthly Labor Review* 118(5, May): 29–36.

———. 2000. "The Effect of Prison Sentence Length on the Subsequent Employment and Earnings of Criminal Defendants." Discussion Papers in Economics 208. Woodrow Wilson School of Economics, Princeton University (February).

Moss, Phillip, and Chris Tilly. 2000. *Stories Employers Tell: Race, Skill and Hiring in America.* New York: Russell Sage Foundation.

Raphael, Steven, Michael A. Stoll, and Harry J. Holzer. 2000. "Are Suburban Firms More Likely to Discrimination Against African-Americans?" *Journal of Urban Economics* 48(3, November): 485–508.

Stoll, Michael A., Harry J. Holzer, and Keith R. Ihlanfeldt. 2000. "Within Cities and Suburbs: Racial Residential Concentration and the Spatial Distribution of Employment Opportunities Across Sub-Metropolitan Areas." *Journal of Policy Analysis and Management* 19(2): 207–32.

Travis, Jeremy, Amy Solomon, and Michelle Waul. 2001. *From Prison to Home: The Dimensions and Consequences of Prisoner Reentry.* Washington, D. C.: Urban Institute Press.

Uggen, Christopher, and Jeff Manza. 2001. "The Political Consequences of Felon Disenfranchisement Laws in the United States." Paper presented at the annual meeting of the American Sociological Association. Anaheim, Calif.

U.S. Department of Commerce, Bureau of the Census. 1993. *National and State Population Estimates, 1993.* Washington: Economics and Statistics Administration, Bureau of the Census.

———. 1994. *National and State Population Estimates, 1994.* Washington: Economics and Statistics Administration, Bureau of the Census.

————. 1995. *National and State Population Estimates, 1995.* Washington: Economics and Statistics Administration, Bureau of the Census.

U.S. Department of Justice, Bureau of Justice Statistics. 1993. *National Prisoner Statistics, 1993.* Washington: Bureau of Justice Statistics.

————. 1994. *National Prisoner Statistics, 1994.* Washington: Bureau of Justice Statistics.

————. 1995. *National Prisoner Statistics, 1995.* Washington: Bureau of Justice Statistics.

————. 1997. "Lifetime Likelihood of Going to State or Federal Prison." *Bureau of Justice Statistics Special Report.* NCJ-160092. Washington: U.S. Government Printing Office.

————. 1999. *Compendium of State Privacy and Security Legislation: 1999 Overview.* Washington: U.S. Government Printing Office.

U.S. Department of Labor, Bureau of Labor Statistics. 2000. *Current Employment Statistics (CES), 2000.* Washington: Bureau of Labor Statistics.

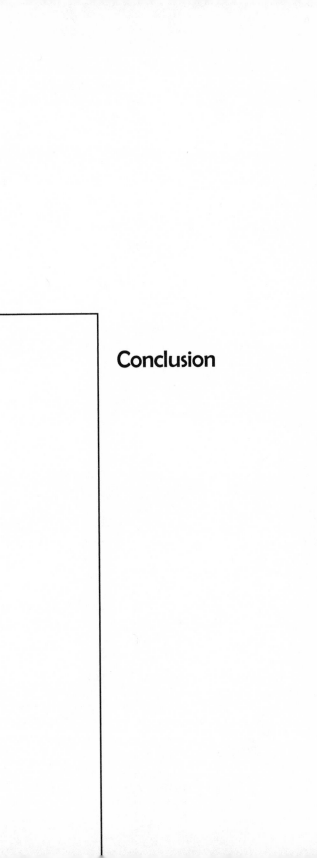

Conclusion

Jeremy Travis

9 Reentry and Reintegration: New Perspectives on the Challenges of Mass Incarceration

The steady growth of imprisonment in America over the past generation has created an unprecedented social and policy challenge: the reintegration of large numbers of individuals who have spent time in America's prisons. This challenge has been largely overlooked amid the intense political and philosophical debates over our sentencing policies that have accompanied the inexorable rise in the rate of imprisonment in this country.

It has not always been so. In the golden age of indeterminate sentencing, which lasted from early in the twentieth century until the mid-1970s, the goal of prisoner reintegration occupied a prominent place in the rhetoric, and often the reality, of American jurisprudence (Tonry 1996). Under the indeterminate sentencing model, judges were given wide statutory discretion to sentence defendants to an indeterminate number of years in prison; rehabilitation was a stated goal of sentencing; parole boards decided the actual time of release from prison, basing their decisions in part on a prisoner's readiness to return to free society; parole agents then supervised the released prisoner during the remainder of his or her sentence, during which time the parolee was expected to meet certain conditions designed to reestablish positive connections with family, the world of work, and other institutions of civil society. Reintegration was an explicit objective of the supervised transition from prison to community. For half a century, every state in the union and the District of Columbia subscribed to these ideals.

Of course, the reality of practice during the golden age did not always (or even often) match the lofty aspirations of the indeterminate sentencing model. But this shortcoming does not obscure the larger point: our sentencing jurisprudence viewed prisoner reintegration as an important objective of the criminal justice system.

The seismic changes in sentencing policy that began in the 1970s fundamentally altered the landscape of punishment in America. Since that time, a dizzying succession of sentencing reforms adopted by federal and state legislatures has undermined the indeterminate sentencing framework. Mandatory minimums, abolition of parole release mechanisms, "truth-in-sentencing" laws, "three-strikes-and-you're-out" schemes, sex-offender registration provisions (sometimes for life), drug tests, electronic surveillance technologies, and a vast and uncatalogued network of "invisible punishments"—the collateral sanctions for felony convictions—have forever altered the reality of punishment in America (Travis 2002b).

True, indeterminate sentencing (including the use of parole boards as release mechanisms and parole officers as supervisory agents for post-release terms) can still be found in a substantial number of states. But the concepts of rehabilitation and reintegration no longer hold the majority market share in the competition for ideas that provide an intellectual foundation for our sentencing jurisprudence. Other concepts—just deserts, retribution, incapacitation for purposes of crime control—are now more likely to animate the next wave of sentencing policy.

The net result of these shifts is the existence, at the turn of the twenty-first century, of a patchwork of sentencing philosophies and practices across the nation. It seems likely that the national discourse over the purposes of sentencing will continue to resemble the jurisprudential Tower of Babel created by the undermining of the indeterminate sentencing ideal. What is less clear is whether this fragmentation of sentencing policy prevents development of a policy consensus that prisoner reintegration should be the goal of any and all sentencing philosophies.

Neither the new reality of mass incarceration nor the absence of a new dominant sentencing philosophy should stand in the way of a renewed focus on the challenges of prisoner reentry and reintegration. Stated affirmatively, the reality of reentry and the challenges of reintegration create a common ground on which the philosophical differences that have created the current cacophony of sentencing policies can be put to one side and policies designed to improve outcomes for returning prisoners, their families, and their communities can gain broad support.

I hasten to make two qualifying observations at the outset. The argument developed in this chapter is not an acceptance of the current reality of imprisonment in America. For a number of reasons, ranging from moral to pragmatic, I agree with those who believe that our level of incarceration is unacceptably high. Nor do I believe that the future is bleak. On the contrary, recent U.S. Department of Justice data show that the rate of incarceration has leveled off and is declining in some states (U.S. Department of Justice 2000; Harrison and Beck 2003). In this discussion I take mass incarceration as a fact; in so doing, I both acknowledge the current reality and purposefully choose not to engage, here, the important questions about the wisdom of our current punishment policies.

UNDERSTANDING PRISONER REENTRY IN THE ERA OF MASS INCARCERATION

Ever since prisons were first built, prisoners have made the journey from prison to home. For some, this journey has been relatively straightforward: they have prepared themselves for the return home, been welcomed by family and community, and made positive connections to peer groups, jobs, and everyday life in the community. For a variety of reasons that are poorly understood, most of these returning prisoners ultimately find their way to a law-abiding, productive life (Maruna 2001). For others, the journey has been difficult, full of challenges and risks, as the returning prisoner has struggled to navigate the tricky waters of discrimination against former offenders, families that are ambivalent about the prisoner's return, employers who cast a wary eye at the years in prison, and the temptations of substance abuse and criminal acquaintances who offer a return to antisocial activities. These returning prisoners may succeed, perhaps after some failures; they may not. For a third group of returning prisoners, the prospect of returning to a crime-free life was never highly likely. Within a short period of time, they are back in the criminal life, often returned to prison in a matter of months.

Little has changed in this picture since America embarked on the grand experiment in mass incarceration that has increased the per capita rate of imprisonment fourfold since the early 1970s. Prisoners still make the journey from prison to home, with similar patterns of success and failure. As in the past, the population being released from prison remains mostly men, often with histories of substance abuse, poorly educated, coming mostly from poor, inner-city communities. Some dimensions of the reentry phenomenon are the same as they were thirty years ago. Yet in another sense much has changed, and the consequences for our society are profound.

First, consider the sheer volume of the reentry population. In 2001 more than 600,000 individuals left state and federal prison, about 1,600 a day. In 1977, by contrast, about 150,000 prisoners were released from state and federal prison (Travis, Solomon, and Waul 2001). This increase in the reentry population tracks the increase in the number of prison admissions (see figure 9.1).

Second, the prisoners coming home today have been in prison for

Figure 9.1   *Sentenced Prisoners Admitted and Released from State and Federal Prison, 1977 to 1998*

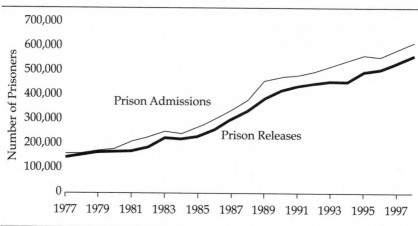

Source: Travis, Solomon, and Waul (2001), based on Bureau of Justice Statistics National Prisoner Statistics.

longer periods of time. The average amount of time spent in prison by those released between 1990 and 1998 increased from twenty-one months to twenty-eight months, an increase of more than 25 percent in eight years. As various sentencing reforms take hold—particularly so-called truth-in-sentencing laws that typically require a violent offender to serve 85 percent of his or her sentence before being released—the distribution of average sentences served in America has shifted considerably. Between 1991 and 1997, the proportion of soon-to-be-released prisoners who had been in prison for more than five years rose by more than two-thirds, from 13 percent to 21 percent. The proportion of prisoners serving a year or less dropped in half, from 33 percent to 17 percent (Lynch and Sabol 2001).

These longer prison sentences have significant consequences for the processes of prisoner reintegration. By sheer passage of time, the ties between prisoners, their families, and their networks of support in their communities have attenuated. Perhaps, for some prisoners, the passage of time and the erosion of community contacts are beneficial. One can imagine, for example, that putting time and space between a young man and his gang network might help him keep his distance from negative influences upon his return home. For some prisoners, the natural aging process will have a beneficial effect as the additional months or years in prison place them beyond the age when rates of criminal offending are the highest. Among the men they interviewed, Kathryn Edin, Timothy

Figure 9.2   *Prisoners Participating in Prison Programs Within Twelve Months of Their Release, 1991 and 1997*

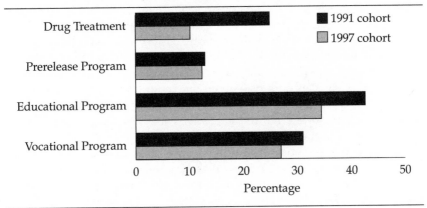

Source: Data from Lynch and Sabol (2001); U.S. Department of Justice (1993, 2000).

Nelson, and Rechelle Paranal find some support for the positive effects of aging within the solitude of prison (chapter 3 in this volume). Overall, however, the more reasonable conjecture is that longer sentences make for more difficult adjustments after release from prison. To the extent that familial and community supports enhance a prisoner's chances of successful reentry, weakening the links to those support systems is inconsistent with achieving the reintegration goal (Lynch and Sabol 2001).

Third, the prisoners who are returning home today, at the height of the mass incarceration phenomenon in America, are less prepared for life in free society. According to the Bureau of Justice Statistics, the rates of participation in several categories of in-prison programs have dropped significantly over the decade of the 1990s. In 1991 almost one-third (31 percent) of the prisoners scheduled to leave prison in the next year had participated in a vocational program in prison. By 1997 that participation rate had dropped to 27 percent. In 1991, 43 percent of the exiting cohort had participated in an education program; by 1997 that rate had dropped to 35 percent. In 1991 one-quarter had participated in a drug treatment program; by 1997 that participation rate had dropped to 10 percent. In both years, only 10 to 12 percent had participated in formal prerelease programs designed to prepare prisoners for the transition from life in prison to life in the community (Lynch and Sabol 2001; U.S. Department of Justice 1993, 2000) (see figure 9.2).

Setting aside questions about the effectiveness of these programs in actually connecting released prisoners to jobs on the outside, reducing relapse to drug or alcohol abuse, or assisting in the practical aspects of successful reentry, the larger point still remains. Over the decade of the 1990s, as American prison populations were expanding significantly, the investments made in the kinds of programmatic interventions designed to advance the goal of prisoner reintegration dropped significantly. Even more telling is the fact that these participation rates were low to start with, no higher than the 43 percent who had ever participated in an education program (Lynch and Sabol 2001). Finally, the low participation rate in "prerelease" programs—about one in ten exiting prisoners participated in such programs—powerfully underscores the low priority given to preparing prisoners for the challenges they face when they return home (Lawrence et al. 2002).

Fourth, the prisoners returning home now, at the height of the American experiment with mass incarceration, are drawn from—and therefore overwhelmingly returning to—a relatively small number of communities. This geographic concentration of the reentry phenomenon can be viewed from several perspectives. From a national perspective, the concentration is found in a small number of states. Slightly fewer than half of the returning prisoners are released by the prisons in five states. California alone, with only 12 percent of the U.S. population, accounts for about a quarter of all releases from state prisons. From a state perspective, the phenomenon of prisoner reentry is increasingly concentrated in "core counties," those that include the central city of a metropolitan area. In 1984 the proportion of prisoners released from state prisons who returned to these core counties stood at 50 percent. By 1996 that percentage had risen to 66 percent. Of course, as the number of releases has also increased over this period of time, the overall flow of individuals going from those neighborhoods to prison and back again increases substantially as well (Lynch and Sabol 2001).

The concentrations of prisoner reentry are felt most acutely at the neighborhood level. This point is illustrated in an examination of the effects of incarceration in Brooklyn, New York. Eleven percent of the block groups in that borough of New York City account for 20 percent of the population, yet they are home to 50 percent of the parolees (Cadora and Swartz 1999). Data from Cuyahoga County, Ohio, which includes Cleveland, make a similar point: less than 1 percent of the block groups in the county accounts for approximately 20 percent of the county's prisoners (Lynch and Sabol 2001). Finally, these concentrations of incarceration's effects can be understood in their aggregate effects on the life cycle of the neighborhood's young people. In the high-concentration blocks of Brooklyn, New York, about one in every eight parenting-age males is sent to prison or jail each year. In the counterpart blocks of Cleveland, between 8 and 15 percent of the young black males are incarcerated on any given day (Travis, Solomon, and Waul 2001).

These neighborhoods are already historically disadvantaged in terms of economic distress, high crime rates, poor social services, and family functioning. So the significant increases in arrests, removals, imprisonment, and return of large numbers of individuals, mostly males, have placed severe additional burdens on the capacity of those communities to do what communities should do—namely, exist as places where individuals, families, and civic institutions can thrive.

The population of individuals leaving prison today is different in several critical respects from those who left prison a generation ago. There are significantly more of them, by a factor of more than four. They have been in prison longer. They are less prepared for the inevitable journey home. And they are returning in larger numbers to a small number of communities in America.

REENTRY AND REINTEGRATION
PERSPECTIVES ON IMPRISONMENT

The new reality of mass incarceration in America poses a number of profound questions for research and policy development, questions that have not received sufficient attention. One can view the increase in imprisonment as a social experiment on a grand scale. In essence, as a nation we have embraced policies that have had the result of increasing, fourfold, the per capita rate of imprisonment in America over the past generation. As with other social experiments, we should ask the obvious question: What have been the effects, positive and negative, of these new policies?

Given the clear fiscal costs of this experiment—state corrections budgets in 1997 were tallied at $44 billion, up from $9 billion in 1982—one would think that there would be a rich research literature on the benefits (and nonfiscal costs) of increased incarceration. Given the relatively predictable effects of various sentencing reforms on future prison growth, one would think that the policy debates over punishment enhancements would include assessments of their fiscal impact, alternative strategies that might achieve similar results, and the opportunity costs of different sentencing policies. Yet with rare exceptions, this kind of analysis has been absent from the public discourse over the wisdom of our experiment with increased incarceration.

Scholars and practitioners have recently been adopting a "reentry perspective" to unpack the effects of the growth in incarceration rates in America (Burke 2001; Hammett, Roberts, and Kennedy. 2001; Travis and Petersilia 2001; Wilkinson 2001). In essence, this framework views sentencing and corrections policies from the perspective of the individuals who pass through America's prisons, their families, and their communities. This analytical device begins with the recognition of an iron law of corrections: except for those who die in prison, all individuals sentenced to imprisonment come back. "Reentry," then, is the inevitable result of imprisonment. Reentry is not a form of supervision, like parole. Reentry is not a goal, like rehabilitation. Reentry is not an option.

The reentry framework recasts some age-old debates in the criminal justice field (Travis and Petersilia 2001). For example, a number of corrections administrators are using the reentry reality to refocus the role of prisons in our society (Wilkinson 2001). Since most prisoners eventually come home, the policy question that should be addressed in every aspect of prison management is this: "How can prisoners be best prepared for the inevitable return?" This question leads to a series of new goals for corrections professionals. For example, providing drug treatment in prison is certainly commendable but is quite incomplete without ways to reduce the high rates of relapse experienced by individuals with histories of substance abuse once they leave prison. Facilitating family contacts for prisoners may be desirable, but visitation programs miss the larger challenge of helping prisoners and families work through the complex dynamics of the prisoner's return home. Encouraging participation in job readiness programs may be good correctional practice, but creating a link to the world of work on the outside is the ultimate test of success. In the words of one criminal justice expert, a focus on prisoner reentry is an "elevating goal" for the corrections field (Burke 2001).

The reentry framework redefines the social responsibilities of prison managers in an even more fundamental sense. Today, about one-quarter of the more than six hundred thousand prisoners released annually from America's state and federal prisons are released unconditionally. They are not on parole, are under no legal obligation to meet special conditions following their release, and report to no parole officer. In a very real sense, prison administrators, under current practice, discharge their social obligations when these individuals leave prison. Yet from a reentry perspective, those administrators have a broader social obligation: to prepare prisoners for the inevitable return home, in most ways no different from those who leave on parole supervision. The prisoners leaving under no supervision, as well as their families and communities, have the same interest in successful reentry as those who leave with supervision. The fact that unsupervised prisoners are not subject to legal constraints may impede the state's ability to require certain behaviors, but the larger social interest in reconnecting these prisoners to positive and productive activities in their communities still exists.

In this way, the reentry perspective operates to define corrections policies that are independent of sentencing policies. Imagine a pure determinate sentencing state, with no system of parole supervision, in which all sentences are complete when the prisoner leaves prison. Does the corrections department in that state have no obligation to prepare the prisoner for the return home? Merely stating, in legislation, that prisoners are released unconditionally does not change the social reality of reentry.

The reentry framework also creates a basis for interrogating sentencing policies. This bridge between sentencing policy and prisoner reintegration is an established but underappreciated aspect of the traditional indeterminate sentencing scheme. In that worldview, parole boards and parole agents are responsible for increasing the odds of successful transition from prison to community. But mandatory minimum and other determinate sentencing laws do not answer the question, "What is the state's responsibility for minimizing the harmful effects of the return from prison to community?" One answer to that question might be that the state has no such responsibility: those risks are born entirely by prisoners, their families, and their social networks. For some prisoners, that laissez-faire policy might indeed be the appropriate societal response. But the broad brush of determinate sentencing does not make such individualized distinctions. An example from the other end of the spectrum illustrates this point: why should there be no legal supervision over a violent, mentally ill, drug-addicted prisoner who completes a fixed sentence and is simply shown the prison door? One need not engage in a debate over the efficacy of the rehabilitation ideal to acknowledge that society is the loser if some returning prisoners are simply released back onto the street.

As these examples illustrate, the reentry perspective creates a natural linkage to a related, important discussion about the goals of the criminal sanction. Reduction of recidivism is certainly a core objective for criminal justice interventions, imprisonment included. Yet another objective quickly comes into focus: successful reintegration of those who have violated the law. At times, these goals overlap. Connecting a former prisoner with a job may reduce the likelihood that he or she will violate the law again. The same job also serves reintegration purposes. It connects prisoners to the habits of work, provides economic benefits to their families, adds their taxes to the public coffers, and gives them status in their communities. Yet recidivism reduction and prisoner reintegration are more often quite distinct goals. Assisting a returning prisoner in establishing a healthy relationship with his or her family upon return from prison may or may not reduce the prisoner's propensity to reoffend, but a successful familial reintegration is likely to have a number of positive effects on the overall well-being of the family.

In sum, the reentry perspective, and the closely allied focus on the goal of prisoner reintegration, provides the foundation for productive discussions about the role of prisons in our society, the purposes of sentencing, and the goals of criminal justice intervention. Because these discussions are not tied to specific sentencing schemes, yet can be used to question the wisdom of any particular sentencing scheme, the reentry perspective offers a broad common ground in the current cacophony of sentencing philosophies.

REENTRY AS A PRISM FOR SOCIAL POLICY

The reentry perspective can also serve as a prism that refracts other social policies outside of the traditional criminal justice domains of sentencing, corrections, and the role of the criminal sanction. The following section explores three issue areas that lie outside the domain of criminal justice policy—family, workforce development, and public health—to illustrate the power of the reentry perspective.

When viewed through the reentry prism, these policy domains take on different dimensions and contours. The common powerful insight is the realization of the high degree of overlap between these domains and criminal justice policy. Consider these consequences of the era of mass incarceration: In some communities, a significant percentage of minor children have a parent in prison. Many low-skilled workers (particularly minority males) have spent time in prison. Substantial portions of the American population facing significant health risks pass through the criminal justice system each year. In some areas of social policy, the criminal justice reality casts a long shadow.

The reentry perspective defines a common ground of overlapping policy interests between unlikely allies in different arenas of public policy. Family practitioners in communities of high concentrations of arrest, incarceration, and reentry can benefit from new partnerships with criminal justice agencies. Workforce developers might realize that the prison experience is one shared by many of their clientele and create alliances with prison administrators. Health professionals seeking to reduce community health risks might find common cause with corrections health care administrators. In this way, the reentry perspective holds the potential for creating new partnerships between criminal justice practitioners and their counterparts in other areas of practice.

Family Policy

More than half of the inmates in state prisons are parents of minor children. As prison populations have grown, so too has the number of children with a parent in prison. In 1999 there were 1.5 million minor children with a parent in prison, an increase from 1 million in 1990.

Today, 2 percent of the country's minor children have a mother or father in prison (Mumola 2000).

Seen through a racial lens, the nexus between children and incarceration looks even starker. In 1999, among minor African American children, 7 percent had a parent in prison. Even this statistic, which simply reflects a snapshot of a moment in time, does not capture the full effect of incarceration on parenting patterns. Given the lifetime probability of nearly 30 percent that an African American male born in 1991 will spend at least a year in prison, the reality of imprisonment penetrates deeply into the father-child dynamics of the African American community (Bonczar and Beck 1997). A final calculation would make the point even more sharply: In neighborhoods of high concentrations of removal, incarceration, and reentry, such as those blocks in Brooklyn described earlier in this chapter, where one in eight parenting-age males goes to jail or prison each year, what percentage of minor children has a parent who has ever been incarcerated? Even this calculation would not begin to assess the effects of removal, incarceration, and reentry on family formation, parent-child relations, and prevailing notions of parental responsibility in those neighborhoods (see chapter 2 in this volume).

A reentry perspective adds new richness to these analyses of the impact of imprisonment on families and children (Visher and Travis 2003). A more dynamic view would focus, for example, on the effects of incarceration on the prisoner's family life over the life course of the criminal case, beginning with arrest, through incarceration, and ending with the parent's return home. For some families, the arrest of a parent may be a blessing: removing a violent or emotionally oppressive mother or father may improve the well-being of the family unit or enhance the safety of individual family members. For other families, the arrest of mother or father may signify the removal of a breadwinner and force the family into poverty or dependence on others. From the basic perspective of where children live, Elizabeth Johnson and Jane Waldfogel (chapter 5 in this volume) show that women's incarceration is more disruptive than men's, as more women than men lived with their children before incarceration. For some incarcerated parents, the time spent in prison proves a turning point in their relationships with their children, allowing for more constructive interactions than were possible during the time when the parent was deeply involved in criminal activities (see chapter 3 in this volume).

The return from prison to family presents its own challenges. How are parent and child best reunited? How should the passage of time be acknowledged? Is there a risk that the reflexes and coping mechanisms adopted to handle life in prison have left the returning prisoner less capable of being an effective parent? Is there a heightened risk of domestic violence and child abuse as the returning prisoner reacts to his or her new reality?

A reentry perspective would also inquire into the impact of imprisonment and reentry on parenting arrangements for the children left behind (Braman and Wood 2003; chapter 5 in this volume). To what extent have the children been cared for by the other parent, grandparents, or foster parents, and what effects do these arrangements have on their development? What percentage of children in foster care and kinship care are there because of the incarceration of a parent? How can those social service systems be equipped to respond to the psychological and emotional needs of this unique category of clients? How should decisions about family reunification be made when the mother or father is returning from prison? How should the parent-prisoner be involved in these decision-making processes?

These avenues for further inquiry are paralleled by new opportunities for policy collaboration (Rossman 2003). For example, one could imagine new partnerships between departments of corrections and child and family welfare agencies, which are clearly warranted by the findings, in chapter 5 in this volume, of the multiple risks that children of incarcerees face. Corrections professionals, aware of the importance of family influences in increasing the chance of successful reintegration for returning prisoners, might forge new alliances with local service providers who could attend to the needs of a prisoner's family (children in particular) during incarceration. One direct result of these alliances might be new programs to enable prisoners and their families to stay in touch, perhaps using the Internet and video communications technologies to overcome the distance between prison and community. Corrections professionals and family specialists could find ways to assist prisoners and their families in working through the complex dynamics of reunification, much as family practitioners handle similar dynamics in child custody proceedings. When there has been a history of domestic violence within the family, corrections professionals could work with victim-serving organizations and police personnel to make sure that violence does not recur upon release and to ensure victim safety should the need arise.

Workforce Development

A second policy arena—workforce development—demonstrates the value of a reentry perspective. The qualitative interviews presented in chapters 3 and 4 of this volume all illustrate the centrality of the lack of viable employment options to the decisions by men to engage in crime, either simultaneous to or in place of legal work. As with the foregoing discussion of family policy, one can start with a number of key indicators of the overlap with criminal justice policy. About 13 million Americans—7 percent of the adult population and 12 percent of the men—have felony convictions (Uggen, Thompson, and Manza 2000). Under state and federal law, the fact of their felony conviction explicitly bars them from a long list of jobs (Petersilia 2003).

In other instances their criminal record may serve as a de facto bar. As Harry Holzer, Steven Raphael, and Michael Stoll show in chapter 8 of this volume, employers are far more reluctant to hire former offenders than comparable groups of disadvantaged workers (also see Holzer, Raphael, and Stoll 2002). An audit using matched pairs of individuals applying for entry-level jobs has found that a criminal record was associated with a 50 percent reduction in employment opportunities; for African American applicants, the reduction was 64 percent (Pager 2002). The shifts in the American economy further compound these barriers. The kinds of jobs for which former prisoners are most likely to get hired—blue-collar and manufacturing jobs—are decreasing as a share of the workforce. The jobs for which former prisoners are least likely to get hired (jobs involving contact with children, the elderly, and direct customer contact) are increasing as a share of the workforce (Holzer, Raphael, and Stoll 2002; chapter 8 in this volume).

The reentry perspective forces a focus on the temporal relationship between work and prison. In a 1991 survey of prisoners the Bureau of Justice Statistics has found that most prisoners in the sample had jobs when they were arrested. Three-quarters were working—just over half had full time jobs (U.S. Department of Justice 1993). There is no similar data on these individuals when they leave prison. There is no data, for example, on the unemployment rate of former prisoners within a month of leaving prison. This lack of knowledge makes it difficult to assess the impact of reentry on participation in the workforce.

Nor is much known about the job-seeking and job retention activities of prisoners when they return home. According to an exploratory study by the Vera Institute of Justice documenting the experiences of forty-nine individuals leaving prison in New York state, most returning prisoners who found work were either rehired by former employers or had help from family or friends. Relatively few found jobs on their own (Nelson, Dees, and Allen 1999). If these intriguing findings were to hold up in a large-scale study, the implications for employment agencies working with former prisoners could be significant. Might a focus on former employers and natural networks yield more employment opportunities more efficiently than a focus on traditional employment programs?

Some relatively recent research efforts, many of which are reflected in this volume, have shed light on the effect of incarceration on the lifetime earnings of former prisoners. According to this body of literature, as the time in prison increases the likelihood of finding legitimate employment after release from prison decreases (Hagan and Dinovitzer 1999). Viewing the relationship between prison and earnings from a different perspective, other researchers have concluded that incarceration imposes a "wage penalty." In this calculation, individuals who have been in prison experience a lifetime reduction in earnings of between 10 and 20 percent (Western and Pettit 2000).

These provocative and disturbing findings take on greater significance when viewed from a community perspective. Given that the processes of arrest, imprisonment, and reentry now affect at least four times as many people as a generation ago, sentences are now longer than before, returning prisoners are less prepared for return to the workforce, and these effects are felt most acutely in a small number of disadvantaged neighborhoods, the aggregate-level impact of our criminal justice policies, at the community level, is to significantly depress the earnings power of those communities.

Perhaps the reentry and reintegration framework can provide some ideas for new policy approaches that would reverse these negative effects on individuals, families, and communities. One obvious focus for innovation and improvement would be the expansion of the level and quality of prison-based and work-readiness employment programs. Historically, evaluations of the effectiveness of these programs at reducing recidivism and increasing employment rates after return to the community have not generally been encouraging. Yet recent assessments of the research literature provide a more optimistic picture and offer solid grounds for increased investments. Four recent meta-analyses of dozens of individual evaluations of prison-based programs arrive at the same basic conclusion: correctional programming can reduce recidivism and improve employment outcomes (for a review, see Lawrence et al. 2002). Although many of the programs suffer from methodological limitations, the weight of available evidence supports greater investments in prison programs that prepare inmates for work on the outside.

Moving beyond prison-based programs, a more promising investment strategy might focus on creating linkages between the prison experience and job opportunities in the community. In a number of states, private businesses have organized job fairs in prison to interview applicants who are scheduled for release in the near future. Other states have created parallel work settings in prison, resembling the work environment on the outside, with expectations that successful "employees" in prison can continue in similar jobs after release. These private sector experiments resemble their public sector counterparts, such as the Safer Foundation in Chicago and the Center for Employment Opportunities in

New York City, that provide transitional work opportunities for newly released prisoners (Travis, Solomon, and Waul 2001).

In its most ambitious formulation, a focus on improving the employment prospects of released prisoners might borrow a page from the national experience with welfare reform. Over the past several years, the country has witnessed a remarkable shift in policy and practice under the rallying cry, "From welfare to work!" Although the differences between welfare reform and justice reform are considerable, the two reform efforts share this goal: moving individuals from a state of dependency (in one case, welfare, in the other, life in prison) toward a more productive life in the community. Perhaps the rallying cry "From prison to work!" could appeal to a similarly broad coalition of political interests, galvanizing the public and private sectors to tap the potential of the workforce leaving prison each year. These coalitions might address the historical resistance of employers to hiring former offenders, documented in chapter 8 in this volume. The key strategy, borrowed from the lessons of welfare reform, would be to create supportive intermediaries, such as the Safer Foundation and the Center for Employment Opportunities, that would screen returning prisoners, handle non-work-related service needs, and vouch for the reliability of their clients.

Health Policy

A final example is the nexus between public health and prisoner reentry. As with family policy and workforce development policy, the common ground is substantial. Prisoners have serious health problems. About three-quarters of them report a history of drug or alcohol use, frequently both. Half the state prisoners in one study said they were using drugs or alcohol at the time they committed the offense that brought them to prison (Mumola 1999). One-quarter report histories of injection drug use (Hammett, Roberts, and Kennedy 2001). Sixteen percent report a mental or emotional condition or an overnight stay in a psychiatric hospital (Ditton 1999). In chapter 5 in this volume, Johnson and Waldfogel find that 54 percent of women and 13 percent of men incarcerees in their study reported having been sexually abused, which is likely to present mental health issues even if the person does not report such.

The health profile of the prison population shows that prisoners suffer from a number of diseases at rates significantly higher than the general population. The overall rate of confirmed AIDS cases among prisoners is five times that found in the general population (Maruschak 2001). For HIV the rate is five to seven times greater, and for hepatitis C nine to ten times higher, than that of the general population (Hammett 2000).

Rather than merely examine this snapshot of the population, as informative as it is, a reentry perspective instructs us to look at the movement of individuals, and their health problems, through the institutions of imprisonment. According to research conducted for the National Commission of Correctional Health Care, in 1997 between 20 and 26 percent of the national population infected with HIV or AIDS, 29 to 32 percent of those with hepatitis C, and 38 percent of those with tuberculosis were released from a correctional facility (including both prisons and jails) that year (Hammett, Roberts, and Kennedy 2001).

The health profile of the prison population poses obvious and critical challenges to prison administrators. They must provide a level of health care that meets applicable constitutional, statutory, and professional standards. As the prison population ages, this health care becomes increasingly expensive. Yet the reentry and reintegration framework imposes a different set of obligations upon prison administrators. Remembering the iron law of corrections—that "they all come back" (Travis 2000)—the policy question is whether the period of imprisonment, combined with a health-conscious period of reentry, can improve health outcomes for prisoners, their families, and the communities to which they return.

Take a simple example: if a prisoner is taking psychotropic medications while in prison, who is responsible for ensuring that he continues to receive those medications (and related medical attention) after release? What organizational arrangements between prison health providers and community health care networks would ensure a smooth transition, from a health perspective? How should parole agencies integrate health professionals into the support network for parolees? How can families be engaged in supporting the health needs of returning prisoners, particularly those who, through the natural aging process or the simple advance of chronic diseases, need substantial care? How can returning prisoners be assisted in navigating the complex system of government benefits, managed health care, and private insurance?

As with the family and employment domains discussed in this chapter, one can hypothesize that marginal improvements in health outcomes for returning prisoners might yield substantial improvements at the community level. If approximately one-quarter of the national population infected with HIV or AIDS passes through a correctional facility each year, then in those neighborhoods of highest concentration of removal and reentry, the percentage is likely to be even higher, meaning that correctional institutions can provide a major point of intervention (Hammett 2000). If those interventions are effective, even at low levels, the aggregate effects on the course of the AIDS epidemic in those neighborhoods could be substantial.

In each of these three illustrations, the public policy questions exist outside the legal framework of our sentencing philosophies and are made more compelling by the fact of mass imprisonment. It may be that those sentencing schemes that require postrelease supervision provide better mechanisms for ensuring compliance with family reunification initiatives, job placement programs, or health regimens, but the absence of postrelease supervision does not make the need for family reintegration, reconnection with work, and maintenance of medical treatment any less compelling.

NEW PERSPECTIVES ON CRIMINAL JUSTICE POLICY

Finally, the reentry perspective raises profound questions about the way our society views the process of reintegration of returning prisoners. Most released prisoners fail. According to the Bureau of Justice Statistics, more than two-thirds (67.5 percent) of a cohort of prisoners released in 1994 were rearrested at least once within the next three years. More than half (52 percent) were returned to prison. The first year out posed the greatest risk: 44 percent are rearrested within that time (Langan and Levin 2002). So the success rate is not high, by any measure.

There is another dimension to the issue of success on the outside. Some prisoners released on supervised parole fail to meet the conditions of their release and are returned to prison. Eighteen percent of all prison admissions in 1980 were parole violators. By 1996 that proportion had almost doubled, to more than two hundred thousand individuals (Blumstein and Beck 1999). Nearly two-thirds of them are returned to prison for a "technical violation," meaning that the parolee failed to meet a condition of his or her supervision. The remaining third were returned for a new conviction (Bonczar and Glaze 1999). The net result is a second pathway to prison, much larger than the earlier one (indeed, now larger than the entire prison admissions cohort in the early 1970s), with unknown consequences for public safety, prison management, and offender reintegration.

The reentry perspective is a useful device for posing fundamental questions about the role of criminal justice supervision in the postrelease process. As mentioned earlier, one can question the wisdom of any sentencing scheme that eliminates postrelease supervision. Yet the more important policy question is, What supervision is best, for whom, and on what terms? Are there some offenses (and some offenders) for which the prison term constitutes the entire extent of the criminal sanction? If so, what are the obligations of prison administrators in assisting the prisoners with a smooth transition to life on the outside?

Viewing these issues from a community perspective adds a rich dimension to the policy challenge. Let us return to the example of Brooklyn, New York, where 11 percent of the block groups account for 20 percent of the population yet are home to 50 percent of the parolees. Would it be more effective to organize the parole caseload geographically, so that a parole officer (or a team of them) was responsible for all parolees in these neighborhoods? If organized this way, and actually located in the community, the function of the parole officer might become quite different. The institutions of civic life in the community—the churches, employers, social clubs, block associations, and extended families—could be engaged in the reintegration process. They could provide "supervision" as well as "services," all at relatively low cost. They could help the returning prisoner, and the parole officer, in assessing the situational risks posed by the neighborhood, serving as navigators through the risky shoals of reentry. Associations of former prisoners could be organized to provide support systems, turning on its head the traditional peroration forbidding parolees from associating with known felons. In short, the existing networks of informal social control could be used to buttress the work of the agent of formal control, the parole officer. (These same networks could also serve those returning from prison who are not under legal supervision.)

From this starting point, one could imagine a number of significant changes in criminal justice policy. For example, I have elsewhere proposed the development of "reentry courts" that would oversee the reintegration process, much as drug courts oversee the drug treatment process for defendants under their supervision (Travis 2000). The U.S. Department of Justice has called for the creation of "reentry partnerships" between community organizations and criminal justice agencies to bring together community assets and stakeholders in innovative efforts to increase the chances of successful reentry. Practitioners and scholars have advocated the creation of "community justice development corporations" that would serve as intermediaries, managing the supervision of parolees, probationers, and others under judicial oversight at the community level (Travis 2002a). In a very real sense, everything is up for grabs—the relationship between the offender and the state, between the community and the criminal justice system, between sanctions (formal and informal) and incentives (formal and informal) that might change behavior. And undertaking these innovations does not require changes in sentencing philosophy.

CONCLUSION

We now live in an era of mass incarceration. So, too, we now live in a time when high levels of prisoner reentry have redefined the landscape of our society. We arrived at this new reality in part because we changed our sentencing policies, in part because crime rates soared, in part because we have aggressively prosecuted a war on drugs. With crime rates at the lowest levels in a generation, we can expect some relief in the size of our prison population. The current fiscal crisis facing most states will spur cutbacks in some of the more punitive sentencing reforms of the past twenty years. But as we look to the near future, we cannot see significant changes in the current fragmentation of sentencing policy. We are thus left with the challenge of responding to the new reality of reentry in the absence of an overarching sentencing philosophy that might give us policy guidance.

The reintegration goal does not depend on a particular sentencing structure for its legitimacy. In fact, the reentry lens can create opportunities for collaboration with new partners from other social policy domains who can assist in the reintegration process. These collaborations, and the research into the consequences of incarceration and reentry, can shed new light on some classic criminal justice questions, such as the pathways of prisoner reintegration. They can also contribute new models for thinking about the relationship between prisoners and the communities to which they return. These new models may, in turn, inform a broader discussion about the response to crime and the pursuit of justice in America.

REFERENCES

Blumstein, Alfred, and Allen J. Beck. 1999. "Population Growth in U.S. Prisons, 1980–1996." In *Prisons*, edited by Michael Tonry and Joan Petersilia. Chicago: University of Chicago Press.

Bonczar, Thomas P., and Allen J. Beck. 1997. *Lifetime Likelihood of Going to State or Federal Prison*. NCJ-160092 (March). Washington: U.S. Bureau of Justice Statistics.

Bonczar, Thomas P., and Lauren E. Glaze. 1999. *Probation and Parole in the United States, 1998*. NCJ-178234 (August). Washington: U.S. Bureau of Justice Statistics.

Braman, Donald, and Jennifer Wood. 2003. "From One Generation to the Next: How Criminal Sanctions Are Reshaping Family Life in Urban America." In *Prisoners Once Removed: The Effect of Incarceration and Reentry on Children, Families, and Communities*, edited by Jeremy Travis and Michelle Waul. Washington, D.C.: Urban Institute Press.

Burke, Peggy. 2001. "Collaboration for Successful Prisoner Reentry: The Role of Parole and the Courts." *Corrections Management Quarterly* 5(3, Fall): 11–22.

Cadora, Eric, and Charles Swartz. 1999. *Analysis for the Community Justice Project of the Center for Alternative Sentencing and Employment Strategies*. New York: Center for Alternative Sentencing and Employment Strategies.

Ditton, Paula M. 1999. *Mental Health Treatment of Inmates and Probationers*. NCJ-174463 (July). Washington: U.S. Bureau of Justice Statistics.

Hagan, John, and Ronit Dinovitzer. 1999. "Collateral Consequences of Imprisonment for Children, Communities and Prisoners." In *Prisons*, edited by Michael Tonry and Joan Petersilia. Chicago: University of Chicago Press.

Hammett, Theodore. 2000. "Health-Related Issues in Prisoner Reentry to the Community." Paper presented to the Reentry Roundtable. Washington (October 12–13).

Hammett, Theodore, Cheryl Roberts, and Sofia Kennedy. 2001. "Health-Related Issues in Prisoner Reentry." *Crime and Delinquency* 47(3, July): 390–409.

Harrison, Paige A., and Allen J. Beck. 2003. *Prisoners in 2002*. NCJ-200248 (July). Washington: U.S. Bureau of Justice Statistics.

Holzer, Harry J., Steven Raphael, and Michael Stoll. 2002. "Can Employers Play A More Positive Role in Prisoner Reentry?" Paper presented to the Reentry Roundtable. Washington (March 20–21).

Langan, Patrick A., and David J. Levin. 2002. *Recidivism of Prisoners Released in 1994*. NCJ-193427 (June). Washington: U.S. Bureau of Justice Statistics.

Lawrence, Sarah, Daniel P. Mears, Glenn Dubin, and Jeremy Travis. 2002. *The Practice and Promise of Prison Programming*. Washington, D.C.: Urban Institute Press.

Lynch, James P., and William J. Sabol. 2001. "Prisoner Reentry in Perspective." *Crime Policy Report*, vol. 3. Washington, D.C.: Urban Institute Press.

Maruna, Shadd. 2001. *Making Good: How Ex-Convicts Reform and Rebuild Their Lives*. Washington, D.C.: American Psychological Association.

Maruschak, Laura M. 2001. *HIV in Prisons and Jails, 1999*. NCJ-187456 (July). Washington: U.S. Bureau of Justice Statistics.

Mumola, Christopher J. 1999. *Substance Abuse and Treatment, State and Federal Prisoners, 1997*. NCJ-182335. Washington: U.S. Bureau of Justice Statistics.

———. 2000. *Incarcerated Parents and Their Children*. Washington: U.S. Bureau of Justice Statistics.

Nelson, Martha, Perry Dees, and Charlotte Allen. 1999. *The First Month Out: Post-Incarceration Experiences in New York City*. New York: Vera Institute of Justice.

Pager, Devah. 2002. "The Mark of a Criminal Record." Paper presented at the annual meeting of the American Sociological Association. Chicago (August 16–19).

Petersilia, Joan. 2003. *When Prisoners Come Home: Parole and Prisoner Reentry*. Oxford: Oxford University Press.

Rossman, Shelli. 2003. "Building Partnerships to Strengthen Offenders, Families, and Communities." In *Prisoners Once Removed: The Effect of Incarceration and Reentry on Children, Families, and Communities*, edited by Jeremy Travis and Michelle Waul. Washington, D.C.: Urban Institute Press.

Tonry, Michael. 1996. *Sentencing Matters*. New York: Oxford University Press.

Travis, Jeremy. 2000. "But They All Come Back: Rethinking Prisoner Reentry." *Sentencing and Corrections: Issues for the 21st Century*. NCJ-181413 (7, May). Washington, D.C.: National Institute of Justice.

———. 2002a. "Invisible Punishment: An Instrument of Social Exclusion." In *Invisible Punishment: The Collateral Consequences of Mass Imprisonment*, edited by Marc Mauer and Meda Chesney-Lind. New York: New Press.

———. 2002b. "Thoughts on the Future of Parole." Paper presented to the Vera Institute of Justice. New York (May 22).

Travis, Jeremy, and Joan Petersilia. 2001. "Reentry Reconsidered: A New Look at an Old Question." *Crime and Delinquency* 47(3): 291–313.

Travis, Jeremy, Amy L. Solomon, and Michelle Waul. 2001. *From Prison to Home: The Dimensions and Consequences of Prisoner Reentry.* Washington, D.C.: Urban Institute Press.

Uggen, Christopher, Melissa Thompson, and Jeff Manza. 2000. "Rethinking Crime and Inequality: The Socioeconomic, Familial, and Civic Lives of Criminal Offenders." Paper presented at the annual meeting of the American Society of Criminology. San Francisco (November 18).

U.S. Department of Justice, Bureau of Justice Statistics. 1993. *Survey of State Prison Inmates, 1991.* NCJ-136949 (March). Washington: U.S. Department of Justice.

———. 2000. *Correctional Populations in the United States, 1997.* NCJ-177613 (November). Washington: U.S. Department of Justice.

U.S. Department of Labor. 2001. *From Hard Time to Full Time: Strategies to Help Move Ex-Offenders from Welfare to Work.* Washington, D.C.: Employment and Training Administration.

Visher, Christy, and Jeremy Travis. 2003. "Transitions from Prison to Community: Understanding Individual Pathways." *Annual Review of Sociology* 29(August): 89–113.

Western, Bruce, and Becky Pettit. 2000. "Incarceration and Racial Inequality in Men's Employment." *Industrial and Labor Relations Review* 54(1, October): 3–16.

Wilkinson, Reginald A. 2001. "Offender Reentry: A Storm Overdue." *Corrections Management Quarterly* 5(3, Fall): 46–51.

Index

Boldface numbers refer to figures and tables.

adoption agencies, 99–100. *See also* foster and agency child care
African Americans. *See* blacks
age: and desistance from crime, 46–47, 250; and fatherhood issues for youth, 59–60; and fragility of adolescent relationships, 81–82; incarceration challenges for juveniles, 76–78, 92; incarceration effects on parental bond, **40**; and incarceration rates, 6, **7**; and turning point lessons, 67
agency care. *See* foster and agency child care
alcoholism and developmental risk factors, 106. *See also* substance abuse
Anderson, Elijah, 81–82
arrested vs. incarcerated individuals, **174**, 175, **176**, 208
Atlanta, Georgia, employer hiring attitudes, **212**, 213–15, **216**
attachment theory, 98–100, 124

birth rates, ethnic disparities in, 78
blacks: birth rate comparison, 78; and disenfranchisement effect, 165, 198*n*2; employment issues for, 46, 227–28, 239*n*11, 259; and gender antagonisms, 81–82; incarceration rates, 4, 5–6; and juvenile incarceration, 77–78; marital-cohabitation rates, 8–9, 25, **26**; parental bonds and incarceration, 36–37, 39, 63; par-

ents as prisoners, 9–10, 257; political attitudes, 190, 194; prior incarceration status biases, **28**; prisoner contacts with children, **11**; in substitute child care arrangements, 116, 120, 123; women's role in family, 21
Boston, Massachusetts, employer hiring attitudes, **212**, 213–15, **216**
Bowlby, John, 98
boyfriends, dealing with mother's new, 62–63, 86–89
Bursik, Robert, 138
Bush, George W., 188
Bushway, Shawn, 207
business cycle and demand for former offenders, 229–32, 240*n*17

child abuse, 93–94, 106, **117**, 118, 119
child development: incarceration effects, 98, 102–7, 123, 124; mental and emotional health problems, 105–6, **117**, 122; multiple risk factor analysis, 104–5
child support payments, 73*n*1, 92, 241*n*27
child welfare systems. *See* foster and agency child care
children: attendance of fathers at birth of, 48, 60; parental incarceration rates, 9–11; and reentry perspective, 256–58, 261. *See also* living arrangements for children; parents; paroled fathers and children; turning points study